In praise of
Leader or Not, Here I Come!

"*Leader or not, here I come is a scary thought for most. 'Am I ready for this bold step' is the question of the hour. Not only is there hope, but content rich help exists for those placed on the cutting edge of today's management and leadership arena. In his excellent book, **Leader or Not, Here I Come**, author, Dennis Nitschke, has developed a step-by-step guide for growing into your leadership role that's so vital in today's competitive marketplace. You and your staff will be motivated with the power that's packed in this life changing book. Leadership growth support is available to you—if you're up to the challenge. Take the challenge.*

—Van Crouch, CEO of Van Crouch Communications,
is a nationally sought after business presenter and
author of books having sold more than 1 million copies.

"*Cabela's, the World's Foremost Outfitters, is proud to be using this book as text for our three-credit Leadership course made available on-line to our 13,000 employees nationwide. Our company, as with any successful organization, needs to grow its leadership capacity using the best tools and support mechanisms available. **Leader or Not, Here I Come** is one of our vital resources.*"

—Sarah Kaiser, Senior HR Manager,
Cabela's Corporate Training Department

"*For success in today's corporate world, leadership skills are more important than ever. Businesses are spending millions of dollars making sure their leaders are equipped for the future and that they have an effective succession planning strategy. Without question, this book serves as an excellent leadership development tool and I look forward to using it with my own corporate staff. In addition, the book adds its own brand of humor, real life exercises, and personal leadership experiences. Both new and experienced leaders will benefit greatly from reading **Leader or Not, Here I Come**. I personally recommend this book for my clients, many of whom are Fortune 500 companies.*"

—Cabot Jaffee, President and CEO of Alignmark
(Orlando based HR Consulting Company)

LEADER OR NOT,

HERE I COME!

Your Ready, Fire, Aim Entrance Into Leadership

DENNIS NITSCHKE

LANDMARK
OPPORTUNITIES, INC.

10 09 08 07   10 9 8 7 6 5 4 3 2 1

Published by Landmark Opportunities, Inc
P. O. Box 326
Lake Tomahawk, WI 54539-0326

Book Cover designed by Douglas J. Thiel, Streamwood, IL

CONTENTS

INTRODUCTION

Remember the childhood game, Hide and Seek? Someone would count to one hundred, while everyone else would scurry about to hide and then shout to the top of their voice...*Ready or not, here I come?* What fun our gang had. If I ran fast and hid well, I could play a long time never getting tagged, having to be "it" myself. There was, of course, a goal area where we could also run to be safe from getting tagged.

Life back then was full of fun and games. However, the games and rules for career advancement and growing in leadership skills are far different than ..."Ready or Not Here I Come!". Today, for many, they find themselves playing the waiting game in mid management, looking beyond their current role in hopes of entering the world of leadership sooner rather than later. For those very individuals, this book was written. Here in your hands is a brand new game plan—called *Leader Or Not, Here I Come*!

This book is written for you; those wanting to move into and through the leadership journey even if it means you must begin while still in your mid-management role. You might be asking yourself, "But how, is it even possible?" "Am I ready for it?"

A long time ago, ten years into my career, I found that my position in mid-management was far from adequately preparing me for what I truly wanted, which was to experience a more meaningful role in leadership. I was told to wait (and hide) until top management felt I was ready for promotion. THEN, they would "move me" into leadership. The problem was, I wanted to begin experiencing and growing in leadership where I was at that time. Being one of those risk taking individuals, I decided to rethink and redirect the "100% safe" pathway to growth. The "Ready or Not" (Leader Or Not) approach was the path I chose to take, but first I had to recognize and address three vital issues:

1. First, I wanted my hidden leadership talents to be recognized and developed openly rather than waiting for them to be discovered. Unfortunately, my supervisors and senior leaders who were classified as "it" on the organization chart never came looking for me unless I did something wrong. I wanted to be tagged as being a future "it" in the organization but was told to remain in hiding.

2. Secondly, there was no safe place (goal area) for me to experience leadership growth because my supervisors never created or planned leadership

growth opportunities for me. The prospects of finding safe and supported ways to contribute to the organization were virtually non-existent. In fact, I was safest when I didn't create any waves at all.

3. Thirdly, no matter how hard I tried or how fast I ran, my potential was not being recognized. While I was appreciated for my mid-management accomplishments, I found myself asking these key questions.... "How much time was I willing to wait before my next career move took place?" "How could I take bolder steps in my current role in mid management and still keep my job?

I knew that I had much to learn about being a solid, high performing mid-manager before senior officials would tag me for the next promotion. At the same time, I learned that growth in leadership could begin while still in my current position and that my role in mid management could actually be enhanced by spreading my new leadership wings in the right ways. My pathway to success required that I create and take part in a new game called *Leader Or Not, Here I Come*. It is this very approach that you'll come to understand and experience by reading this book.

Don't give up on your dreams. Begin by blooming where you're planted for now—even in mid-management.

"Leadership and learning are indispensable to each other."
—JOHN F. KENNEDY

*"Leadership should be born out of understanding
of the needs of those who would be affected by it."*
—MARION ANDERSON

"The first step to leadership is servanthood."
—JOHN MAXWELL

*"I start with the premise that the function of leadership
is to produce more leaders, not more followers."*
—RALPH NADER

*"Be gentle and you can be bold; be frugal and
you can be liberal; avoid putting yourself before
others and you can become a leader among men."*
—LAO TZU

CHAPTER 1

YOUR STARTING POINT

Did you ever watch a track meet and notice how the great sprinters seem to explode out of their starting blocks? Do you think "starting well" comes easy for these runners? Of course not! These runners know that their race can be won or lost in the starting blocks, and they prepare hard and long for that great start. You must keep this in mind as you choose to approach the starting blocks on your journey—not sprint—into leadership. You should be on the lookout for those opportunities that will propel you in the right direction and at the right pace. If you want to succeed in leadership, you'll have to work at it–hard and long. That's *exactly* what this book will help you do. It will help get you started well, today, while you're still in your mid-management position. Use it as your starting block.

On one hand, you must be careful not to "push" your way too quickly into leadership. Yet on the other hand, you may be ready, eager at the starting line, just waiting to be "asked" to perform a more meaningful role. Where's the middle ground? It lies somewhere between these two extremes and it begins with *you making the decision* to grow into leadership as a mid-manager. You must apply both wisdom and an appropriate degree of caution based on your workplace setting, culture, and current role. The fact remains, however, that you can get started today.

Your success is not measured by a stopwatch; it's based on your adding value to the organization in new ways over the long-term. The prize is not acquiring a new job title. Rather, success requires a proper start, defining the right strategies to progress through the journey, and a clear understanding of how your leadership efforts (at whatever level) will help your organization succeed. If you want to finish well, you must start well, perform with quality, endure the challenges, and have the right finish line in sight.

Many of you are probably questioning how to begin this journey into and through leadership. Believe me, it isn't all about your knowledge base, how fast you can make decisions, or how objective a thinker you might be. Instead it starts with your mindset as to what leadership really involves. Be prepared for the risks, challenges, and changes associated with leadership. In addition, be prepared by gaining the right leadership skills and achieving a leadership style that can effectively lead others with sound tactical and strategic actions. There are skills and Leadership Tools that will assist you, but nothing can compare with pure "wisdom" that will evolve over time as you move into and through your leadership growth experiences. Become a leader of significance, one who is prepared mentally, emotionally, professionally, and experientially. Make sure your leadership efforts and motivations are directed at making a measurable difference in the life of your organization and others.

If you're serious about beginning your leadership journey, I'll ask three things of you:

1. Have a sincere passion to acquire **new knowledge** and to develop **new thinking** about leadership. The only way to start and progress through the leadership journey is to be open to new learning and thinking about change, people, and measures of success—forever.

2. Be ready to learn critical lessons of leadership from on-the-job, **applied experiences.** Go beyond reading and knowing about leadership. Choose to experience and learn from it every day.

3. At this stage of your learning, consider yourself an apprentice by **understanding and experiencing leadership "from two steps behind."** Embrace this learning model, and you will be surprised what you can learn by simply watching and serving others from your current mid-management position. You don't begin out-front of existing leaders; you must learn from and with them.

Now, where do you begin? What are the most important mindsets, skill sets, and strategies one must acquire to be successful? What Leadership Tools are available to help you grow? What is this *Leader or Not, Here I Come* concept all about?

Ready, set, and go.

Begin Here

If I were to suggest a starting point, it would be to challenge you to *assess your true motives for wanting to be a leader.* Why pursue a role in leadership? Your answer to that simple question will provide meaningful insight into your future. Your motives will drive your thinking, your thinking will drive your actions, and your actions will determine your outcome. Having the right motives (and goals for success) as a leader is the first step in charting your journey.

Your success in leadership must be measured and driven by something far more important than merely charting your own career pathway to success. Ultimately, your success will occur and be measured by how your leadership directly and indirectly moves "others toward success." It does not begin and end with YOU. Be certain your motives are driving you to make a significant difference in the lives of your customers, work teams, and organization. *Then,* look at how these leadership decisions and actions will affect you and your career. This isn't a humble approach to leadership—it's the smart approach.

I offer the following principle: *Your* career path will follow the significant (positive) impact your leadership has on others; not vice versa. On the surface, this may not make sense to you, but think of the word *Leadership.* It implies actions or outcomes that move those following you to a better place. It's far broader than how many individuals you can get to follow you or your next promotion. It is about results that matter. What do you believe matters most in the long run for the organization, your customers, or your work teams? Are they more concerned about your success or theirs? The point is, it's not all about you. It's about what your leadership does for others and then what these successes might do for your career path.

Each of us has had unique experiences that allowed us to gain great wisdom as we transitioned through different seasons of our careers. In my youth, I was hyper-focused on receiving immediate gratification for all that I did. During my early career years, I sought and fought for recognition and job promotion, at all costs. Later, I measured success and took personal satisfaction based upon the challenges faced and major accomplishments achieved on-the-job. Near the end of my career, I finally began to understand that my greatest measure of success was found in how my leadership was making a meaningful difference in the lives of others and the organization I was serving. As they succeeded, I succeeded—both personally and professionally.

I wish I had learned this last lesson sooner. You see, for most of my career I was trying to define success in leadership based on how it satisfied MY definition. In reality, my success was being based on how OTHERS defined success. Whether you understand this today or not, the truth is based on how others define success and what I call the *"so what" factor.* I believe the workplace is tired of self-serving individuals simply "playing leadership," being too full of themselves. Yes, your career is vitally important as a destination, but your journey into and through leadership will have far greater impact if your focus is on achieving results that matter to the organization, without destroying those around you. If

Be committed to acquiring the right tools for your leadership journey and be committed to improving your skill level with each and every one.

you want to be an effective leader tomorrow, start here with this simple mindset and take the focus off yourself. It will free you up and point you in the right direction.

Your Leadership Toolbox

As we focus on *your leadership journey*, I offer this visual to help you. Each day, visualize yourself carrying a Leadership Toolbox full of the right tools that you can pull out and use as each new challenge requires. Your goal, however, must reach far beyond simply acquiring a half-empty Leadership Toolbox or a box full of the wrong tools. You must acquire the right tools and be proficient in how and when each is most effectively used. It's not about the number of tools. It's about the right tools. Remember, there's not a one size fits all tool that will be perfect for every leadership challenge. As you grow in your leadership role, you will find it necessary to acquire more advanced, high-powered tools. However, begin by acquiring and using a basic set of tools. Do you currently have a Leadership Toolbox? I'm sure you do, but have you assessed what tools you actually have in it? Are they the right tools? Be committed to acquiring the right tools for your leadership journey and be committed to improving your skill level with each and every one. Keep this Toolbox close, keep your inventory current, and make sure your tools are clean and well organized. You never know when the need for each tool might arise.

This book will expose you to more than 60 Leadership Tools that I've learned and successfully applied in my career. Many of these tools will be supported by challenging exercises to guide you in experiencing use of these tools in your workplace setting. Your on-the-job application of these tools will allow you to assess whether or not each is appropriate to include in *your* Leadership Toolbox. Let these tools serve to increase your self-confidence and overall leadership ability. Over time, my goal is for you to grow through new thinking and learning, making you a wiser person able to apply these new tools to the many leadership opportunities/choices that will come to you every day.

I want you to go far beyond simply "knowing about" these tools. It's necessary that you gain a "working knowledge" of each one. Like the sprinter, you get better by daily practicing the essentials of your craft. Consider the contents of your Leadership Toolbox an essential requirement for your role in leadership.

Learning by Applying What You Learn

The challenge I had in writing this book was to offer easy-to-read insights into leadership that would add meaningful, applied knowledge in support of your leadership journey. At the same time, I wanted to write in a style that reflected "home spun" stories and tools all the while helping you develop the proper leadership mindset (or paradigm). There is no quick fix or magic pill that will make you that "stand-out" employee and effective leader; that can only occur over time and with considerable effort. You need to be challenged, learn continuously, recognize opportunity, and want leadership badly enough. I've found that leadership opportunities often come disguised as hard work and it's not necessarily for everyone. If making your "mark" in the workplace and on the organization is your goal, expect to experience the full range of ups and downs of growing into and through leadership. Expect the best, but be prepared for a most challenging (and exciting) journey. It's a process that you grow into. No one simply arrives as a leader.

Leader Or Not, Here I Come has been written to go beyond merely "telling" you about leadership. The book is structured to help *guide you* in your *learning* and *application* of the new Leadership Tools being presented by:

- Expanding your **paradigms and thinking** through the sharing of my experiences (both positive and negative). You must balance your leadership growth process with both concepts and experiences.

- Offering more than **60 Leadership Tools** for your Leadership Toolbox. There's not "one leadership approach for every workplace situation." Equip and customize your Toolbox, as well.

- Challenging you to *apply* these tools by piloting many of them in your workplace through a set of **40 Exercises**. Leadership advice without context is just knowledge; not necessarily learning. *The key to effective learning is to **apply** this knowledge on-the-job,* as soon as possible.

- Encouraging you to **seek a mentor** and then commit to being a leadership mentor to others in the future.

- Linking Leadership Tools to higher level **strategic planning** and to a proven framework for **performance excellence**. While leadership is implemented at ground zero, you must also view and plan leadership for your organization from 20,000 feet. Both are a must.

- Asking you to draft and then revise a **Personal Leadership Statement** that will define your journey and measure of success in leadership.

- Suggesting you commit to follow-through on a *12-Step Action Plan,* which will encourage you to APPLY what you've gained in this book over the next six-month period.

This book offers guidance and a vast array of success tools for your leadership journey. Just add water (sweat equity) and see what grows. A lot of what I've learned and am sharing you've heard before, but it's always good food for growth. I urge you to read the book carefully and think through the lessons and tools being offered. In addition, please complete the Exercises offered because they are NOT intended to be casual "fill-in the blank" questions. Rather, they are designed to facilitate true "learning" by having you actually experience the nature and impact of specific tools. Apply these Exercises in a personal way in your customized workplace setting. Through this approach to learning, I hope to enlighten, reinforce, motivate, and cause focus as you grow and apply your leadership skills, experiences, and commitment. *In this regard,* **the book is all about you.**

Formula for Leadership Growth

Leader Or Not, Here I Come is not a cookbook with highly structured recipes for success, a traditional step-by-step self-help manual, or a compilation of research on leadership theories. There are volumes of excellent leadership resources that I strongly encourage you to read and absorb along the way. However, while many of these valuable resources will add great theory, logic, and new perspectives for your journey, you must also have the proper grounding (start) in leadership before you strive to take giant leaps. "Walk before you run" and "go slow to go fast" are great words of advice for new leaders to grow by and follow.

Here's where this book fits into my "non-scientific" formula for your growth in leadership:

- 25% of your growth begins with a basic awareness and knowledge of applied Leadership Tools that will **prepare** you to move into and through the challenges of leadership (It's what **this book** will do—*it's your starting point*).

- 50% of your growth is through those teachable moments and powerful learning experiences over time—growing in your leadership skills and expanding the opportunities for leadership on your job (It's what you must do today and every day in the workplace—*it's your learning curve and your learning place*).

- 25% will be through *advanced thinking, learning, and seeing the bigger picture* through additional resources and mentors; carrying you to higher levels of effective leadership. You will grow in competence, character, creativity, consideration, courage, and in your career. Over time, you will become wiser in seeing and capturing opportunities to lead—applying the right tools to the right circumstances.

There's one more part of this formula that I need to stress, and it is found in all three parts of this non-scientific formula. *The absolute requirement for effective leadership is that you gain wisdom in each phase of your growth experience.* The best legacy you can leave is that you lead wisely. Be a wise and trusted leader—a leader who matters. *Your learning curve is a forever thing. The key is learning and applying this knowledge with wisdom; it's not just about the knowing.*

Why Learning Leadership From Two Steps Behind?

Earlier in this Chapter, I mentioned the phrase "leading from two steps behind." It's an essential paradigm or mental position from which to begin your journey. Two steps behind does *not* mean being invisible in your leadership role, leading in the shadows of others. It does not mean beginning as a "loser." You already know that leadership will require you to be two steps ahead of most others in addressing needed change and your thinking must be two steps ahead of the current decisions being made. It is critical that your measure of success in leadership be focused on moving the organization two steps ahead. Why then this discussion of working from behind?

Two-steps behind is meant to be a reflection of your attitude toward who gets the credit for successes and why you're choosing to lead. If it's all about you and all for you alone, you're reading the wrong book and you're setting yourself up for a major crash sometime in your career. Self-centeredness may work in the short-term, but will fail you in the long-run. You must remain vulnerable in taking risks and in giving credit. Your success is dependent upon identifying the right opportunities, retaining your focus on the Main Things, and doing the right things for the right reasons—for others. This will require both effective management skills and effective leadership skills. Learn to be a selfless leader.

Leading from two steps behind isn't just a positioning statement for leadership activities; it's also a positioning of your heart attitude. The heart attitude of

Leadership is not an event; it is not a destination—it's a continuous journey.

a true leader sees and is driven toward adding meaningful value to the organization and to others. By its very nature, this positions a new leader two steps behind the spotlight, but certainly not out of the loop or circle of influence. The most effective leaders I've known had an incredible "servant's heart" with immense courage to carry-out the difficult role of leadership. They did not, however, seek center stage. They could see the big picture more clearly than most and I chose to follow their lead because their ideas, actions, and heart served to benefit the overall organization. That's the kind of leader I wanted to be. It may sound naive, but it worked for me. As my organization succeeded through my leadership efforts, I succeeded. Success of the organization defined my success.

Leader Or Not, Here I Come is intended to encourage you as a potential leader, but remember that the race into leadership is not a crown to be obtained. *Leadership is not a position or title—it's a state of readiness and effectiveness.* Realize that you don't have to be the "top dog" to be an effective leader in your organization. You can be a leader two steps behind your CEO or your supervisor—even in your role as a mid-manager. At the 100% investment level, that's where we must all begin.

With all of this said, the concept of leadership from two steps behind might be summarized as:

- A positioning of **your leadership role** in full support of your CEO and other true leaders.

- A positioning of **your heart attitude and your ego**—the need to claim success can get in the way of actually achieving success.

- A positioning of **your success measure** in leadership—leadership is *for* others, accomplished *through* others, and your success is measured **by** others.

Can your ego stand supporting senior leaders even if they get all the credit? Can you be motivated to lead and risk seeing others and the organization succeed based on your leadership efforts—even if you're not always properly recognized for your efforts? I'm not being naive in suggesting that "sharing the glory" is easy for any of us and that there isn't a risk factor involved in letting someone else take the credit. However, leading from two steps behind thinking, at least as a starting point, will benefit you greatly in the long run. It will create a positive reputation and create political alliances that will pay major dividends for you in the future. Remember, leadership is not an event; it is not a destination—it's a continuous journey. Position yourself well to start this journey.

My "Ah-Ha's"

In writing this book, I experienced several startling "ah-ha's." First of all, I discovered an incredible joy in documenting my Leadership Tools and experiences for those of you just beginning or mid-way into your leadership journey and careers. I was (am) committed to being a valuable resource for you to bring about a positive difference in this exciting and challenging journey. This book is about seeing *you* succeed—not me as its author.

The second "ah-ha" was to learn that the concepts I wrote on effective leadership also apply to effective parenting, grand-parenting, my faith walk, and my marriage. Leadership traits and thinking are not limited to the business world. Here's an interesting question to ponder. What if the concepts of effective parenting or an effective marriage are actually transferable back to effective leadership? You mean you might be a better leader by learning from your effective marriage (Note: my wife told me to ask that question!)? While I believe it to be true, someone else can write *that* book. The "ah-ha" is that many of these skills, traits, and mindsets are fully transferable to success in other areas of life. It's because these areas of life and business involve people, their complex interrelationship issues, and how others define success. Their success will have a direct (positive) impact on your success. You see, leadership is far more than the "tactics" you apply. It's about the strategic *"so what"* outcomes you're striving to accomplish through your leadership efforts. You're always in the people business—get used to it.

Big Picture Lessons of Life

As I reflected on what overall advice I might give someone preparing to begin their journey into leadership, I was able to boil my sage wisdom down to eight broad statements:

- View your daily challenges/trials from a higher vantage point. Remember your objective is to drain the swamp; don't let those alligators get to you.

- See that having choices is a good thing; then be fully aware of the daily choices before you. Choices are good!

- Have more fun along the way than what you originally thought appropriate. Smile more and frown less. If you wear your intensity or frustrations on your shirtsleeve, you're an easy target for manipulation.

- Formulate your decisions or changes based on driving toward something bigger. Make opportunity your driver, not fear. Benchmark against your passions, not the status quo.

- Go beyond making decisions based solely on what's logical—trust your instincts more.

- Understand the importance of leaving a leadership legacy *through* others.

- Focus on your journey, not just the destination.

- Receive that feeling of success and personal value from seeing OTHERS succeed.

I urge you to remember these eight sage lessons of life and incorporate them into your daily living, in addition to your leadership journey. You will need common sense and high-level perspectives during tough times, as well as, the good times. Each of us wants to grow in leadership but we must also grow in balanced ways—at home, with friends, and so on. Effective and meaningful leadership is needed in all aspects of life. See the big picture and define "significant positive impact" in all that you do.

Enjoy the Journey

Look forward to what you're about to experience. Proceed with confidence and courage. I've found that entering any new learning situation in a state of fear is a bad thing. On the other hand, you cannot perform with excellence if you have a flippant attitude or take related challenges too lightly. Take a deep breath and venture forward one step at a time, taking each step with your eyes wide open, realizing that leadership is as much about learning as it is about doing.

As long as you're not part of a totally dysfunctional and unhealthy organization, your senior officials will *want* you to grow and make you part of their succession planning strategies. They *need* you to make operations at the mid-management levels better today and to see you preparing to play a greater leadership role tomorrow. Keep your eyes on the future and remember not to make this journey all about you. Expect some mistakes, but require growth from these mistakes. Deliver your best efforts consistently.

Leader Or Not, Here I Come is based on the principle that—whatever business you're in, your role in leadership will always be in the "people improvement business" that results in organizational improvement. It's not about manipulating people. It's not about you "winning" while others are losing. It's not about being bold, brash, and direct in making decisions. Rather, it's *through others* that your leadership talents will materialize and it's *for others* that the effectiveness of your leadership will be measured.

Some of you more logical and sequential thinkers are already looking for that sure-fire 1, 2, 3 step guide that will ensure your success in this leadership journey. Forget about it! You don't need a cookbook approach and I know of no guaranteed step-by-step formula. You need to experience the leadership journey one step at a time and remain flexible in where to take that next step. Do not be fearful of leadership; be proactive and remain a positive thinker. Leadership skills often develop in the least likely manner. Be ready to grow every day.

Although I can't give you a step-by-step pathway to success, I *can* provide you with a listing of numerical references I've made to "Leadership Tools" in various chapters of this book. These tools need to be fully understood and become part of your Leadership Toolbox. Here are some Lessons for you to grow from, beginning with Leadership Tool #1:

#1: The "one main thing" is to keep the Main Things the main thing. (Chapter 3)

#2: It's Management and Leadership—together forever. (Chapter 3)

#3: The Three R's—Relationships, Relevancy, and Responsiveness (Chapters 5 & 8)

The Three C's—Customer, Change, and Competition (Chapter 7)

The Three 3's Assessment—Start, Stop, and Continue (Chapter 8)

#4: The Four-Step Shewart Cycle of Plan-Do-Check-Act (Chapter 2)

#5: The Five-Level Skill Development Approach (Chapter 2)

The Five Levels of Leadership (Chapter 12)

#6: The Six-Sided Leadership Rubik's Cube (Chapter 4)

#7: The Seven E's to address in Political Positioning (Chapter 7)

#8: The Eight Drivers in Managing Complex Change (Chapter 7)

#9: The Nine Key Result Areas for Performance Excellence (Chapter 11)

#10: The Ten Basic Truths Learned From Watching Geese (Chapter 12)

#11: The 11 Core Values of Highly Effective Organizations (Chapter 4)

#12: The 12 Leadership Competencies (Chapter 4)

#20: The 20 Workplace Success Nuggets (Chapter 8)

#40: The 40 Exercises for your Application (Throughout the Book)

Your organization not only *needs* but *requires* improved leadership today and into the future. It's a matter of survival in the global marketplace. Be that leader when called upon. I trust you'll know the when, the why, and the how.

Welcome to *Leader or Not, Here I Come!* I challenge you to take time during this reading to reflect and then apply what you're learning. Remember, the start of your leadership journey begins with learning the key concepts and tools and then experiencing/applying them on your job. Once the journey has begun, gain proficiency in using the tools and concepts, obtain wisdom along the way, measure your growth and success, and then be a mentor to others. Seek to leave that leadership legacy others will want to follow.

"The task of a leader is to get his people from where they are to where they have not been."

—HENRY KISSINGER

—✦—

*"My own definition of leadership is this: The **capacity and the will** to rally men and women to a common purpose and the **character which inspires** confidence."*

—KEN KESEY

—✦—

"Leadership is not magnetic personality; that can just as well be a glib tongue. It is not making friends and influencing people; this is flattery. Leadership is lifting a person's vision to higher sights, the raising of a person's performance to a higher standard, the building of a personality beyond its normal limitations."

—PETER DRUCKER

—✦—

"Gifted leadership is when heart and head—feeling and thought—meet."

—DANIEL GOLEMAN

—✦—

"Leadership cannot really be taught. It can only be caught."

—HAROLD GREEN

—✦—

"Much of leadership is about finding balance between two often conflicting activities; asserting authority and responding to the needs of others."

—KATHY LUBAR

CHAPTER 2

ARE YOU READY FOR THE JOURNEY?

As Norm in the TV series *Cheers* says: "In this dog-eat-dog world, do you ever feel as though you're wearing Milk Bone underwear?" This is, no doubt, how some of you feel on your job today. It's easy to feel like a victim in this complex, demanding world of work, wearing that Milk Bone underwear and having a bulls-eye on your back. "Why in the world would I want to venture into a leadership role? I'm getting kicked in the pants too much already."

This book is written to help you gain the confidence and skills required to venture into applied leadership—beginning with new thinking about your role(s) and a broader set of Leadership Tools. Remember, we're talking about a journey into and through leadership, not a destination or detour around the lessons of applied leadership. Your career is a journey; a continuous process of learning and improvement. In the same way, leadership development is a vital part of that career journey; it's a continuous process of learning and improvement. Where you are today on the job will NOT carry you to where you want to go. Be prepared to learn, risk, fail, risk more, learn more, succeed, and continue growing. It's a journey and an ongoing educational process.

Do You Know These Mid-Managers?

I've found that the soft underbelly of many organizations, in fact, lies at the mid-management level. This is not a matter of mid-managers being unqualified or unmotivated. Rather, it's a problem that falls right onto the laps of top management to address. You've been promoted to mid-management because you did your previous job well and you have "potential." You have a passion to perform at higher levels, but top management may not have adequately prepared or supported you in your desire to move into a leadership role. As mid-manager, you're being evaluated annually based on doing exactly what your job description reads; being recognized and rewarded for "managing" people and things. You're a work in progress in terms of management and leadership skill development, becoming seasoned (defined as growing a thicker skin), and gaining confidence in your actions. The unknown question is: will your hard work actually move you forward or will your efforts merely keep you treading water?

Unfortunately, many of you might be enduring that endless process of maturing into leadership through ineffective or non-existent mentoring and second-guessing from well-meaning peers or supervisors. Your growth plan is limited to what you're learning on-the-job, taking learning cues based on the management and leadership styles of those above and around you—which may or may not be a good thing. Pressures on the job mean you don't even have time to take a breath in your role as manager and you certainly don't have a clear learning path to move ahead in building your leadership skills. Do you know any mid-managers that might be in this position?

This is why, in writing this book, I've targeted you in *mid-management.* You clearly understand the need for and are seeking opportunities to mature and become more effective on the job. Yes, you want to advance in your career, but you need to earn that advancement by doing the best job possible—beginning today. I've been there, feeling frustrated and stressed on the job. In addition, I've been confused with my role as manager, my interest in leadership growth, and the level of support I'd receive (or did not receive) from top management. I may be wrong but I'll bet many of you have already attempted to step out into leadership but have been blocked or discouraged along the way. Hello Milk Bone Underwear!!! In my opinion, mid-management is one of the most difficult positions in the organization. Do you ever feel like staying in bed in the morning, wanting to pull the covers up over your head? Calling in for a "sick day" is not an acceptable strategy for growing into leadership.

I fondly refer to you in mid-management as the *"Toasted Cheese Sandwich Crowd."* Yes, I may be a cheese-head from Wisconsin but I believe this description fits for many of you.

You're being pressed and toasted from above by senior officials expecting more from you. You're being pressed and toasted by staff directly reporting to you expecting you to move mountains to improve their work barriers. Guess what? You're having the cheese-filled stuffing squeezed out of you, running out over the sides like a toasted cheese sandwich. You know your role in mid-management is vital but you want to grow in leadership to become a more important part of your organization's growth. You don't want to be a toasted cheese sandwich forever.

You don't have time to think much less plan, and your energy level is often down to near zero. The "people issues" are becoming a bother and a pain. You're tending to become more efficient and demanding as you "manage" your team—

not lead them. Everyone seems hyper-focused on the latest crisis and urgent task-level activities rather than on effective planning, continuous improvement, and achieving key results that will make a significant difference in the success of your team and the organization. Help!!!!!!! *If YOU'RE not leading others from two steps behind; you're leaving your team five steps behind.* The same is true for you. If you're not receiving leadership, maybe you too are being left behind.

Follow the Leader

Do you have what it takes to be an effective leader? It goes without saying that your *attitude* during this journey is the most critical predictor of success. What is your current attitude or thinking concerning your leadership role and how will you achieve your preferred vision? Does your attitude have you wearing that milk-bone underwear or do you see yourself having buns of steel—able to take the hits and continue the journey?

While I will be referencing the many trials and tribulations during your journey, I want you to see a light at the end of the tunnel. That light doesn't have to be another train; it can be your preferred future.

Let's begin freeing up your attitude by recognizing that you are NOT limited by your present circumstances or your present career position. The minute you feel you are without choices or are trapped in the job is when you become at risk for that dreaded "workplace burn-out and bum-out." YOU DO HAVE CHOICES and your professional future will be guided by the choices you make today. If you're unwilling or feel you're unable to assume leadership over your own choices, how will you be able to lead others (generating the required "follower-ship") into and through major change and challenging leadership issues? Remember, choices are good! Your journey must begin with a positive and proactive ATTITUDE as step one.

EXERCISE #1: Let's begin by looking at those in leadership positions within your organization. I want you to identify those in your organization that you feel are truly "great leaders" and those who might be the obvious "weak leaders."

- Write down at least five attributes and characteristics that separate the great leaders from those who might be "less than great."

- Describe the impact those great leaders have on the overall organization. How do these leaders positively impact you and your department(s)?

- What attributes do you most admire in these great leaders? How do YOU measure up in terms of "living" those desirable attributes you identified in these great leaders?

I'm asking you to reflect on the important attributes you see "lived" in these great leaders and the undesirable attributes you find in the weaker leaders. If you need help in defining "attributes," consider how trustworthy the various individuals are, how they problem-solve, how they generate follower-ship, or their ability to communicate effectively. Do the words attitude, character, competence, focus, and will come to mind? What constitutes "leadership" in your mind?

No doubt, you can easily identify the positive role models within your organization. Isn't it interesting how easy it is to identify effective leadership when you see it and take time to reflect upon it? On the other hand, you can also easily identify and learn a lot from weak leaders. We're all examples—either good ones or bad ones. Don't forget that your team and peers are watching you each day, as well. Do they see you as having potential to become a great leader? Learn from and attempt to model the great leaders in your organization and strive to grow in spite of (not model) the weak leaders.

I'm quite sure that your CEO is an effective leader, because survival of the organization is depending upon it. True senior leaders of an organization recognize that part of the organization's future depends on growing new and even more effective leaders. They, in fact, need you to grow in leadership. On the other hand, you as a mid-manager need effective senior leaders who recognize and support your role as both an effective manager and an effective leader.

The relationship between management and leadership roles, responsibilities, and levels within the organization can be very complex, and will vary greatly based on organizational circumstances, history, personality, workplace culture, and style. I will address ways that management and leadership relate in Chapter 3, but for now, simply know that your role as a manager is vital as is the need for you to grow into leadership. The organization is not one-dimensional; your role in the organization is not one-dimensional either. *The Key is to position yourself as a mid-manager "in transition" to becoming tomorrow's leader.*

The saying that "we're often over managed and under led" is true for many organizations because, too often, senior officials are more focused on their management role as opposed to their leadership role. Think back to identifying the weak leaders in Exercise #1. Aren't some of them actually functioning as senior-level managers rather than senior leaders? For some, they still see their managing role as being easier and clearer than their role in leadership.

Those still functioning as senior-level managers (not leaders) have a direct impact on your role, often leading to your being micromanaged and under led. This over-focus on managing often creates a leadership gap. This can be both good and bad for you. Being under-led is terrible. However, being under-led does create an opportunity for you to venture carefully into leadership. Bottom line is, *Leader or Not, Here I Come!*

Your decision is whether or not you wish to help fill this leadership gap. If the answer is YES, your management and leadership roles must be customized based on the strengths (and weaknesses) of those around you—including the roles being played by your senior officials. Effective organizations need both management and leadership functions performed with excellence yet in a coordinated manner. All levels of the organization must address this leadership coordination and performance excellence challenge. In short, this challenge presents a set of leadership opportunities for you.

Three Interrelated Roles

Since the focus of this book is on effective leadership, it's necessary to address how the roles of management and leadership relate. That is, how are they similar, how are they complementary, and how do they differ? In addition to addressing these questions, I'll be introducing a relatively new form of leadership—one that tends to be found primarily in highly effective organizations. I refer to this new role as the Change Leadership Model and will address it in Chapter 6.

Here are the three interrelated roles that will be reviewed in the next few Chapters:

- The traditional view of management.

- The traditional view of leadership, in partnership with management. The role for traditional leaders is to have managers focus on advancing and then implementing needed change utilizing the influence and authority of their management position.

- The "change leadership" model, which is found in most highly effective organizations. This role does not require the influence or authority of a management position—it's available to anyone and everyone in the organization. Change leadership does not substitute for the traditional leadership role; it supplements it.

Highly effective organizations need all three roles performed with excellence:

- The management function performed with excellence by mid-managers.

The leadership process involves having others "catch" the change vision as they (and the organization) let go of an old vision.

- The traditional leadership role performed by both managers and leaders

- The change leadership model performed by individuals at all levels throughout the organization.

In contrast, poorly run organizations get hung up on and tend to focus on managing people, things, and processes. They consistently function from the top down, with the leadership resting solely at the very top of the organization chart—with most senior officials being senior "managers" rather than leaders. Truth is, these organizations tend to be simply over managed and under led.

Whether your primary role is that of mid-manager or a senior leader, the impact that effective leadership has on the organization is the same. That is, effective leadership will have a positive, measurable, significant impact on the organization. If you are successful in exercising leadership effectively as a mid-manager, it will ultimately affect your career positively—trust me!

Are You Ready?

Leadership opportunities thrive throughout every organization. I challenge you to come to work each day prepared for leadership and discover those leadership opportunities when they present themselves. You'll know it when you're called upon to deliver. Is this something YOU can decide to do or must it be blessed from top-level leaders? If you're waiting for an invitation or permission, you may have a very long wait. Obviously, timing and opportunity must be right for you to jump into a leadership situation. The key questions, however, are: Do you see the right opportunities to lead? If found, are you ready to jump into this new role, using all the wisdom you've acquired to date? Be prepared to get the job done when called upon; be prepared to provide the needed leadership effectively. *Leader or Not, Here I Come!*

Start From Where You Are Today

I've found that for effective, meaningful change to occur in almost any situation, individuals, as well as, organizations must FIRST have an accurate and complete understanding of where they are TODAY. You're not only *going toward* wherever the proposed leadership initiative or change will take you, you're *departing from* where you are today. The leadership process involves having others "catch" the change vision as they (and the organization) let go of an old vision. It's been said that every breakthrough must begin with a break from. That's a two-fold tool for your Leadership Toolbox; know where you're going from AND going toward.

Leadership requires much more than the decision to take a wild leap of faith into change. You must have a common understanding of today's realities, understand the opportunities found in the new vision, and use drivers from both perspectives to draw others toward this new vision. THEN you can begin to proactively plan and take the actions appropriate to move from this starting point toward your leadership vision and strategic goals. Unfortunately, too many individuals and organizations become impatient, wanting to begin by taking future-oriented action steps, overlooking the critical step of accurately assessing where individuals and the organization are today. Leadership is "not the art of who can take the first bold, macho, action steps." You don't just move ideas—*you must move people* and *move the organization*. The unasked question often preventing staff from moving forward is: "Why should I move (change) from something I now do well, in order to do things I don't know how to do?" If you want to be successful in change, you'd better answer that question directly and early in the change process.

What Is A Paradigm?

Before going further, perhaps I need to clarify the term "paradigm." It is a word I use frequently in this book. Paradigm means a perception, assumption, or frame of reference that drives how you view your world and/or workplace situations. A paradigm is a mental picture that defines reality for you and it's the "mental filter" you use to make decisions as to what changes will or will not work. You have many paradigms, which may reflect an accurate or inaccurate perception of reality. However, they're your paradigms and you will stick with them until new circumstances or additional knowledge opens you to new thinking.

Here are three examples of paradigms that reflect faulty thinking:

- When Christopher Columbus set sail for the new world, most thought he'd sail off the end of the earth. Obviously, new knowledge changed people's paradigm.

- For me, I believed in Santa Claus until I was eight years old. "What, you mean Santa isn't real???"

- For some mid-managers and team members, they believe that only senior officials have a role to play in leadership. If that's the case, I guess we're all robots and "yes" men and women.

These are examples of paradigms—and all three reflect wrong thinking. Can someone survive in the workplace with wrong or outdated paradigms? The answer is probably yes, but will these paradigms move them and the organization forward in a highly competitive marketplace? The long-term answer is NO. Wrong paradigms hurt progressive, growing organizations, and serve to support the status quo.

Senior leaders, teams, and managers need common paradigms from which to begin the change process. Achieving these common paradigms and understanding of realities will save you many sleepless nights and needless stress as you press forward into leadership. Your approach to change must include strategies to shift the paradigms and understandings of staff over time. This is a Leadership Tool and strategy you need to remember.

There are two paradigm shifts or barriers that must be addressed:

- The paradigm among many staff is that complacency or maintaining the status quo is an okay thing. Go back to the unasked question on staff willingness to change as referenced above. It must be answered and addressed directly to obtain needed staff buy-in.

- The paradigm held by many senior officials is a belief that once an action toward the desired change has been initiated, their job is completed. Their job requires them to go far beyond simply getting the ball rolling. Effective monitoring, continued support, and follow-through often falls off the table for these officials.

Many senior officials and staff are either fearful or unable to change their paradigms, even in the midst of crisis. That's why, for too many organizations, the term "frozen in place" is alive and fully functioning.

Effective leadership begins with YOU having accurate and positive paradigms regarding your role in leadership followed by your ability to help others develop a common understanding of today's realities. These Leadership Tools are often overlooked, and both are critical to your success in leadership. Based on your paradigms (whether accurate or inaccurate), your attitudes, motives, behaviors, and actions are exposed and seen by others. You cannot lead others if you feel you're unworthy or believe you can't lead as a mid-manager or you're unable to shift others off their current paradigms. Change involves change—within yourself and your ability to help others change. No one said it would be easy, but it is doable and it is required.

The P-D-C-A Cycle

One Leadership Tool to help you enter and work through the process of change is the Shewhart Cycle for continuous improvement. This tool involves a four stage cycle of actions to greatly enhance the likelihood that change will be effectively implemented. This Cycle is built on the paradigm of meaningful planning, testing the planned change, followed by careful implementation, and the concept of making continuous improvements during and after the process of change.

The Shewhart Cycle has four stages: Plan-Do-Check-Act (P-D-C-A). The following illustrates how the PDCA Cycle would be applied to change:

- "P"—PLANNING. Documenting a change and change process that clearly defines where you want to go, why the change is needed, and how you will get there. This involves effective communication, collaboration, and a plan of action that will successfully move others toward a given change. The planning must include a complete set of strategies to move individuals and the organization toward the desired change. It involves the assessment of current realities, effectively communicating the new vision (after the change), and the process of transitioning individuals and the organization toward the new vision.

    Identify and clarify the areas of major change required to reach the vision.

    Determine the data required and collect the appropriate, accurate information to form targeted strategies and actions necessary to accomplish each of the major areas of change.

    Plan the change process steps and communicate effectively with those responsible for action.

    Deploy (communicate) the Plan and vision throughout the organization.

- "D"—DOING. First pilot the change to determine the effectiveness of the actions and strategies as outlined in the Plan. This could involve formally beginning the full change process or testing the change with a control group or obtaining ongoing feedback from a broader group of stakeholders and customers.

Conduct the piloted (change) process.

Those responsible for success of the change should carry out duties according to the Plan.

Monitor the pilot activities carefully and obtain feedback.

- "C"—CHECKING. Monitor results of the pilot conducted in the DOING stage. Carefully identify all improvement opportunities in processes, communications, planning, progress, or direction. As appropriate, be prepared to modify the original change PLAN.

  Collect and analyze feedback and data on the piloted change process.

  Ask the question: "Will the change be successful and the desired results be achieved?"

  What secondary changes need to be added to achieve the results desired?

  Plan subsequent changes and communicate with those responsible for action.

- "A"—ACTING. Formally implement the process of change based on what was learned from the DOING and CHECKING stages. The ACTING stage is designed to make final improvements in the planned change, formalize and implement the change processes to completion, and set up measures and strategies to ensure long-term success.

  Implement the changes with a greater degree of confidence.

  Document the impact this change has had against planned impact.

  This ACTING Stage must continue indefinitely, including re-visiting the PDCA Cycle regularly to discover and implement ongoing improvements in processes and actions.

The success of this Cycle, however, begins with proper PLANNING. If you do not Plan your future actions based on a thorough understanding of the issues, current realities, change strategies, responsibilities, support systems, and success indicators, your leadership improvement path is likely to be a hastily designed Plan followed by do, do, do, do (over). You end up a bunch of "do-do." If the proposed change is important enough for the organization to seriously pursue, then it's important enough for you as a leader to follow the PDCA Cycle—and do it right.

EXERCISE #2: Apply the P-D-C-A Cycle to your leadership quest by writing down your answers to the questions or statements below. You are now beginning to prepare for your leadership journey by laying out a "plan" followed by a commitment in order to clarify and re-direct your decision-making process as necessary along the way.

- Objectively identify your current leadership strengths and weaknesses. Then identify the greatest opportunities for you to improve in your areas of greatest weakness. (Assessment of CURRENT REALITIES)

- Where do you want your leadership career to take you in the next three years? (Short-term VISION for your leadership journey)

- What are the key strategies, action steps, and timelines you envision to accomplish your personal leadership vision and how will you measure your success in leadership? (PLAN)

- The next two questions are future oriented. To the best of your ability today, are you committed to answer "Yes" to the following action steps (Yes or No)?

  > Are you willing to commit to implementing or at least piloting the action steps in your Plan and, over time, noting what's going right and what's going wrong? (DO)

  > Based on what you learn from piloting these implementation steps, are you prepared to make strategic and tactical changes to your original Plan? (CHECK).

  > Are you prepared and committed to act on this growth plan? (ACT)

The PDCA Cycle is an important tool for your Leadership Toolbox because the processes of change and continuous improvement are essential elements of effective leadership. Plans and actions must be continuously monitored, improved, and updated if progress is to be made toward your vision of success. *Make sure you plan and implement effectively as you seek continuous improvement in change as well as your leadership—always.*

Now that you have at least a working knowledge of PDCA, consider applying it to a major project you are undertaking on the job. I encourage you to learn it well and apply it often.

Test Run—See the Leadership Opportunities

EXERCISE #3: This Exercise requires a focused, serious discussion with your supervisor concerning key opportunities for change and improvement in your areas of responsibility.

- Write down the three to five of the most significant changes or improvements *you* could make that would have the greatest, positive impact on your team's performance and serve to benefit your organization the most. Think big!

- Then, have a discussion on this topic with your supervisor, *without sharing* the list of three to five items you've identified. Write down what *your supervisor* feels are the most critical changes or improvements YOU should make to help your team's performance?

- Next, share your initial list with your supervisor and discuss the similarities and differences between his list and yours.

- The goal of this Exercise is for the two of you to reach agreement on one common listing of three changes *you* should be making—and why.

This may sound like an obvious discussion with your supervisor, one that should be done as part of the annual goal setting process or personal evaluation process. But this *is* different. The focus is not on the organization's goal attainment—it's about you making personal improvement changes in order to improve your team's performance. Since this is something that you and your supervisor have jointly prepared and agreed upon, you'll most likely have her or his support during the implementation process. You'd be surprised how seldom targeted personal improvement discussion and collaboration actually occurs in the workplace. Equally rare is full accomplishment of the three changes or improvements identified in a timely manner. In addition to the leadership opportunities identified, this Exercise serves notice to your supervisor and others that you're taking the risks necessary to step out into leadership.

After reaching agreement on these initiatives, you may want to prepare a PDCA Cycle for each of the top three change improvements agreed upon. You will then have a planned approach to successfully implement and monitor these change processes.

EXERCISE #4: Okay, you and your supervisor have identified a set of significant change initiatives you are both committed to implementing. I challenge you to take this Exercise one step further. Have this same discussion with your team.

Repeat the process used in Exercise #3 above. You'll open up a world of opportunity of NEW thinking and change for your team members. Your role as manager should involve far more than controlling and managing progress toward established goals. It should also include identifying and seizing opportunities for change and continuous improvement that add significant value to your team, as well as, to other departments.

Your role in leadership involves changing what and how individuals and teams THINK.

Ask your team to identify three to five changes YOU could make to help the team's overall performance. Do this without sharing the list you and your supervisor developed.

- Write down the specific changes your team identifies as priorities—and why.

- What actions need to take place to secure the support of your team members in these changes?

- Write down the areas of support and assistance you will need from your supervisor and other departments to accomplish these changes—and why.

Through these two Exercises, you have experienced how to drive change and continuous improvement in YOUR actions and outcomes while still in your current role as mid-manager. What you've done is to drive collaborative dialog and change in thinking about common priorities and actions—beginning with YOUR thinking and actions. In addition, you've prepared a plan of action to achieve broad-based buy-in to accomplish these priorities. This is a reflection of your ability to create the proper paradigm and the common understanding discussed earlier.

The result of effective management is changing what individuals and teams DO. Your management role is made far more effective if it's tied to leadership. *Your role in leadership involves changing what and how individuals and teams THINK.* The Leadership Tool being advanced at this time is to begin changing your own "thinking;" then to change the thinking of others, and finally to act on this planning to achieve the desired results.

The Hidden Risks in These Exercises

In the last two Exercises, you've placed yourself at risk by asking both your supervisor and your team how YOU need to change to make things better for others. There is one major problem that could arise, however. What if the list your supervisor suggests in Exercise #3 is in direct conflict with what the team suggests in Exercise #4? You're about to enter the second level of leadership, sometimes known as the "Twilight Zone." That is, leading the process of achieving one common prioritization of changes between you, your supervisor, and your team. For success, you need this alignment of understanding and support. What you don't want is a conflicting set of three action priorities. Do not set yourself up for failure.

If you're successful in negotiating one common plan of action with your supervisor and your team, you've provided effective leadership and exhibited needed communication skills. If not, you've experienced a real-life learning curve. Without alignment and agreement on these changes, you're setting yourself up for some serious lessons in damage control and crisis management. Remember, a common plan of direction and action are critical first steps in experiencing effective leadership. While change can occur without this alignment, it's obviously much easier with it. If leadership is not coming from the top of the organization chart, then you do it from two steps behind.

Now here's the "oh-oh." Let's say you've successfully received agreement on three change initiatives and the common plan of action. Now what? You've raised the expectations of your supervisor, peers, and team. They're watching to see what you will do with this input and listing of opportunities for improvement. It's crunch time; it's time to deliver.

- If you do nothing, you've wasted everyone's valuable time and lost credibility.

- If you begin the planning and implementation processes to move toward these changes, you'd better have your full set of management *and* leadership tools close at hand so you can follow through in achieving what you've started.

    You, your supervisor, and your team need to seek the required degree of buy-in and support from others. (e.g., IT, accounting, HR, your peers)

    If you are unable to implement the changes within an acceptable timeline, be proactive in sharing honest feedback on your progress and your learning experiences (not excuses, but knowledge gained), and be prepared to offer a well thought-out, alternate approach.

    Staff can accept that problems and modified planning are part of any improvement process (the PDCA Cycle). However, what staff will not accept is poor communication, misleading or blaming excuses, or lack of a meaningful correction plan.

- If, however, you do succeed in implementing the changes agreed upon, you've grown in your thinking, skills, and credibility. Just as importantly, you've positioned yourself properly for the next level of opportunity that WILL come your way. Finally, I urge you to document the "impact" implemented changes actually had on you and your team's performance. Communicate this documentation appropriately. Without documentation of the "so what" factor, you have not closed the leadership loop. Finish what you've begun and make sure that the changes you've implemented are appropriately communicated.

It sounds so simple, doesn't it! We all know the challenges and risks involved, but I encourage you to take these risks with your supervisor and your team. In this Test Run, you:

- Went public ASKING for input and support.
- Balanced diverse interests and opinions to form a common set of actions—achieving agreement on priorities with key stakeholders.
- Solicited help from others for the greater good.
- Managed the planning and follow-up modifications through the PDCA Cycle.
- Monitored and managed the change process implementation.
- Documented and communicated the "so what" factor.

Take this test flight; spread your wings. Like it or not, you're on the "learning bubble." You cannot reach for "change leadership" while sitting inside your comfort zone.

Tricks or Tools?

This journey into leadership will require a deeper understanding of the workplace dynamics, the real and priority needs of your team, your organization's goals, and your own growth in this leadership quest. This book is not about parlor tricks, short cuts, smoke and mirrors, or fast-talking. Learning to be an effective leader does not have a short-cut. It's about YOU choosing to be proactive in assuming greater leadership and learning as you apply the basic tools of leadership day-by-day. It requires both a revelation in thinking AND a hard knocks learning approach with experiences based on trial, error, and growth. You can't go "around" these trials and errors; you must go through them. Look for those daily opportunities to apply the tools and paradigms being advanced in this section.

Five-Level Skill Development Approach to Learning

Each day, you must look for opportunities to APPLY the tools and perspectives you're learning. I suggest you consider the following five-step approach to learning and experiencing leadership growth:

1. Be committed to going beyond "business as usual." Have the paradigms that keep you open to new opportunities and the concept of change.

2. Improve your communication strategies, styles, and skills in addressing change. Staff needs to "understand" the expectations being placed on them during and after the change, and the anticipated outcome once the change is successful.

3. Transfer your change vision and passion effectively through your communication, actions, and forms of recognition with those who must help you move change forward. Do things that will allow others to "catch" your vision and "buy-into" your future change initiatives.

4. Focus on the few, right priorities and be there to support your staff as they take on added duties and risks relating to change. Be certain you are there for them when things go "bump in the night."

5. Elevate and continually improve the overall level of your own job performance. You must walk the talk—daily—in every way.

EXERCISE #5: The Five-Level Skill Development Approach referenced above addresses ways you can increase your effectiveness in advancing change and implementing improvements. While these points may appear obvious, they do represent "moments of truth" as you pursue opportunities for improvement in your day-to-day leadership journey.

- Re-read the five points above. Do you agree or disagree with each of these five skill areas? Why or why not?

- Write down two change challenges you are currently experiencing.

- Among the Five-Levels above, how many have you successfully applied as you move forward in the two change challenges just identified? Which of the Five-Levels is the most challenging for you—and why?

Two Additional Dimensions of Leadership

As you address each of the 40 Exercises in this book and begin applying new Leadership Tools on-the-job, there are two additional dimensions of leadership you need to factor into your decision-making and actions.

- *Leadership is an art, not a science.* It's an art because leadership involves people doing things for and with other people—requiring effective people-to-people relations. I've seen many talented individuals "fall out of leadership" because they believed they've found the one "system" that fits every challenge. WRONG!!! You must customize your approach, communication, and strategies to every leadership challenge because you're dealing with hard working, talented, and sometimes skeptical people. In developing your art of leadership, I suggest you focus on:

  Having the right mindset.

  Having a willingness to get outside your own comfort zone.

  Knowing how to identify and then do the right things.

  Measuring your success in terms of having the maximum positive impact on the organization and on others.

- *Become a student in learning the culture issues that affect individuals and teams.* The interpersonal dynamics within your organization will have a critical impact on your leadership success—both good and bad. Each organization has its own culture, tone and tempo, which adds to the challenges of leadership. Do not underestimate the history, personalities, and comfort zones that staff have experienced and fallen into. We call these things "culture" but they represent a huge barrier you have to overcome on your way to the future. Understand the culture, and treat it as a real and important consideration in the change process.

I believe there's a direct correlation between workplace culture and how people, processes, paradigms, and plans are actually aligned. If there are major problems with inefficient processes or self-centered managers or poor leadership, you WILL have a chaotic workplace culture. Merely aligning staff, processes, and plans will not, in itself, create an effective culture and new paradigms. The answers are found in creating deeper leadership strategies—not surface quick fixes. No organization will achieve the level of high effectiveness without a highly effective workplace culture. This requires "artfully" applied leadership.

Ready, Fire, Aim

Moving into leadership is easy—simply take the first step, with wisdom. To move "through" leadership, however, requires a long-term commitment, investment of time and energy, and taking risks by making changes in YOUR leadership paradigm and Leadership Toolbox. It's about possessing the right thinking, tools, and framework for doing right things, in the right ways, for the right reasons—and doing this through and for others. The question is, when WILL you be ready to lead? When is the right time?

To answer these questions, I might draw a comparison to someone debating whether or when to buy a new laptop computer. Computer pricing and technology is changing constantly; "maybe you should wait until next year." Likewise, if you're hesitant about learning to lead, I guess you could always wait until next year. However, what will be lost in the form of "opportunity" and "timing" for both you and the organization if you delay spreading your leadership wings?

You're probably not alone in questioning your readiness for the leap into leadership. At the personal level, your decision to act represents a battle of desire versus fear versus opportunity. Which is your driver? Is your desire and confidence in stepping out into leadership greater than your fear of the challenge (fear of failure)? What's the opportunity to gain or lose? If you're genuinely fearful, the fear of failure will invite your failure. Your passion (with wisdom) must be at a level to drive your entry into leadership. Otherwise, you're better off waiting until next year.

At the 100% level, you WILL have questions or concerns about taking those first steps into leadership, and that's OK. However, fear of leading is not healthy. One lesson I learned is, having an objective awareness of the complexities of your organization and the risks tied to moving into and through leadership is healthy. At the same time, having an objective awareness of your readiness and willingness to venture into leadership is also required. While this "awareness" is very important, it must be factored into your "personal risk tolerance" when presented with an opportunity to assume leadership. If you wait until all conditions are perfect and you're fully ready to lead, it WILL be too late. I'm not talking about READY, AIM, AIM, AIM—then FIRE. While this may be the preferred approach as to your comfort level, it's not how leadership opportunities generally present themselves.

For most of you, the likely track into leadership will follow a Ready, *Fire*, Aim approach rather than Ready, *Aim*, Fire. This "ready or not" approach to begin your journey usually accompanies the flow of major leadership opportunities that you'll be discovering. Opportunities for leadership will appear at the most unexpected times. Are you going to buy that computer now? Are you going to take this opportunity and run with it…now? The choice is before you…now! While a detailed, well thought out, and approved plan of action is highly desirable, don't expect it to be part of your leadership opportunity package. That's why effective leadership is rare. It's because the organization is moving in one direction and most often the opportunity is coming at you from another direction. When these two forces intersect, you must make the decision—whether to jump into leadership, or not. This is called risk or "crunch time."

For many, the opportunity for leadership will occur something like this. It's a normal day at work and, while the pace is hectic, you're still able to take it in stride. Then, out of the blue, a leadership opportunity or management crisis will present itself and you'll find yourself at the threshold of jumping into that leadership role. Believe me, it will feel like READY, FIRE, AIM. Your decision could place you at some risk, you have not necessarily been anointed to lead, you have not thought out your best plan and frankly you would rather someone else step forward to lead. However, you're the one on the bubble today. Expect to win many and lose some—but don't get paralyzed by it. Without risk there can be little opportunity and without opportunity there will be NO leadership.

The lesson here is to prepare you for the timing and the way you will most likely be thrust into that leadership role. Readiness is often more a state of mind than it is a state of preparedness. This may be a somewhat negative thought, but even if you're not 100% successful in this one leadership opportunity, you have gained new and rich leadership experiences and sent the signal to others that you want to grow into leadership. Remember, with any failure comes wisdom and with wisdom rests hope and with hope you will find opportunity. If security and safety are what's driving you, stay in bed and stay out of the temptation to be a leader. It's not a cakewalk experience or a role for the faint of heart. Be prepared to *Ready, Fire, Aim*, even if you're not completely equipped..

The Leader's Two-Step

Let's be straight forward about this leadership thing. If you're not helping your organization move forward, you're allowing the organization to slide backward. There is no such thing as an organization being stationary over time. This is due to the fact that your competitors are closing in and your customers are not afraid of moving to your competition. You're either providing leadership to position the organization for future growth and success or you're allowing the organization to maintain a status quo or back-sliding position. The organization must WANT the high ground position and WANT leadership—your leadership. Creativity and willingness to change comes from within individuals and must be found throughout the organization. It requires intrinsic motivation for individuals to step forward—from within, for all the right reasons. While you and other leaders may want change, how do you get the critical mass to want it as well?

You may see a leadership change opportunity and desire to step forward but your supervisor or senior officials may be doing the "sideways two-step" and not supporting you. In addition, you may find other managers taking "two-steps backwards" allowing you to sink or swim alone. While you may have the willingness to lead, you WILL have occasions when you're forced to be "two-steps out front," and it can be very lonely and frightening out there. Be aware of this two-step dance that WILL undoubtedly be performed by those around you during your journey. I can't protect you from this leadership dance; but I *can* give you tools to improve your approach and strategies to achieve the desired change. Be a student in the art of leadership and learn to survive the two-step dance during the change process.

Approach the process of change by first exploring the need to change yourself. Then, boldly build it outward to relationships, teams, your organization, and then to other organizations. What you really want is for the team and others to say is that, "we did a great job on our own" or "that change was actually easier than we thought it would be." YOU don't have to get direct credit and, in fact, do you really need it? You fulfilled your role as a leader by moving others to follow your change idea. Together, change was implemented. By osmosis, you will get the credit deserved—but from two steps behind. What did you do? You were a leader and saw the organization and others succeed. Isn't that an honorable goal to start with? It isn't false or fake humility. It's about positioning your strategy to lead for, with, and through others. Let THEM celebrate the success of leadership with you. As they succeed, you will succeed.

We often feel trapped into doing what we've always been doing and having a genuine fear about stepping out in public to take real risks. It's lonely out there on that leadership limb. If you defer or take a two-step around that opportunity to engage in the art of leadership, what have you gained? What have you lost? Only you can answer those questions, and they're very situational. Think of this. When you're on your deathbed, what will you truly value in your life? Success should be defined more broadly than simply "outliving your pallbearers." While survival on the job is vital, so is realizing your potential and experiencing your dreams. Live your leadership dream by keeping that bounce in your step, that grin on your face, and that tune in your head—people will wonder what you're up to. Make yourself better every day so you will add value to your organization and to others when that leadership opportunity comes. It isn't really a dog-eat-dog world out there. It merely contains some narrow, misguided, difficult people and circumstances to overcome. Get beyond yourself, rise above those difficult people and circumstances, and grow your personalized brand of effective leadership. Guess what—you'll win, and so will others. Be prepared to lead.

With all of this said, the base-line question is: *Are you ready for this leadership journey?* You must answer that question and act on your answer accordingly. It is not an exercise to be completed; it's a choice, a decision, and a commitment to be made. There is no right or wrong answer. It's simply a matter of what's best for you at this time. If it's right—take the challenge. It's your career!

"Management works IN the system; Leadership works ON the system."

—Stephen Covey

⤙⤚

*"Leaders must be close enough to relate to others,
but far ahead enough to motivate."*

—John Maxwell

⤙⤚

*"People ask the difference between a leader and a boss.
The leader leads, and the boss drives."*

—Theodore Roosevelt

⤙⤚

*"Control is not leadership; management is not leadership;
leadership is leadership. If you seek to lead, invest at least
50% of your time in leading yourself—your own purpose, ethics,
principles, motivation, and conduct. Invest at least 20% leading
those with authority over you and 15% leading your peers."*

—Dee Hock

⤙⤚

*"Leadership must be based on goodwill. Goodwill does not mean
posturing and, least of all, pandering to the mob. It means obvious
and wholehearted commitment to helping followers. We are tired of
leaders we fear, tired of leaders we love, and of tired leaders who let us
take liberties with them. What we need for leaders are men of heart
who are so helpful that they, in effect, do away with the need of their
jobs. But leaders like that are never out of a job, never out of followers.
Strange as it sounds, great leaders gain authority by giving it away."*

—Admiral James Stockdale

CHAPTER 3

MANAGEMENT AND LEADERSHIP— TOGETHER FOREVER

Producers "do it." Managers "delegate it."

Leaders decide what "it" is.

The above heading references the role of producers, managers, and leaders, making "IT" seem so simple. While not found in highly effective organizations, many organizations simply have a delineation of roles that looks something like this: front line employees who do the front line work, managers who bark orders and make front-line decisions, and leaders who have little or no direct contact with those working on the front line. In contrast, highly effective organizations often go out of their way NOT to define leadership by a corner office location or position title or years of experience or academic credentials. They find ways to develop a common understanding of what "IT" means to the producers, managers, and leaders. To them, "IT" spells success. To achieve this success you must have real leadership to involve the total organization in this quest.

If, internally, all staff in an organization can define "IT" in the same way, we'd see everyone moving in a similar direction, focused on the right things, and having a common understanding of the role producers, managers, and leaders will play. All these roles must be interrelated and aligned, doing the right things in the right way, at the right time. Leaders must provide needed direction and support for producers and managers as they accomplish "IT." Whatever "IT" might be, *everyone* in the organization must know it and be driven toward achieving that point of focus and success.

One thing that I've learned over the years is that *every* organization is perfectly aligned to achieve what it's currently achieving—whether that's high performance or dysfunctional performance. What do you do if the organization now wishes to achieve something new, like raising itself to the next level of competitiveness or performance? A new "IT" is needed, and that will require both leadership and management to act in concert supporting those on the front line who actually produce and deliver the products and services. It must *result* in a *realignment* of the roles, thinking, acting, and outcomes for all staff. You cannot have half the organization still functioning under the old system while the other half is changing to move toward a new vision. That organization would be perfectly aligned (or misaligned) to achieve backsliding. The operative positioning for success in *any* organization wishing to move to the next level of performance is "achieving proper *alignment* of its plans, people, processes, and paradigms." This would include having the roles of managers and leaders being closely aligned and driven toward the same "IT."

Producers Don't Just Get "IT" Done—They Make *You* Look Good

I will be focusing on the role of managers and leaders throughout this Chapter, but first I must make a strong case for the caring, connecting, and mentoring of your front line staff; the Producers. I'll simply say—"you're not seeing the big picture if you don't see and treat these individuals as your greatest assets." Understand that your front line staff are far more than the "worker bees." They can and will make you look very good or very bad. You want to be successful? Make sure they're successful, but don't confuse their success with keeping them happy at all times and at all costs. Your goal is to gain and then retain their respect and trust—not their love.

Treat them well because you sincerely care about their success—and the impact they have on success for the organization. Connect with their real needs and ideas because you need to learn a great deal from them. Mentor them so they too can grow. I'm sure you know peer managers who are so full of themselves that they have no room to recognize those on the front line who are working so hard to make them look so good. With all humility, include the following tool in your Leadership Toolbox: *Honor your team members, individually, and collectively, as you work to see them succeed and then, together, work to move the organization toward success.*

Differences Between Organizations and Leaders

You already know that not all organizations are created equal or perform at equal levels of excellence. Neither do managers and leaders. Big surprise! We come in all sorts of shapes and sizes, with our own set of strengths and weaknesses as well as styles and strategies. We often find ourselves functioning in less than favorable circumstances or in dysfunctional workplace cultures or even without the necessary base of experience in which to operate successfully. But what makes some organizations successful and some unsuccessful? I've found the big difference between organizations can almost always be traced back to the caliber of their leadership. If you want to move your organization forward, you must have true leaders who can lead change and move staff paradigms and the organizational culture forward. Leaders should always remember they're in the "people improvement business" no matter what business they're in, and this people improvement business desperately needs effective leaders.

How often do you hear senior officials say "our people are our most important asset?" Okay, now ask their employees if they feel they're the most important asset. You may get a different answer.

EXERCISE #6: In highly effective organizations, you'll find that staff at all levels know, in a hundred different ways, that they're its greatest asset. How about your organization?

- On a scale of 1 to 10 (with 10 being a national leader in terms of organizational commitment to employees), rate how staff feel *your organization* is committed to its employees. Write down why the average employee feels that way; what is being done (or not being done) to generate that specific employee rating?

- How do you feel personally? On that 1 to 10 scale, rate this level of commitment and write down why you feel (or do not feel) like a most important asset?

- How would your "team" respond if asked to rate (on that 1 to 10 scale) *your* level of commitment to them—how your actions reflect that they're the greatest asset? Why would they give you that rating? I hope you're prepared to ask them that question directly.

We have all experienced or seen managers who do the two-step stomping all over their staff, demoralizing them and often humiliating them in public. And these managers think they're making a positive difference in helping the organization achieve its goals? Your staff IS the organization's competitive advantage and represent *you* on the front line when push comes to shove. They have choices, whether managers believe it or not. The proper care, feeding, and growing of your staff is a vital tool for your Leadership Toolbox. Use them or lose them.

Focus On The Main Things—It's What the "IT" Is.

The next Leadership Tool I'm advancing is the primary theme I'll be repeating throughout the book. Remember it well, because I will not let you forget it. The tool is: *the main thing is to keep the Main Things the main thing.* This may or may not seem profound to you now, but believe me it is a significant tool. It tells you what the "IT" is for leadership—it's the Main Things.

We often get so bound up in details, the tasks of the job, and the way we've always done things that we forget or lose sight of accomplishing the Main Things. Every day you work hard but are unable to hit the mark of true management effectiveness and growth in leadership. Part of the challenge may be the need for better time management tools or priority setting skills, but daily matters such as too many phone calls or meetings or task-level crisis issues can easily take over your day. How do you recognize and make progress in addressing the Main Things? Here's a hint on what **not** to do. You will never achieve success for the organization by simply working harder or focusing on meeting compliance rules or being the one who never creates any waves. Keeping busy and out of trouble on the job should not be confused with success.

What IS required is that you and your staff get outside of your comfort zones. It's about moving well beyond the status quo. It's about changing to achieve the Main Things. Be deliberate in defining how you measure your success on the job. Are you spending more time and effort trying to keep out of trouble or being well liked—or are you focusing on accomplishing the Main Things for the organization? Even though it may feel like you're "pushing the rope" some days, don't be afraid to hyper-focus on moving your team and the organization toward the Main Things.

What Are the Main Things?

To move toward the Main Things it's obvious that you must first gain greater understanding of what the Main Things might be for your organization. Then you can integrate this knowledge into your daily decision-making, action, and planning. Beyond *your* gaining this understanding, do others also know and understand what the Main Things are? Wouldn't it be great if everyone you worked with had a common understanding of and commitment to achieving the Main Things?

EXERCISE #7: There is a need to go beyond managing processes and people and the traditional goal-setting activities. Staff needs to clarify and reach a common understanding on what the Main Things are for their team and the organization. In this Exercise, I want you to write down:

- The three to five "Main Things" you believe that *your team* must focus on for the organization to succeed. Think creatively here—don't look at the Job Descriptions.

- Ask your team the same thing—record their answers.

- Ask your supervisor the same thing—record the answers.

- Are your answers the same as your team's and your supervisors?

- Summarize the areas of agreement and the differences.

- What changes must you and your team make to accomplish these Main Things?

I'll bet there are major differences in thought and understanding on the Main Things, aren't there? If you, your supervisor, and your team do not have a *clear and common* understanding of what the Main Things really are for your organization, is it any wonder why we find our hard work and decision-making often in conflict with others? However well intentioned, your ideas for change, priorities for improvement, and daily conflict resolution challenges are made far more difficult (and almost impossible) because your organization never developed a *clear and common understanding of the Main Things.* Yes it's a difficult and longer-term issue, but the urgent needs of our jobs often out-shout the truly important needs. This sounds so simple but is so often lacking. The Leadership Tool is: Know the Main Things and focus on moving toward them.

EXERCISE #8: Survey your supervisor and your team to identify the Main Things your *organization* was created to do by virtue of its Vision and Mission. Compete the following:

- First, *you* write down your understanding of three to five Main Things your organization was created to do.

- Next, ask your supervisor and your team that same question. Write down their answers and analyze whether there is a common level of understanding on these Main Things for the organization.

- Create one listing of the three to five Main Things the organization was created to do.

- Compare the list from Exercise #7 (above) with this listing from Exercise #8. Discuss with your supervisor and team the priority Main Things *your team* must focus on to achieve the Main Things for the *organization.*

- Now, on a strictly personal basis, *write down what the three to five Main Things are that will make the significant difference as you advance along your career path to success.* It may not be easy to identify just three to five Main Things, but give this exercise serious thought. Share these written thoughts with your supervisor if appropriate and use it to open new lines of communication and support for your career goals.

With the understanding and perspective gained through this Exercise, allow it to drive more of your daily thinking, actions, and priority setting. Begin by reflecting on one or two of the Main Things for both the organization and for your team. How might this new knowledge influence what you're currently doing, how you're doing it, and the significant impact a handful of key changes might have on the organization and others? How might you effectively communicate this understanding and perspective with your peers to possibly refocus their priorities as well? This initiative can change your meeting agendas, your communications, your way of thinking, your decision-making, and priority setting. It's a perspective that you *will not* have if all you see are the daily personnel and production crises.

You're starting to see and understand the bigger picture; the things that will make a significant difference. You're thinking more like a leader and as such, *expect* to see new opportunities unveiled in the near future. Be prepared to *act* (lead) as required based on the circumstances and opportunities before you in both your role as a manager and your emerging role as a leader.

Keep Your Eyes (and Your Car) on the Road

Here's an illustration of how your role and actions will change based on your line of sight—that is, your ability to see the Main Things more clearly. Remember when you learned to drive a car, and your eyes tended to focus on the road ten feet in front of the hood? Your steering actions were quick, jerky, unsure, and sometimes random. Your main thing at that time was to keep the car on the road by reacting to your shortsighted field of vision. As your driving abilities matured over time and you gained new skills, your line of sight moved further ahead of the car hood, more toward the horizon on the road. You began to see the bigger picture. While you were still able to see things to the side and ten feet in front of the car, your eyes now focused 1000 feet in front of the hood. You became a much safer driver because you could see both those potential dangers from oncoming traffic sooner and those urgent dangers jumping out from the curb.

You could smooth out your steering and add greater confidence to passengers as a result of having a far-sighted field of vision and context for your driving actions.

The Main Things changed from keeping your car on the road to being a skilled, proactive, and safe driver based on your new field of vision. You became more mature in your role and added value to those in your car and those in other cars. Your thinking, skills, and field of vision directly influenced your actions and performance. This is why you and your organization must have a clear and common understanding of the Main Things. Your main role is no longer attempting to keep the car or organization on the road. You want to drive safely *and* reach the desired destination. Your organization needs mature, skilled leadership, *and* better management. As you discover and build strategies and skills around the Main Things, your managerial and leadership actions will be of greater value to all parties. You'll be a better mid-manager, *and* future leader. What's your line of sight and vision field at the workplace? Is it at the tactical level (10 feet) or at the strategic level (1000 feet)? It will make a difference in your actions and priorities.

Management "AND" (not versus) Leadership

There are obvious differences between the terms Management and Leadership. But are these functions contradictory, are they adversarial, are they complementary, are these roles changing over time? The answer to all these questions is yes! From a traditional and practical sense, leadership is defined as doing the *right things*. Management is defined as doing *things right*. These are good definitions to start with because they highlight that the two roles have a different focus and function. While different, these leadership and management roles must function in a complementary manner and are both essential to the overall success of the organization. They are not independent roles; rather, they both are required to be performed with excellence and they are definitely interdependent.

Where would your organization be if it didn't honor the role played by effective mid-managers? It would have chaos, poor and inconsistent actions throughout, high employee (and CEO) turnover, wasted budgets, and undoubtedly, dissatisfied customers. Power games and those retiring on the job would control the operation. Organizations need that conductor of the orchestra to have the team function as the sheet music intended—to be delivered as originally written (processes, procedures, and timelines) with the intended "Main Thing" results achieved. Without the orchestration of effective management, you would have a perfect plan for failure.

Assess the tone,

tempo, and timing

when attempting to

balance priorities and

introduce change.

On the other hand, you can get so wrapped up in the daily grind of management trying to do things right that it's easy to lose sight of the Main Things, *the right things.* Enter the role of effective leadership, providing the sheet music for the orchestra (management) to follow. But how do you do both, and do both with excellence? I'll discuss this concept later in the book but my response to that question is that "it depends." It depends on your assessment of the tone, tempo, and sense of timing within the organization and your personal motivation to stretch and grow. *Your challenge is to know when and how to transition in and out of leadership as the need arises*—all the while having a job description and box on the organization chart that shows you as a "manager."

The greatest time commitment you face must be on your role as manager. There are major cycles in your daily, monthly, and yearly schedules that consume 120% of your time. You also experience those things that go bump in the night that require immediate action and full attention for short periods. On the other hand, there may be times of the week, month, or year, you have brief periods of time to plan and pursue needed improvement and change. Take these opportunities for leadership whenever you get them. Hone your skills, see appropriate opportunities, and take time to observe quality leadership in others. Remember, you're on a leadership journey and you're still "transitioning." Take time for leadership growth when and if you can—and then make it a priority to learn and grow along the way.

Over time and with experience, you'll gain greater wisdom to discern which tasks are *urgent* and which are *important.* This wisdom will influence your decision-making and communication skills, which are necessary to "balance" the array of priorities facing you. This is why I encourage you to assess the tone, tempo, and timing when attempting to balance priorities and introduce change. Here is a Leadership Tool to remember: *The right idea for change presented at the wrong time will be a "dead on arrival" idea—98% of the time.* On the other hand, sometimes a simple suggestion at the right time is a surprising success. With experience, you'll gain confidence in your decision-making, timing, and communication skills. You'll learn to view management and leadership as working together and know when to do either (or both). One is not good and the other bad. You must respect and devote focus to both.

It's Not Always Perfect

Have you noticed that management and leadership do get on each other's nerves once in a while? It's a little like marriage relationships, in that you respect and need each other but there are times you don't necessarily enjoy your spouse, right? On the job, when you're pressed as a manager with daily time deadlines, isn't it maddening to have some senior official come down to make a new (and seemingly unreasonable) request that must be completed by next week? At the same time, it's hard for that senior official to understand why it's taking you longer to get something done this month when it normally takes you only half that time. You respect and need each role, but you don't necessarily understand what is driving each other every day. An oversimplified solution to this dilemma is to achieve "balance and trust" in your relationships through effective communication and improved understanding of priorities. While you get frustrated with that senior official from time to time, it is important to remember that this person is likely suffering from pressure above him/her? The challenge is to be a better manager and a better leader where you are today, and get yourself prepared to be an even better leader tomorrow—when you're in that senior official position. All you can do is to learn, apply, fail, improve, and grow daily.

Leadership is not about the reward or recognition *you* receive; it's about *doing the "right things" for the right reasons to accomplish the Main Things.* Secondly, *leadership is not defined by position within the organization* and certainly not limited to the CEO in that corner office. Perhaps the bigger question is whether you're prepared to respond to a leadership challenge when it's presented. It's not about the medals or recognition you receive for your efforts. It's about the results you achieve for the organization through the efforts of others.

Traditional Definitions

Management

Management, as I learned a long time ago, revolves around planning, budgeting, and controlling the staff and resources you're responsible for. Managers make sure the "IT", or the Main Things, actually get done. They delegate and manage operations. In comparison to leadership, I view the role of management functioning more like an automobile engine that needs to be closely monitored, fueled, repaired, and finely tuned to run at peak performance. The function seems to focus on process flow, process improvement, and production (with quality). It's like driving your car by seeing the road perhaps 1000 feet in front of you, versus leadership whose looking 2,000 feet or more down the road. Compliance and consistency are highly valued and measured.

Too many organizations function in a crisis mode almost 100% of the time. Their focus is short-term and cycle-driven. Accordingly, the priority for many managers is to keep the team performing their tasks at peak efficiency and effectiveness, with success measured in short-term segments. "Now" or "immediately" or "yesterday" are often the timelines for results. Is this a critical role—absolutely. Most managers try their utmost to personalize the job for team members and initiate incremental improvements in processes and results for the organization, but the focus tends to be more at the tactical or operational level. It's tough being a good manager in light of the press for "doing more with less."

Management, like leadership, must be delivered at two levels: *at the operational level and at the strategic level.* I don't want to overlook the critical role effective managers have in supporting or even leading key operational change. They are needed for their contributions well beyond the operational functions, but are most often blocked from expanded leadership roles due to time constraints, operational culture barriers, and office egos. I urge you not to become discouraged if you don't find strategic leadership opportunities on the job first thing tomorrow. Remember that the tone, tempo, and timing for this opportunity will likely change in the future—be patient and opportunistic. In the meantime, grow as you learn, and be ready to lead when called upon.

Leadership

Leadership has more to do with higher-level direction and that vision thing—deciding what "IT" is and setting strategies to achieve the Main Things for the organization. The focus is on making the necessary decisions and changes that will drive the organization and teams toward success as the organization defines success.

The focus of leadership is on the organization-wide issues and opportunities to achieve longer-term results. Even when functioning at this strategic level, effective leaders stay close to managers for guidance and support as decisions are made on significant opportunities for improvement and change. Leadership, at the operational level, works closely with managers and is aware of the major barriers managers face in achieving the Main Things. Real leadership must focus on the vital few Main Things and, with the help of managers, rely heavily on the ability to influence others to implement new direction. Without effective managers, leaders would have to revert to the power of their position to move others to accept the desired changes.

To me, effective leadership tends to be softer and harder to explain than management, and requires a broader paradigm and skill set. Ideally, leadership functions in more of an influencing and nurturing manner, in that the basis for success relies on:

- Keeping the workplace culture (individuals) ready for change;

- Focusing on the Main Things and building relationships for follower-ship;

- Working both inside and outside the organization—to produce the desired change;

- Monitoring changing conditions that affect existing Main Things.

Once a direction for major change has been communicated, I sometimes find leaders falling short in their role in that they move on to other issues and challenges too quickly. It's critical that leaders remember to follow-through with the implementation process and to have documented the full impact this completed change actually has had on achieving the Main Things. While it's important to document the positive impact changes have made, it's also important to document why expectations may have fallen short. *Accountability is essential for the "bottom line of leadership"* and serves as a valuable learning tool for future leadership decisions. One final word of advice: Be generous in sharing the credit for all successes. Your rewards (both personal and professional) will follow as you see others succeed.

Both leadership and management are essential and must work together effectively. The ideal balance is for the two functions to ebb and flow together as internal and external circumstances require. They are separate roles but they are also joined at the hip. Together, these two functions must work to properly align the plans, the people, the paradigms, and the processes to accomplish results that will move the *organization* toward achieving the Main Things.

I urge you resist the temptation to become discouraged if you don't find strategic leadership opportunities on the job first thing tomorrow. Remember that the tone, tempo, and timing for this opportunity will likely change in the future—be patient and opportunistic. In the meantime, grow as you learn, and be ready to lead when called upon.

What's Your Vantage Point?

Earlier in the Chapter, I addressed the process of learning to drive a car to illustrate how your focus or line of sight affects leadership. As a leader, you need to be looking ahead, seeing the big picture from a different perspective than that of a manager. Stephen Covey, in his book; *Seven Habits of Highly Effective People,* tells of the jungle Safari Manager, having the power of his position, years of experience, and a big machete as tools to carry out his management role. He's in front of the team hacking and cutting away the jungle brush so the team can move forward in an effective and efficient way. The manager is doing his job safeguarding the team, warning of snakes, quick sand, and other dangers/barriers he observes as the team moves forward. He works to keep the team motivated and moving in a consistent and timely manner. The team trusts and respects the manager. This person is, after all, the *manager,* doing things right to keep the team on task and on schedule, doing what he was hired to do with excellence.

The jungle Safari Leader, on the other hand, has climbed to the top of the tallest tree to see if the Safari team is actually headed in the right direction or is even "in the right jungle." Assuming the safari is in the right jungle, the leader's view from the higher vantage point helps the Safari Manager and the team get to its targeted destination in the best path possible. The added value provided by this leader being "up a tree" is the seeing of new, unanticipated dangers if they continue heading in the current direction—even before the manager can see this danger. The leader is supporting the Safari Manager by making sure the team is doing the *right things,* and plays a vital role in the team's ultimate success.

From this illustration, you can see how much wasted effort can be saved and ultimately how much more productive the team can be with the manager and leader working together. It's not just a matter of the manager and team working harder that will determine success. It's not a matter of how high a tree the leader can climb. It's management working within the right framework as guided and modified by effective leadership.

The team is following you, the effective manager, as they should. They've come to trust and respect you in working through the endless details and complex interactions in your workplace jungle. Your role requires that you understand and monitor the work of your team from "ground zero" and understand the impact your team's work has on other departments. You fight the fights on behalf of your team with others in the organization—most often behind the scenes.

Should you always listen to counsel from that leader who's up a tree? Yes, if you want to keep your job, but do so with the right degree of wisdom and learned judgment. You'll know when you can interject new ideas and offer an alternative approach to a problem. Remember, it's best for the organization when management and leadership are working well together—do your part in ensuring that this partnership is working effectively.

On the other hand, are you allowed to or can you afford the time to climb that tall tree to do some leadership sightseeing on your own? Your job is *far more* than just keeping the team efficient and focused, pleasing your supervisor, following rules, and advancing work through the processes in the right way. You must play your part in making sure the Main Things for the organization are accomplished. Begin by being the most effective manager possible, being an effective advocate for your team, respecting your supervisors, growing into that effective leader, and committing to see that these actions help the organization succeed. The organization needs both effective management *and* effective leadership from you. The organization needs *you* to do your job with excellence daily and to add value as appropriate.

Not All Are Leaders

This traditional view of leadership builds directly upon the role of management. Have you noticed that the term "leader" is automatically used to describe the role of any senior official? I would point out that, in some cases, top officials are still performing primarily management duties like you except at a different level. These senior officials are really not providing leadership on the Main Thing "things." They're still managing people and processes. We automatically tie the term leader to higher positions within the organization, but should we? Perhaps we need to explore different uses for the term leadership. Don't trust job titles. Rather, look at the "so what" factor as to the (positive) impact someone is having. While the term "leadership" might be used in someone's job description or title, what leadership contributions are that individual actually making to the organization that make a significant difference? Is she/he actually managing 90% of the time as a senior manager or actually providing senior-level leadership.

Leadership by a true senior leader might be seen as working maybe 80% of the time from a really tall tree in the workplace jungle, where your current role might have you working 20% of your time from a somewhat shorter leadership tree. The senior leader sees more of the big picture, using this vantage point to add creative judgment, taking higher profile risks when necessary to advance a new change idea, clarifying and communicating the context for next steps, developing external partnerships, and changing or bending some rules (legally) as required. Watch this effective leader carefully and learn what you see. If appropriate, establish a mentor relationship or at least discuss your observations with your immediate supervisor. When you find effective leadership, learn and grow from it!!!!

What I'm suggesting is that leadership is not limited to a position or title, but the call for true leadership is even greater the higher one goes in an organization. In Chapter 4, I'll go into detail on the traditional view of leadership, which closely aligns with the concept of leadership and management—together forever. Traditional Leadership is a valid, vital, and serious role. However, leadership is also needed from throughout the organization. You'll see in Chapter 6 that leadership is not required to be a prescribed function or title in highly effective organizations. *Leader Or Not, Here I Come* needs to be more commonplace throughout the organization if growth and leadership development are deemed important.

Initial Description of Effective Leadership

To introduce and begin to explain the basic elements of effective leadership, I offer these three broad concepts as to what an effective leader does in partnership with the management function:

- *A Leader provides direction and shows the path to follow*—climbing that tree in the jungle, providing guidance to managers saying, "we need to go over there," "here's why," "here's how you can get there," and "here's how I'll help you." Sometimes, the team needs to move in a different direction (minor shifts); other times it needs major shifts, even to a new jungle— changing what they do and how they define success. This direction setting and communication role, however, does carry with it an accountability requirement. If the leader moves everyone to a new jungle, it sure helps if it ends up being the "right jungle."

- *A Leader aligns the paradigms, people, plans and processes at a high level*— supporting managers in decision-making, removing barriers and providing resources throughout the change implementation process. It's more than saying "we need to move this direction" and is certainly much more than writing a new plan that goes on a shelf somewhere. The leader must go much deeper by linking the plan to the necessary level of staff and budget support, modifying processes as required, and removing "people barriers"—all focused on moving others to achieve the desired results.

You don't just whip people into shape. Rather, you must create the workplace paradigms and culture that guide and support them. The leader creates the system to allow others to succeed which in turn helps the organization succeed.

- *A Leader gets things done through others, by preparing and empowering them:*

  Clarifying and giving context to move others (and teams) in the right direction.

  Daring to look at new opportunities, processes, and changes, taking the "hits" that come with thinking outside the box.

  Supporting (aligning) individuals with the proper budget, staffing, training, communication, information, and process improvement in which to succeed.

  Reducing competition and barriers between departments and individuals; building teams and partnerships.

  Mentoring the creativity and leadership skills of others and creating the opportunity for them to lead from two steps behind.

Can you be both an effective manager and an effective leader? The answer is a resounding **YES!!!** It really should not be an either/or question. It should be an **And** statement. Finding the right path, aligning the resources to go down that path, and getting things done through others are the essence of leadership. Start there. I believe the world is full of good managers (although many are ill-prepared and under-supported) but the world is incredibly short of effective leaders. As Admiral Grace Hopper stated, "manage things…lead people."

Are You a Quality Leader?

If I were to ask you the question "are you a quality leader," how would you answer? Many of you would say "Yes, I am—of course!" Now, what if I asked you to defend that response? How would you prove your "Yes" answer? Would your team members confirm your "yes" answer to this question? Before reading further in this book, I'm asking you to complete the following Exercise, describing your current role as an effective leader and your leadership vision.

EXERCISE #9: As a former educator, I believe it's essential to conduct a pre-test and a post-test to document that learners/readers have actually gained the desired knowledge or at least improved based on this course of study. Here's the

Exercise. It's a pre-test assignment for you to complete at this time, with a post-test scheduled for you in Chapter 12 of the book.

Whether or not you answered "yes" to the quality leader question, I'm challenging you to answer these questions in a way that reflects the following statement: "Yes, I am a quality leader." Document your current leadership qualities that would support a "Yes" answer, describe your career vision (where you want to go into leadership), and identify measures of success in this journey. This may be difficult, but I assure you it's a great starting point for growth.

- Document your current leadership qualities: Identify and list the top 10 elements, attributes, and/or qualities you believe would define your current leadership strengths.

- Write the vision for your leadership journey; what accomplishments or career path do you envision for yourself in the next five years?

- Identify three measures of success you will use to assess your growth in leadership.

Okay, begin writing, keep in mind that this will remain a draft only. Date this paper and ask someone close to you to review it and give you feedback. You'll be asked to review this draft in Chapter 12 and to write an updated version of your *Personal Leadership Statement* at that time to document a more specific Action Plan for your leadership journey. Please don't get hung up on the format, length, wording, or even your ego. Simply capture the key concepts that come to mind today—be open—and honest.

This Exercise is designed to have you do a first assessment and begin documenting your own strengths and leadership vision. It's only a start, but it's important to have a benchmark from which to measure your growth—both personally and professionally. I hope you will continue reassessing and measuring your progress over the years.

I firmly believe that both individuals and organizations become what they choose to measure and reward, so choose your measures of success carefully. Your leadership plan, qualities, and rate of growth are yours and yours alone. Own it and continue learning and moving toward that leadership vision. What you want others to see *in* you must become a motivating and guiding factor in your daily actions and decisions. *Become that leader you truly desire for others to see in you.*

We all started our journey into leadership slowly and learned from our successes *and* our mistakes over time. The key is to understand where you are today and to have a vision for your journey. Your steps into leadership must not be forced or taken simply because you've overcome a fear of risk-taking. Be driven by the passion to venture into leadership and the desire to see both the organization and your team succeed. Retain that enthusiasm for your job, your staff, and for your personal growth—it will separate you from the "nearly great" leaders and keep you on that cutting edge of effectiveness.

The ONLY way an organization can achieve its Main Things is if leadership and management work together effectively and consistently. Do not let the different roles confuse you. Highly effective organizations demand excellence at all levels and expect leaders and managers to work together—forever.

"Leadership is practiced not so much in words
as in attitude and in action."

—HAROLD S. GREEN

～

"Look over your shoulder now and then
to be sure someone is following you."

—HENRY GILMER

～

"A leader takes people where they want to go.
A great leader takes people where they don't
necessarily want to go, but ought to be."

—ROSALYNN CARTER

～

"Leadership is based on a spiritual quality;
the power to inspire others to follow."

—VINCE LOMBARDI

～

"Never mistake knowledge for wisdom.
One helps you make a living;
the other helps you make a life."

—SANDRA CAREY

CHAPTER 4

THE LEADERSHIP RUBIK'S CUBE

(The Traditional Leadership Role)

Lessons in leadership occur many times and in many ways during our lifetime. I had a close friend who entered retirement thinking his days at home were going to be relaxing and wonderful. What happened six months into his retirement makes me believe he was lounging around the house too much. One day his wife took a leadership opportunity to tell him that having a retired man sitting around the house was like keeping a grand piano in the kitchen. Both he and the piano were pretty to look at but both were always in the way. Being a quick study, he immediately decided to transition from full retirement into semi-retirement. Bam!!! A late-career shift that resulted in a happier home. Clearly, we learn lessons in leadership throughout our life.

With that said, have you ever known senior officials who were a lot like having a grand piano in the organization—they were pretty to look at but in the way? We need effective leaders; however, it requires the leader to be part: genius, psychologist, futurist, minister, lobbyist, athlete, salesperson, politician, gunslinger, teacher, and gambler. There are thousands of books written about leadership each year and hundreds of thousands of practicing leaders. We have tons of resource material but most of us are still "practicing"—we never take our training wheels off practicing the art of leadership. Leadership is sorely needed, and too often sorely delivered.

In this Chapter, I'll overview the "traditional" role and context for leadership. I'm using the term "traditional leader" as a positive term; one that is widely used and deeply valued. I see this definition and role as closely tied to your mid-manager position. It relates to your functioning as a change agent in the traditional sense, whereby you are a manager with an idea for change, you influence others to accept it, you decide to act, and then you remain involved leading the change implementing process. In other words, change is implemented with the help of your mid-management position. This is how leadership is traditionally viewed, and it properly defines leadership in most organizations. You carry the change idea from conception through completion. Leadership and change is made easier because you have ready access to all various resources, including your access to information and budgets, your visibility and influence within the organization, and the power of position. This traditional leader role is critical, so learn to do it well, use all resources at your disposal, perform it consistently, and do it effectively.

I considered using *The Leader In Each of You* as the subtitle for this book because I believe the essence of leadership begins from within. You don't begin by changing or controlling situations or circumstances around you; begin with YOU. To carry this concept to another level, *begin with who you are rather than what you're doing.* There's a growing wave of books and seminars telling you *how* to be more effective by improving your behavior or use of buzz words or your dress for success or your customer service smile or your position power. They're partially correct but too many of them base success on effectively "manipulating" others or situations in the name of leadership. The art of manipulating or controlling people is not leadership—it's simply the goal of tricking or forcing others to change in order to make yourself look better. Manipulation is a lose-win strategy, and not a valid strategy to follow if you're serious about leadership.

We know that leadership is not a title or even a position within the organization. Neither is leadership limited to someone having a great idea for change. Leaders must be prepared to move that great idea for change by getting the work done *through* others in ways that build team, success, ownership, and future organizational capacity for change. Yes, action on your part is required but it all begins with where *you* are—your mindset, style, and set of skills.

The Six-Sided Leadership "Cube"

Do you remember that fun little toy so popular about 25 years ago called the Rubik's Cube? It's still around and you can spend hours rotating its six brightly colored sides attempting to move each of these six colors to the same side of the cube. Frankly, I would get very frustrated with the time and energy it took to get the "job done" but success in aligning the Cube was rewarding—if spending hours with a plastic cube has redeeming value. But in some ways, this illustrates how leadership functions; it's like attempting to solve that Rubik's Cube because:

- It takes a set of unique skills and a lot of patience;

- It requires a clear vision of the end result that anyone and everyone understands;

- It requires confidence that you can succeed in aligning the multi-dimensional challenges of Leadership by using a creative and win-win strategy;

- You cannot be only half complete when doing the Rubik's Cube. It's all or nothing;

- Likewise, you cannot be a "complete" leader if you only get the leadership function "half right."

Okay, you *did* the Rubik's Cube successfully and you now want to *do* the leadership thing. The point is, placing your focus on the *doing* is only half of the job—and it's the second most important part of leadership. It's the first half of the job that I believe too many individuals overlook and, in the long run, serves to discriminate good leaders from poor leaders in highly effective organizations. It's first about *being,* then about *doing.*

Now I can already hear the shouts of hard-line managers saying enough of this "soft stuff and fluff" on leadership. Flat out, they hate this talk and will disagree with my approach to long-term, effective leadership. In their minds, leadership is *only* about the *doing.* Can't you hear them saying things like: "We need to get the job done at all cost, just do it, focus only on the bottom line, play hard-ball." You've heard them, right? Perhaps you agree with them, but understand me well. Leadership is a journey, and a long journey. Choose carefully how you envision your role in leadership today because, to a large extent, it serves to define how you will function tomorrow. I guarantee you will not suddenly change your operating style as a *doing* tyrant four years down the road after your second promotion. The leadership style you choose today is the one you'll have four years from now and long thereafter. The leopard will not change its spots.

Your leadership style and competencies *will* ultimately drive your success, your legacy, and personal stress level. The Leadership Tool I'm advancing is: *Be* before you *Do.* As Yogi Berra said: "When you come to that fork in the road—take it." You are at a crossroad. Are you the *doing* leader or are you a *being* and *doing* leader? Welcome to personal choice and the world of leadership.

The Six Sides of Leadership

As you ponder the *Being* and *Doing* decision, I'll explain in greater detail my six-sided Leadership Rubik's Cube. The six sides are:

"Being" Sides

1. *Paradigm*—How you perceive your leadership role, your commitment to being a change leader, your mentor model, your definition of success, your attitude toward empowering "others," and your passion to succeed. It's your mental model of effective leadership.

2. *Integrity in your approach* to leadership (and people)—Your core values, belief in others, your consistent follow-through on commitments, and your character traits that will instill follower-ship from others. Are you trustworthy? It's who you are way down deep.

"Doing" Sides

3. *Setting Direction*—That vision thing communicated to others with clarity. An ability to set priorities based on change opportunities to advance the organization. Creating a common understanding of the "Main Things" and supporting others in achieving these Main Things.

4. *Creating a Positive Work Culture*—Building individuals and teams, creating buy-in to change, having a strong customer focus, being accountable for your actions, valuing risk-taking in others and for your-self, and keeping the organization agile enough for change.

5. *Getting the Desired Result*—Persistence and skill in influencing others and managing the change process within acceptable timelines. Having a bias for action, but an appreciation for people and processes. Being accountable for results achieved and measuring the actual impact of the change. A set of competencies that achieves desired results by aligning people, paradigms, plans, and processes.

6. *Building for the Future*—Measuring and rewarding the right things; building capacity in processes and in people. A short-and long-range plan to move the organization forward and the building of new leaders (sustainability of the organization).

The premise is that these six sides work together and work best if they flow in sequence from #1 to #6. For example, you cannot achieve the Desired Results without first setting the Desired Direction. Likewise, you cannot create a Positive Work Culture unless you, as the leader, function with Integrity as an example for others. In a similar manner, a true leader must first *be* before she/he can *do* (effectively).

EXERCISE #10: Before presenting the Leadership Cube in Chart form and going into detail on each of the six-sides, I have a personal Exercise for you to complete. Based on the brief definitions listed above for each of the six-sides, write down your answers to the following questions:

- How would you rank the order of your strengths in performing each of the six sides from 1 to 6? List your greatest strength as #1 and the side you need to grow in most as #6.

- Looking at your top two strengths, what might be three opportunities you can identify where you could fully utilize these strengths in leadership within the next three month period?

- Looking at the two areas needing the most growth, what are actions you could take in the next three months to build those areas into strengths?

With this Leadership Rubik's Cube in mind, I will first address sides #1 and #2. These are the two "*Be*" sides of leadership. They're the "to *Be* or not to *Be*" aspects of sustaining your future in leadership. Trust me on this. Many highly competent senior officials and mid-managers have had their leadership paths cut short due to their having serious deficiencies of Paradigm and/or Integrity. Forget about credentials or charisma if the individual cannot be trusted or has "the town bully" as his/her role model. After addressing the *Be*-sides, I'll covers the remaining four sides (#3, 4, 5, and 6); the "*Do*" sides.

Please understand that the *Do* sides can get you into leadership but the *Be* sides are necessary to *Keep* you there.

The following illustrates the Leadership Rubik's Cube in chart form:

THE LEADERSHIP RUBIK'S CUBE

You Must "Be" Before You Can "Do"

BE

Paradigm—How you perceive and perform your role.
(**Attitude**, Passion, & Personal Role Model)

Integrity—**Character**, Core Values, Style, & Genuineness.
(What you feel you think, what you think you say, and what you say you do)

DO

SET DIRECTION

Understand the "Main Things"
Set Priorities
Internal & External Opportunities

BUILD FOR THE FUTURE

Strategic Planning
for The Main Things
Sustain the
Organization
Develop New Leaders
Manage Change
Drive Improvement

VISION, MISSION, & CORE VALUES

CREATE POSITIVE ENVIRONMENT

Build Trust & Respect
Build Teams
Communication
Be a Role Model

GET DESIRED RESULTS

Decision-Making/Action
Set of Competencies/Skills
Empower Individuals
Align Paradigms, People, Plans & Processes

Paradigm For a Change
(Leadership Cube Side #1: The Leadership Paradigm)

Remember the story and movie entitled *How the Grinch Stole Christmas?* Near the end of the story, the Grinch had a change of heart, a change in paradigm (or attitude) that allowed him (or it) to see Christmas in a whole new light. Like the Grinch, the first step for many of us is a paradigm shift to see our perceived roles, thinking, style, and success in a whole new light. It *isn't* about accumulating budgets, facilities, people, or power. Rather, it's about seeing the "big picture" through new eyes and defining success through the eyes of others, not yourself. Don't be that mean, old, negative, self-centered, ugly Grinch. Be that transformed Grinch, having a new heart, attitude, and paradigm. At the end of the story that Grinch not only restored the Christmas celebration, he added new value to the joy of Christmas due to his new paradigm. People don't follow you simply because of your good looks or even because of a good idea. The "new Grinch" wasn't any better looking, but the "Who's down in Whoville" now wanted to follow him. The passion to make a positive difference, add value, and achieve the Main Things are the essence of effective leadership. It gives you direction in taking steps in the *doing* sides of leadership. That's the right road, the high road, to becoming an effective leader.

Pareto Principle

Did you ever hear of the 80/20 Pareto Principle? It's a concept I've found to be true in many situations, and having a working knowledge of this Leadership Tool is very useful in addressing challenges in the workplace. Basically, the Pareto Principle tells us that 80% of our success in resolving a problem is found in addressing the 20% "right" issues, the Main Issues. Focusing on the remaining 80% of the issues will not bring you to the point solving your problem.

An application of this concept to leadership might be that, given an opportunity to implement change, 80% of your success will be found by your focusing on the right 20% of process issues and people issues. Conversely, 80% of these process and people issues will impact only 20% of your being successful in implementing the change. So...what do you want to focus on? Probably, it will be the smaller number of key processes and people issues that make a significant difference in the change process. The unspoken question is, what are the key 20%? Over time and with experience, you'll be able to identify that 20% with greater accuracy—it's situational.

Here's my spin on using the Pareto Principle as it relates to your leadership growth. It's that *80% of the key to your being an effective leader is found in your attitude toward the organization,* your team, and your own role. It begins with your paradigms. To look at it another way, *only 20% of your success as a leader is due to your skills and knowledge.* WOW!!! The greatest key to your success lies in the 80%—your attitude. I believe the following to be true:

- Knowledge is 8% of our ability to change

- Skill is 12% of our ability to change

- Attitude is 80% of our ability to succeed at change (belief is the self-concept)

"Status Quo" People

Have you ever observed efforts being made to rally the troops by negative thinking individuals or those who hate their jobs or someone who does not respect team members—and yet they expect positive results? Guess what? The only follower-ship those persons generate is grumbling, digging in of heals, fear, a compliance response, and a possible revolution. These individuals are not leaders—they're acting more like "thugs."

There's another set of individuals who have a bad attitude when it comes to change. These individuals can be found at any level throughout almost any organization, and they're usually defined as "gatekeepers." Gatekeepers are the organization's keepers of the status quo and guardians of the fences/walls/silos that exist for protection of themselves or those they serve. What these people tend to focus on are the tactics and mechanics of issues, creating confusion and anger between individuals and departments. They block creative thinking and change *unless* they've come up with the change idea. The way things are today is just fine with them.

Both the negative thinking managers and gate keeping individuals seem to generate serious attention because they feed upon the fear and intimidation of people. There is no uplifting attitude or positive momentum generated. Rather, it's like dragging an anchor when you're trying to move others toward change. Unfortunately, fear and negative paradigms seem to shout louder than the passion others have in seeing individuals, teams, and the organization succeed. These are not positive examples of the proper "attitude for leadership." It's not hard to guess why tension and frustration seem to follow these individuals when change is being considered.

Proactive leaders, on the other hand, tend to generate followers (not out of fear) but out of a clear vision, a passion, and an effective communication system.

These leaders are not defenders of the status quo. Rather, they have a contagious "attitude." Their attitude is reflected in their passion about pursuing change opportunities that advocate for customer satisfaction and achievement of the Main Things. Attitude is an easy identifier of an effective leader. What's your attitude and paradigm toward individuals, your team, your peers, your supervisor, your job? Watch your attitude—it's showing, and it's a major predictor of your success.

Proactive leaders, tend to generate followers out of a clear vision, a passion, and an effective communication system.

Effective leaders develop and hold follower-ship over the long run. They are more than a one-trick pony, having simply one great idea or achieving success only once or twice in "leading others." Instead, these leaders have gained the reputation and trust of others based on *who they are*, as well as, *what they've done* over time. They achieve success consistently. Along the way, they develop and exhibit skills that serve to generate voluntary *followers* for a given change. They're able to push through the negative thinkers and gatekeepers.

Your paradigm is one of the two major drivers that are reflected in the *Be* side of leadership. It will ultimately predict your leadership success and form the basis for your actions. Do not overlook who you must first *Be* before you *Do*.

The Badge of Integrity
(Leadership Cube Side #2: Integrity)

POINTS TO PONDER:

- "Integrity without knowledge is weak and useless, and knowledge without integrity is dangerous and dreadful."

  —Samuel Johnson

- "To be persuasive we must be believable; to be believable we must be credible; to be credible we must be truthful."

  —Edward R. Murrow

- "A person who is fundamentally honest doesn't need a code of ethics. The Ten Commandments and the Sermon on the Mount are all the ethical code anybody needs."

  —Harry S. Truman

EXERCISE #11: Complete this Exercise in a confidential manner—keep the names and job titles "for your eyes only."

- Think of (do not write down) three individuals from anywhere within your organization you see consistently exhibiting high integrity. Write down three to five attributes or qualities that best describe each of these high-integrity people that made them so easy to identify.

- In contrast, think of three individuals who consistently exhibit a *lack* of integrity.

- Write down three to five attributes or qualities that make them stand out in the crowd as a negative example.

- Write down how you see these identified high and low integrity attributes affecting staff around these individuals.

- *Are you modeling the high integrity individuals you identified? Would others identify you as a high integrity individual? Yes or No, and why?*

I'll bet not all of the high integrity and low integrity examples are found in top management. *Integrity isn't something you inherit on your way up the organization; it's something you "live" daily.* You either have it—or you don't.

It's relatively easy to identify such general qualities as honesty, trust, strong value system, emotional consistency, respect for others, and balanced strength of character. There are probably other qualities you identified such as being open in communicating, consistently following-through on promises, having courage to do the right things in the right way, and making "mature and well thought-out" decisions. Integrity traits or qualities do not have to be rocket science but they certainly make a difference in how people are viewed, trusted, and followed. The key is to observe, learn, and then try to emulate those positive factors that make true leaders, leaders.

Organizational Integrity

We tend to think of individuals when thinking of integrity issues, but *individual integrity, taken collectively by enough of the "right" (or wrong) individuals, converts to organizational integrity.* Some organizations simply do not have integrity at their core, and these organizations are at serious risk of surviving. Just reflect on those recent examples where we've seen major scandals in corporate offices, churches, legislative halls, and in charity organizations. The issues were largely related to integrity. What if you have high personal integrity but find yourself working for an organization or senior officials who have no integrity? This would be a difficult place in which to spread your leadership wings, wouldn't it. Do not be misled by those in the workplace who tell you that "having integrity in the workplace is a sign of weakness" or you're just being a "goody two shoes." Just because others lose their integrity balance, you don't have to. It's a strength that will carry you through tough times and you *will* emerge the victor in the long run.

Integrity Action Steps

Integrity is a leadership virtue—grow it and encourage others to follow you in this journey. To help you in this integrity quest, I'm offering a set of tools or strategies on how you might position your thinking and actions to help build trust in the workplace. These **Five Integrity Action Steps** may prove difficult to implement, so I encourage you to move slowly until you have the confidence and maturity required to take each step:

- *Lead with a Trust Model rather than a Distrust Model.* Function and make decisions based on a model of trusting others until they show you they cannot be trusted. Trust the words and actions of others and trust that they will support and follow-through on actions when they say they will. Most individuals can be trusted. However, watch carefully those few who will double-cross you. In addition, you will have some co-workers who see a trust model as a sign of weakness on your part, especially that macho crowd drawn to power games. For effectiveness over the long run, you cannot lead from a distrust model—unless individuals prove to you that they cannot be trusted.

- *Be transparent with your beliefs, feelings and actions.* Warning: you must use good judgment and not to wear *all* your feelings on your shirt sleeve *all* the time—it can be draining on others and serve to discredit you in some situations. A controlled openness in the sharing of your beliefs, feelings, and actions is linked to leading with trust and humility. Here is where wisdom comes into play. There are appropriate moments when you can share your feelings openly, but this must be the exception, not the rule. Your team *expects* you to be under control, but with a well-placed showing of "being human" you can increase your effectiveness. In doing so, you show others that you trust them in those instances, and probably 95% will respond in kind with trust. The other 5% will take advantage of your seemingly weak position. Just make a mental note to function in a more cautious mode around these individuals.

- *Be consistent with your reactions.* Let others know what pleases you and what displeases you. If they respond by doing things that please you—recognize it positively and do so consistently. If they respond by doing things that displease you, as promised, allow your displeasure to be consistently communicated (appropriately). Try to avoid the ups and downs of emotion and surprises for your team members. They have enough problems and stress without having to second guess or roll with your emotional swings and reactions.

- *Be genuine, authentic in your communications* with others, and communicate often on matters of importance to them individually and collectively. Try to avoid springing surprises on them by "filling in the communication gaps" from top management and other parts of the organization, as often as feasible. Place yourself in the position of your team members—you too need open, honest, and frequent communication to do your job effectively. Be that communication link for your staff, but don't waste everyone's time communicating on non-essential topics.

- *Keep your promises and follow through* in doing what you said you would do. This is a major breaker of trust and integrity. If your staff can't count on you to follow through, consistently, you've given them the perfect reason to distrust what you say.

These Five Integrity Action Steps are important personal leadership traits, as well as, valuable Leadership Tools. I suggest you attempt to live them at both the personal and professional levels.

Building Trust

You understand and would like to lead by these Five Action Steps to build integrity and higher levels of trust within your team, but where do you begin? I'm glad you asked! The following are six strategies I've found critical in building a more trusting culture and an overall team commitment to integrity:

- *Be a positive example.* Exhibit your own core value system of openness and honesty, and communicate in an open and frequent manner—daily. Encourage others to follow this example. Your staff are watching your every move.

- *Deal directly with destructive attitudes and practices of those 5%* of co-workers wanting to stir up trouble for their personal gain. You cannot let those negative, dysfunctional influences destroy the positive culture you're trying to develop. You will lose trust if obvious negative examples are left to function—in your face. There is a hard side to leadership, as well as, a soft side.

Integrity is the rock upon which effective leadership can be built.

- **Show genuine appreciation for jobs well done,** and discuss "teachable moments" directly and quickly when things aren't being done well. In all cases, this communication must be done in a manner that reflects a caring attitude about the success of others and the organization. While this may be seen as effective management, it's also effective leadership because you're building team, trust, expertise, and succession planning for the organization.

- **Listen well when others are communicating,** taking seriously their comments and input. Watch carefully the body language and non-verbal communication individuals are making. Effective listening is essential to building trust, respect and a positive culture.

- **Directly address the barriers** (policies/procedures/staff) that inhibit or prevent effective performance in a timely manner. Your team needs you to champion changes to modify or remove these barriers.

- **Be clear in giving direction and in placing expectations.** Hold yourself and others accountable for results based on these expectations. If you make a serious mistake, take the risk of admitting it—the trust level, from your team, will go up.

I believe your best source for learning and understanding is to receive direct feedback from trusted co-workers and those who have a stake in your success. Seek mentors, look for positive and negative examples to learn from, ask others their opinions about integrity, and be willing to receive honest feedback about how you're walking the talk. Integrity isn't a fancy buzzword or something for wimpy leaders. Instead, it's the rock upon which effective leadership can be built.

What a Leader Does
(Leadership Cube Sides #3, 4, 5, & 6—DOING)

Sides #1 and #2 of my Leadership Rubik's Cube are like the hidden part of an iceberg—the mass that remains under the surface. The remaining four sides of my Cube tend to be above the surface and are the more visible aspects of leadership. Sides #3, 4, 5, and 6 are the *Doing* sides that are grounded in the proper leadership Paradigm and Integrity. These four remaining sides of my Cube are extremely interdependent and build upon each other. Learn them well.

Here are the remaining *Doing* sides of the Leadership Rubik's Cube (Sides #3, 4, 5, and 6):

#3. **Set Direction**—the ability to clearly see, plan, and communicate the leadership path to achieve organizational success.

In *setting direction,* you must not only identify where it is you want others to follow, but you must create and communicate a clear and convincing picture of how this movement will benefit their work and the organization.

Have a clear vision and purpose—identify, communicate, and have the passion to achieve the Main Things. This clear vision will position your specific change ideas into context of the larger organizational vision.

Instill this vision in others—clarify and add personalized context in how others see their roles and how their value increases as the change is implemented. Go beyond their general "understanding" of the vision. Their buy-in to a vision will facilitate buy-in of future actions.

Have a Plan—know the pathway, strategies, and major steps to achieving the desired results. In the process of planning, honor and meet established timelines. Understand and resolve the major challenges to be faced as soon as possible, and develop the detailed outcome measures that will define success.

Show the ability to set priorities; and focus—help others distinguish between the urgent and the important aspects of the job. Know what needs to be done and in what sequence.

Recognize and maximize both internal and external resources to bring about needed change. Understand the words *synergy* and *partnership.*

Be more than customer-focused; be *customer-driven,* with decisions and actions driven by what adds true value as defined by the customer.

#4. **Create a Positive Culture**—be a builder of collaboration, a *nurturer of people-building processes,* a developer of effective policies and processes that are user friendly and efficient, and a destroyer of silos between people and departments.

You must walk-the-talk in creating a new and better *workplace culture*. Dare to be that *culture change agent* even if your supervisor and your peers are creating different cultures. It won't be easy but you can break that negative culture chain within your team if you're committed. I should note, however, that a negative culture throughout the organization may, in cases, be well beyond your ability to impact in the short run.

Build trust, respect and commitment with others.

Inspire, coach, and build success in others.

Create and nurture effective teams and develop talents in individuals.

Effectively communicate with and recognize efforts and accomplishments.

Be a role model for others; create "follower-ship" by walking the talk.

#5. **Get Results**—be a *doer* who is accountable for achieving results that add value to customers, the organization, and to the team; moving toward the Main Things.

You need to be *committed to and accountable for results*. Remember that all actions have consequences; there are even consequences for inaction. Achieve results through the following actions:

Be effective in problem-solving.

Communicate a passion and commitment that's catching and inspiring.

Have a sense of timing and the ability to set meaningful priorities.

Exhibit effective decision-making; achieving maximum buy-in from others.

Effectively align paradigms, people, plans, and processes.

Have a bias toward action.

Be accountable for results and follow-through.

Get work done through others—*empowerment* with a purpose.

#6. **Build for the Future**—be a construction expert keeping the organizational foundation solid (sustaining the organization) *and maintaining* a grasp of the desired future. Be a *builder* of people, visions, customers, sense of community, meaningful success measures, and desired results.

In building for the future, your leadership role must be an example for others to follow. Commit to continuous improvement, measure your progress in achieving the Main Things, learn more about strategic thinking, and excel at being a change agent as opportunities present themselves (and they will).

Develop new leaders—with new visions and succession planning.

Have commitment to continuous improvement.

Effectively plan and communicate the plan.

Maintain strategic-level thinking and actions.

Be an effective change agent—stressing win-win solutions to the extent possible.

Keep the Main Things the main things.

There are hundreds of books written on the *Doing* side of leadership, but how might I summarize the final four sides of my Leadership Cube in a series of one sentence statements? Good question. Consider the following:

- *Be an effective leader who skillfully sees and communicates where individuals, the team, and the organization must move to be successful (the right jungle).*

- *Have relationships, style, and integrity, which will support and encourage others to move forward (follower-ship) toward a common vision.*

- *Be ultimately accountable and recognized for achieving the desired results (the "so what" factor) while sharing the credit to the extent appropriate.*

- *Build a framework for sustainability of individuals and the organization (and team) by moving others toward achieving the "Main Things."*

I encourage you to read more, observe more at the workplace, listen and learn effectively daily, be mentored, and practice, practice, practice. I stress the need to *Be* before focusing on the *Do*. However, do not understate the importance of *Doing*. Points #3, 4, 5, and 6 above are vital sides of that Leadership Cube and I challenge you to grow in these skills and in your thinking, as well.

If you grasp both the complexity and simplicity of the Leadership Rubik's Cube, you'll see why effective leadership is rare in some organizations and why it's so badly needed in *every* organization. There is a pathway for you to follow as you venture into and through your leadership journey. That pathway begins with you. Leadership requires a selfless approach, a building of team, a culture of trust, a bias for action, and an assurance that actions will build a better and sustainable future for the organization. For this to occur, you must *Be* and *Do* what is required for effective leaders—the six sides of leadership.

It's not all about *you* and your success as a leader; rather, *you* must be the catalyst that helps move *others* toward personal and organizational success. As others succeed, you will succeed. Leadership is sorely needed but too often sorely delivered. Be that positive force and a role model of an effective leader. *Be* a genuine person and *do* the main things of leadership with excellence. Your organization is waiting.

*"A good leader inspires others with confidence in him;
a great leader inspires them with confidence in themselves."*

—UNKNOWN

⌒

*"Wisdom is knowing what to do next;
skill is knowing how to do it;
and virtue is doing it."*

—DAVID STARR JORDAN

⌒

*"Leadership is much more an art, a belief, a condition of the heart,
than a set of things to do. The visible signs of artful leadership
are expressed, ultimately, in its practice."*

—MAX DEPREE

⌒

*"The main characteristics of effective leadership are
intelligence, integrity or loyalty, mystique, humor,
discipline, courage, self-sufficiency, and confidence."*

—JAMES L. FISHER

CHAPTER 5

THE KEY TO THE CUBE

When I turned sixteen and obtained my drivers license, I couldn't wait to wash the family car, make plans with my friends to drive them to "anywhere," and even save my money to fill up the gas tank after the night of driving was over (maybe it took all of $2 back then). I could obtain my Dad's permission, stand by the car touching it, and even have my friends over to sit in the car, but I was missing one thing. I didn't have the key from my Dad to actually use the car that night. I needed the key to turn the engine on and that would allow me to fulfill my dreams for that evening. So close to total happiness and success, but so far away.

Sometimes opportunities in leadership occur just that way. You can see opportunities to lead, the leadership success is so close you can almost touch it, you have permission to lead, and you know the six-sided Leadership Rubik's Cube so well you could write a book about it. But something is missing—you're unable to lead effectively. You do not have the *"key"* to turn the leadership engine on. In this case, no matter how badly you want to be an effective leader, you're lacking that "certain something" that prevents you from taking that wild leadership ride. If you know all "about leadership," then why can't you complete the Cube (*Paradigm, Integrity, Set Direction, Create a Positive Work Culture, Get Results, and Build For The Future*)? What's missing is the *key* that will make leadership work.

What is the key to leadership anyway? It's a set of *personal* and professional attributes or qualities that "turn on" the *being* and *doing* sides of the Leadership Cube. Having the key goes beyond being nice or kind or smart. It means you're prepared to lead with character, confidence, commitment, and consistency. By their actions, leaders invoke follower-ship and success. These leaders might be defined as "people-people," doing the right things for the right reasons, in the right ways—through others. At their core, they're dedicated to seeing others and the organization succeed and they know how to lead others to achieve that desired goal. They have the qualities and competencies (*the key*) that will turn on the leadership engine.

I believe most of you, by virtue of seeking to grow in leadership, possess most of the qualities and competencies required to lead. All that some of you need is further skill-building and some encouragement to learn through those tough teachable moments in leadership that will force you to grow.

Key Qualities and Attributes

The key to the Leadership Cube consists of you having the proper *attitude, character, competencies, focus,* and *will.* These five attributes or qualities serve to drive the long-term effectiveness of your leadership *being* and *doing* and are interwoven into each of the six sides of the Leadership Rubik's Cube. Your Paradigm (Side #1), for example, is directly influenced by your attitude, character, and your perception of what's important (focus). Your ability to Set Direction (Side #3) is directly influenced by your competencies and is driven home by your focus and your will. Your ability to Get Results (Side #5) is driven by your competencies, integrity, and will. It's your attributes and qualities that are the keys to turning on or turning off your leadership effectiveness.

Key to the Six Sides—Lessons Learned as a Child

The five attributes or qualities I'm advancing are the same ones I learned in my youth. Some of these learning lessons came through challenging personal experiences. I didn't learn them from some well-known leadership book or motivational speaker. I learned them from my parents, friends, family, co-workers, and experiences. Think of it. Where did you form your character or learn how to focus on priorities? These attributes are discriminating factors that separate an effective leader from someone who's going to be an okay manager or leader—forever.

The following are some of the early lessons that have helped me throughout my career:

- As a kid, my parents often warned me to *"watch my attitude"* or there would be consequences in the form of discipline. I learned quickly I needed to shape up and fly right, even if I didn't always feel like it. I discovered over time that I could work to control my attitude, and it was usually to my advantage. Pouting or crying or getting angry didn't work with my parents (or with my work team). I learned I had to watch and control my attitude if I wanted to work through difficult situations. Creating an atmosphere of guilt or anger will never bring success in leadership. In a hundred different ways, your staff knows when you have a "bad attitude" toward situations, problems, the organization, or regarding them.

- I was taught early and often that my strength of *character* went before me in terms of my friendships, marriage, raising children, and building a career. As a kid, I was taught not to lie and to be considerate of others. It served to form my reputation, strengthened my relationships, and kept me out of trouble. My character is reflected in what I think, do, and say when no one is around. Can I be trusted, do I work with integrity, can I share the credit for success? My character is a critical attribute in generating voluntary follower-ship by others. If I can't be trusted or I'm unwilling to share the credit for successes, all four of the *Doing* sides of Leadership are negatively affected.

- "Be Prepared" was the Boy Scout motto that taught me to have *competencies* (skills) that would allow me to handle most any emergency. On the job, it seemed the minute I felt I had all the answers or that everything was under control, the lid blew off and I found myself scrambling just to survive the day. The best approach is to expect the unexpected. Be prepared for the hidden challenges and have a broad set of skills at your side to apply in any situation. In this book I call them competencies and Leadership Tools but the point is to "be prepared." While my set of skills have now shifted from those of tying knots in ropes and applying first aid to leading teams and developing strategic plans, I must still learn constantly in order to be prepared for those unexpected "crises" that will face me tomorrow.

- While playing right field in Little League as an eight year old, I was one of those who got bored and would start watching birds in the sky or wave at my parents sitting in the bleachers. Sure enough, that's when someone would hit the ball to right field. I had lost my *focus*, did not see the ball coming to right field, and would find myself back in the dugout warming the bench. Keep your head in the game. Learn to focus on the Main Things, and not get distracted or become uninterested in the details. There are hundreds of distractions you must work through every day. *Focus* is a daily challenge and is required for success in leadership.

- Participation in sports taught me that if the goal was to be the best, my *will* and effort had to be elevated to the highest level. I played college basketball even though I had limited natural skills on the court. I did have one thing, however. I had an intensity to succeed and a strong *will* that pushed me to actually play better than my natural abilities. This strong will drove my focus, skill development, attitude, and at times tested my character. My *will* drove me to new levels of performance.

I know many of you already possess these five attributes. The question is, how well do you exhibit them in a crisis, under pressure, and in those instances when you're unsure in decision-making? This is when your attitude, character, competencies, focus, and will shine through. *It's leadership under pressure that reflects the "real you."* Let's see how you do.

EXERCISE # 12:

- On a scale of 1 to 10, with 10 being "at the 100% level," how well do you currently understand and perform each of these attributes?

    Attitude: _____

    Character _____

    Competencies _____

    Focus _____

    Will _____

- Under pressure, which one of these five attributes are you the weakest? How has (or might) this weakness hurt you in your role in management and leadership?

- Under pressure, which one of these five attributes represents your greatest strength? How has strength helped you in your role in management and leadership?

- Do you think your staff and your supervisor would agree with your ratings? Ask your team and your supervisor to rate you on the five attributes and record the responses. Once you have their feedback, write down what you've learned and your priorities for improvement.

Leadership Competencies to Observe

The leadership competencies (skills) you possess and exhibit, much like character, are seen by others through your *Being* and *Doing* as a leader. Competencies are a key factor in determining your leadership success. Do not underestimate the value of *how* you lead others through the delivery of your competencies. I cannot over-emphasize the importance of your learning to effectively blend the What (competencies) and the How (delivery) to achieve the desired leadership results. You must be *real and authentic* in your thinking, your attitudes, and your competencies. You are not working with a bunch of fools. Staff are far smarter and more perceptive than many senior officials or managers think, and they will not follow a fake unless forced to out of self-preservation or fear. Likewise, they will not voluntarily follow someone who is incompetent. Following a fake or someone who's incompetent or even intimidating is merely an act of compliance—not commitment. It's hardly what I would call leadership.

12 Leadership Competencies

I invite you to review this listing of 12 Leadership Competencies, or critical skill areas, that I've seen consistently exhibited by effective leaders over the years. I readily admit that I'm still working on my skill levels in many of these areas, but that's the beauty of it. Every one of us will always be continuous learners in these competency areas and then learn to apply them as higher-level Leadership Tools on the job. Remember, it's a journey and it requires ongoing learning and application of the knowledge you gain from this book, from others, and from every resource you can tap into. The minute you believe you can stop learning is when you will stop leading.

The following are a set of *12 key competencies that effective leaders exhibit consistently and with excellence. These competencies are an interdependent set of skills that will distinguish a true leader from a "want-to-be" leader.*

- **Paint a clear, big picture Vision of the "Desired State"**—make it simple for others to understand. Let them see the relevance of the changes you're advancing in your shared vision, allowing them to understand the *context of change* and how their efforts will make a positive difference. Let them see their role based upon the clear vision you've painted for them. A good vision must be more than understood; it must be caught.

- **Think Creatively**—discover *new and innovative opportunities* based on your big picture vantage point. Help build a creative and agile organizational culture that can see opportunities when presented, having the *will* to move toward that opportunity in a straight line upward. Think, communicate, and act "outside-the-box."

- **Communicate, Communicate, Communicate**—listen well, *share information openly and often.* Observe non-verbal communication from others and groups, anticipate needs, follow-through, and invite input and feedback from both your internal and external customers. A lack of information creates mis-information—and problems.

- **Balance your logic and emotion**—*reach individuals and teams where "they are," then move them toward where they "need to be."* Keep your focus on the Main Things, yet have compassion for people during the change process. Seek consistency in your reactions to barriers and issues presented to you for resolution. It's essential that you're seen and perceived as predictable and balanced in your actions and reactions.

- **Be hard on issues but gentle on staff**—*make the hard decisions with a focus on changing processes* **before** *you try to change people* (their thinking or their employment status). You need their buy-in throughout the change process. Remember that staff are doing what you've taught them to do before you decided to implement the change. Ease them into change. Support them in understanding the process of change. Understand and address their barriers first, then address the people issues.

- **Be an effective Manager**—*understand the internal processes and interpersonal dynamics,* have technical abilities, work well with peers and other departments, and understand how "getting the job done sometimes means getting it done in spite of others." This includes having the patience, courage, skills required to manage people, processes, and budgets for both short-term and long-term success.

- **First meet the broader "interests" of others; then seek solutions**—*understand and consider the fears and barriers others have regarding change before advancing your own solutions to these barriers.* Communicate, listen, be creative, model leadership, and negotiate with others in a manner that will encourage them to take the required risks. Others will follow if their fears are at least brought onto the table for discussion. Do not start with your solutions. Avoid the "be reasonable, do it my way" strategy.

- **Think longer term**—the big picture view goes well beyond short-term implementation and results. There are those rare crisis issues that resemble a cry of "Fire!" that require immediate action. In most cases, however, the change process resembles trying to turn an ocean liner in the open sea—it takes miles, time, and a consistent hand on the leadership wheel. *Keep the desired results the main focus, but allow the change process time to achieve those results* based on internal and external conditions or circumstances.

- **Be a positive thinker**—have an optimistic, "can do" attitude, seeing the glass as ½ full. *Be an encouraging realist;* not an overly optimistic, Pollyanna thinking, out-of-touch mouthpiece. Encouraging others is essential, but so is being in touch with realities of any given situation. People need a guiding "light" that can "lead" people out of the darkness, but they can see right through a phony who might be offering weak encouragement.

- **Be accountable for your actions**—monitor progress toward desired results, have follow through, and admit mistakes. *Measure the impact changes have on both external and internal customers.* (Note: You need to recognize other departments and teams receiving your products and services as internal customers. Treat them as you would the organization's external customers). Get the job done and be accountable for it.

- **Walk-the-Talk**—*consistently model integrity, ethics, and wisdom.* Like it or not, you're an example—especially during the tough times. You must control your emotions (keeping your cool when those around you are losing theirs), use effective time management techniques, be willing to assume the dirty jobs if required, do what you say you'll do, exhibit pride in and support of individuals and teams during bad times, as well as the good times, and be able to honestly admit mistakes.

- **Share the success/recognition**—be humble enough (smart enough) to *formally and informally thank others for their role in the successes achieved*, to advance those worthy of being promoted, and to recognize the efforts of others in front of their superiors. If you act as though you achieved success on your own, you'll lose respect from others and probably their support when future opportunities emerge. If you share the success and recognition, you're building leadership capacity for the future.

EXERCISE #13: Now that you've learned the critical competencies to be a great leader, rate your leaders. Go back to three of the "great leaders" leaders you identified in Exercise #1 (Chapter 2). Write down your answers to the following:

- Which of these 12 competencies do these three leaders exhibit the most?

- Which of the 12 competencies (if any) do they lack?

- Now rate yourself on each of these 12 competencies based on a scale of 1 to 10, with 10 being you're the "best in the organization." Compare your strengths and weaknesses with those of the three leaders you identified.

- You know what I'm going to ask of you next, don't you! Have your team members rate you on each of the 12 competencies using that scale of 1 to 10. Record the results and write down the two or three lessons you've learned from this feedback.

Remember, growth through real-time feedback is an invaluable Leadership Tool. I refer to this as the "ouch-amen" feedback experience. As you grow from these "teachable moments," you're learning to lead on-the-job. That's what this book is attempting to help you accomplish.

With the proper *"Be"*, these 12 Competencies form the pathway to the effective leader's *"Do."* There are many leadership lessons to learn and new Leadership Tools to acquire along the way. While it will take time, keep the faith. You *will* succeed in time and you *will* lead others toward success. You have to work hard at it—daily. Leadership is not for the faint of heart, but it's also not for the pitbulls in life. It's not something you can just charge into wildly.

There's a careful balance that's required along with good judgment as to the tone you use, the pace at which you move, who you choose to involve, and the sense of timing when deciding to act. The factor I cannot guide you on is *wisdom*. It's something that's situational and learned over time. *Leadership requires wisdom but not all wise people are effective leaders.* As you learn to *Be* before you *Do*, also remember that the key is to find and use the right keys.

The Business Side of Leadership

If I were teaching a course entitled Leadership 101, I would include a unit on the *principles of running an effective business* and would link this study to a set of *principles for effective leadership.* Boiled down to the essentials, there are only a few points of focus that can make a significant difference between survival and success in both running a business and being an effective leader.

Summary of the Leadership 101 Survival Course—The Main Things

The essence of business is that it stays in business and serves its mission with excellence. The formula for survival and success in this competitive worldwide marketplace is that *every business must consistently produce and deliver;*

- *products and services with **excellence**,*
- *that customers **want** and **value**,*
- *with **timelines, prices, and conditions**,*
- *relative to those offered by **competitors**.*

To me, these four points make sound business sense and summarize the basics as to how a business can remain in business and grow. These four points reflect the Main Things. If you don't deliver excellence based on what your customers place the greatest value on and offer these products and services at competitive prices with customer convenience (including meeting customer timelines), you will struggle to achieve even moderate success. How else do you stay in business and beat the competition?

The essence of leadership is that you help move individuals and the organization toward the desired vision by achieving the Main Things. As in the business model, leaders must focus on serving the organization by meeting customer needs and beating the competition. Similarly, my parallel formula for survival and success in leadership is that *effective leaders* **must** *produce and deliver;*

- *leadership competencies delivered consistently and with* **excellence,**

- *that customers, the organization, teams, and individuals* **want** *and* **value,**

- *within customer-driven* **timelines, prices** *(or costs), and* **conditions,**

- *resulting in measurable outcomes that serve to move the* **organization** *forward (by achieving the Main Things).*

How effective leaders exhibit and deliver these four points is as important as **what** is delivered. As in running a successful business, leadership success is based on serving the needs of the organization by meeting customer needs through the work of teams and internal customers.

What Leadership Tools are included in this Leadership 101 Course?

- It requires that you give maximum effort in pursuit of *excellence* in *all* that you say and do. Focus your efforts on those vital few things that add the greatest value to the organization, to your external customers, and to your team—that 20% as reflected in the Pareto Principle. **Deliver excellence where it creates the greatest value.**

- How do you know what your customers and team truly *want* and *value?* At the end of the year, **what will be the major achievements that, if realized, can be documented as helping move the organization forward?** This is the "so what" factor I've referenced several times. In the final analysis, your job as a leader is to create results that make a significant difference. Look beyond the task-level issues you're dealing with today, and visualize how you can add the greatest value to each of these:

    Key Stakeholders—did the organization move toward its stated goals as a result of your actions and did you appropriately recognize the team effort it took to achieve these results?

External Customers—do they still want you as their provider of products and services they value? Is your market share expanding?

Team—were you there when things went "bump in the night" and did you effectively prepare, engage, and recognize the success accomplished together?

*You see, it isn't about making **you** look good; it's about how **we** achieved success.*

- **Deliver what's expected, requested, and unexpected within established timelines and conditions.** You don't set the parameters or define success, your customers do. As in football where it's all about blocking and tackling, here it's all about listening, planning, and delivering. It requires *communication, follow-through,* and *accountability.* Many well-intentioned managers get caught short in this area. If you say you'll do something, do it when and how you would want it done unto you. People want and need leaders they can trust, who deliver, and who lead by example.

- Advancing the *organization* relates to viewing your leadership role from a higher vantage point, perhaps 20,000 feet. What are the Main Things you can impact positively? **You need to communicate the context of proposed change to your Team** (individually and collectively) and to your peers. How will their new roles and actions impact the Main Things? How will their roles change when the change is fully implemented? Is the organization better off because of your team's efforts? Give your team recognition and feedback as they deliver in response to your leadership.

A Look At Your Own Leadership

EXERCISE #14: Let me challenge you further. What if I asked you to describe what it is that you do? I'm not interested in what your job description says, but rather the description of your current job *in your own words*—looking at it from that 20,000-foot level. Write down your answers to these questions honestly:

- What is it that you do on your job (using your own words)?

- Why do you want to do this work (what is your true passion)? I hope it's not just for the money or security. What is it about your work that really trips your trigger, and why?

- In what ways do you consider your team indispensable; making a significant difference?

- What would happen to your team and the organization if *you* were no longer in your current position?

Would You Be Re-Hired?

Let me really drive these points home. If you had to apply for your job again tomorrow, would you be re-hired? Why or why not? Uh, oh! Did I hit a job security nerve? Are you making a positive difference in the lives of those around you or not? At the same time, are you fulfilling what drives you the most internally—your true passions? It's important that each of us take time periodically to refocus and recalibrate the job "so what" factor and the personal "what makes me tick" factor. In every aspect of our lives, way down deep, I believe we're driven by wanting to make a positive difference and in some way leave an honorable legacy. Know where you stand today, and chart a course toward where you want to go. Do not live in fear of whether you would be re-hired for this job. Rather, make yourself indispensable and be proactive in knowing you have a plan to move forward in your leadership journey.

Make your self indispensable and be proactive in knowing you have a plan to move forward in your leadership journey.

EXERCISE #15: This Exercise is designed to help you meet the management and leadership needs of your team. Using the 1 to 10 scale as before, write down your answers to the questions below in terms of how you direct your team. At what level are you providing your team:

- Assurance that they're the right individuals doing the right activities at the right time?

- Needed training and support to maximize their success on the job?

- Personal and timely support in helping them do their work to the best of their ability?

- A clear understanding about what they must *not* do on the job?

- Regular feedback as to how they're doing and how they can continually improve?

- Trust that you're a constant and positive advocate for them when things go "bump in the night?"

Members of your team want you to lead them in making a positive difference on their jobs. As you know by now, as they succeed you succeed.

Other Strategic and Tactical Leadership Roles

We've reviewed the keys to our six-sided Leadership Rubik's Cube, 12 Leadership Competencies, and examined the impact of your current leadership on your team. Much of what I've presented was the more strategic aspects of leadership, but there's an equally important vantage point and role. *You must **also** be a leader at the tactical level. That is, you must be available, knowledgeable, diligent, and specific in working with the operational aspects of change.* A leader does not just sit on high, shouting directions on how to get to the right jungle. She/he is a full partner as the team moves in a given direction, staying in touch with the operational issues and barriers faced by managers and front line staff. You must become an even greater *buffer* and *advocate* for your team and others, taking the hits and blows from negative gatekeepers, other departments, and even your supervisor to keep the momentum and initiative moving forward. You provide invaluable leadership simply by allowing your team to make progress in spite of others outside the team. They may not even see your bumps and bruises, but it's a critical role you must play. While these roles will never be found on your job description, they're examples of the front-line, tactical duties you must provide as a leader (and a manager).

The following are some leadership roles that may fall somewhere between the tactical and strategic definitions. One key role is to gain and keep the support of senior officials for the initiatives being undertaken by your team, using different communication and documentation approaches. While you must customize your approaches when working with different officials, by all means use the most accurate and timely information possible. Never use half-truths; your credibility is essential. I've known some managers/leaders who believe keeping a low, invisible profile on these initiatives is a good thing. The attention span of many senior and mid-management leaders is often very short. You'd be smart building into your strategies the provision of brief, regular updates on progress, barriers, timelines, costs, and projected impact on all initiatives. An "out of sight, out of mind" strategy can end up being having an "out of sight, out of a promotion" impact. Being a visible target can be a risky thing but being invisible to the right officials is even more risky. Develop and apply a set of proactive strategies on how you can effectively communicate your leadership initiatives to senior officials.

Another tactical role for you is to link and partner with other departments and peers as appropriate. Reach out to them *before* you begin advancing your change initiative. The practical and political advantages of reaching out in partnership and sharing ownership on an initiative can far outweigh the effort involved. If you want to be successful, make this a group project with willing partners. Do not make this a win-lose war or play the "gotcha games." I suggest that you seriously consider taking a partnership approach if local conditions and personalities allow for it. If you can, you are helping you and your team succeed in the long run.

It probably goes without saying that, as you are promoted over time from the front line up to the CEO chair, your skill sets must change along with the size of your office. As a front line manager, you need probably 90% of your skills and focus to be on the tactical, operational processes, and technical areas. On your way up, you need to increase your interpersonal skills and strategic-thinking skills to the point where the CEO devotes perhaps 90% of the time to these new roles. Your transition from tactical to strategic thinking and action must be part of your career planning and skill building goals.

For you just entering the path of leadership, I encourage you to do so with vigor and confidence. Use your mid-management role effectively. You have a serious and vital leadership role to play as a mid-manager. Make yourself invaluable (not just valuable) to others and to the organization. Don't be one of those individuals who couldn't lead a group in silent prayer. However, even some of these individuals were able to grow into effective leaders over time. When appropriate, do not be afraid to take the offense when providing leadership; don't just play defense.

This approach may shake up some staff, but then again that may be a good thing. In the long run, however, the results of your efforts will be the final measures of success. The proof is in the outcome. And, the proof of your leadership is found in your having the *Key* to the *Cube*. Do not forget the supporting (key) role your *attitude, character, competencies, focus,* and *will* play in your solving the Leadership Rubik's Cube. This is far more than a game puzzle to be solved; it's about what *you* must do as a leader to achieve success for others and the organization. It's about you creating a legacy and a pathway to even higher levels of leadership and personal success. Remember, discovering and applying the Key to the Cube is up to you.

"No institution can possibly survive if it needs geniuses or supermen to manage it. It must be organized in such a way as to be able to get along under a leadership composed of average human beings."

—PETER DRUCKER

⟞⟝

"Leadership is getting someone to do what they don't necessarily want to do to achieve what they want to achieve."

—TOM LANDRY

⟞⟝

"This is the world of white water where we have to change to survive; where we have to develop to thrive; and, paradoxically, where the very act of change increases the risk that we won't survive."

—RANDALL WHITE, PHILLIP HODGSON AND STUART CRAINER

⟞⟝

"Change is hard because people overestimate the value of what they have—and underestimate the value of what they may gain by giving that up."

—JAMES BELASCFO AND RALPH STAYER

⟞⟝

"The very highest leader is barely known by men.
Then comes the leader they know and love.
Then the leader they fear.
Then the leader they despise.
The leader who does not trust enough will not be trusted.
When actions are performed without unnecessary speech
The people say, 'We did it ourselves.'"

—LAO-TSE

CHAPTER 6

THE CHANGING FACE OF LEADERSHIP

(The Change Leader)

One of the important lessons I've learned over time is how to multi-task and find ways to make my work more efficient. A practical example of that comes with getting older. It now takes great effort for me to bend down to tie my shoes in the morning, so I've learned to use that opportunity to see what else I can do as long as I'm already down there. It's a big deal, and I can see the world from a different perspective. There's a downside, however, because the blood rushes to my head, my face gets red, it's a pain in the back, it's usually accompanied by a lot of grunting and groaning, and I'm forced to be very efficient getting more things done "now that I'm down there." My efficiency change is that I now wear more deck shoes rather than wing tips; it feels so good to simply slip into my shoes. Efficiency in management and leadership is a good thing too; the groaning and having your face turn red is not something you want your team to see. Since I've already taken us down that path of "traditional leadership" in Chapter 4, let's see what else we can review now that we're down here.

I'm introducing what I consider to be an emerging form of leadership, capable of supplementing (not replacing) the Traditional Leadership Model. I refer to this emerging form as the "Change Leadership Model." Your understanding of this expanded view of leadership can add great value to your organization, to the traditional leadership process, and to your leadership journey. Be open in examining this new thinking and seek opportunities to experiment with it. I do not want this to make the blood rush to your head, be a pain in the back, or be the cause of great grunting and groaning, but leadership requires you to sometimes work from a different paradigm. While Change Leadership may not be possible to introduce into your organization at this time, at least be aware of the concept, how it works, and look for opportunities to apply it whenever possible. This may be one of those Leadership Tools you pack away for application in the future. I guarantee it's a great tool if you can apply it successfully.

Introduction to Change Leadership

Effective leaders have learned to appreciate the importance of instilling self-confidence and reassurance in team members and peers before, during, and after the change process. You must aggressively seek buy-in and partnership with other internal stakeholders—beginning with your supervisor and extending to other departments. Do not underestimate the importance "others" will play in moving your idea forward. The bottom line is *that staff needs to have as much buy-in and belief in the value of this change as do you, their leader.* These individuals must be *with* you rather than saying: "let's watch to see what happens" or "we're forced to blindly follow the chosen leader because we have to." In reality, your staff does have a choice in what they believe and who they will follow. Sometimes, believe it or not, they may even choose to follow someone not classified as a manager or a leader simply because they believe in the idea or the individual.

The greatest motivators for developing follower-ship are: the *quality of the change idea* and the *quality of the change agent.* While important, it's not always the power of your management position. Highly effective organizations have taken this concept to what some may consider an extreme level. These organizations have developed a culture that encourages and actually *empowers employees at all levels* to seek and share their ideas for change and improvement—and *to become* "*leaders.*" This goes well beyond the traditional suggestion box approach or paying people an incentive for improvement ideas or following the Traditional Leadership Model. ***All employees are empowered to lead change. These organizations have unleashed the capacity and the power of a significant and traditionally untapped resource.*** They allow and require their managers to risk managing with the humility and security to empower members of their team and others to be leaders. This goes beyond having an organizational culture shift; it's a major paradigm shift. I refer to this as an emerging leadership model as "Change Leadership."

Talk is cheap and you probably want to know some of the organizations that apply the Change Leadership Model. The following are names of several highly effective organizations having received the National Malcolm Baldrige Award between 1990 and 2004. These organizations have infrastructure processes and internal cultures that not only *allow* staff input beyond what the *average organization* does, they aggressively seek this input and advancement of change ideas from throughout their organizations as part of their improvement and growth strategies. You may want to research how and why several of these organizations have implemented Change Leadership.

- Ritz-Carlton Hotel Company (now part of Marriott International)

- IBM Rochester
- Federal Express Corporation
- Xerox Business Services
- Motorola Business Services
- Eastman Chemical Company
- Merrill Lynch Credit Corporation
- University of Wisconsin—Stout
- Community Consolidated School District 15
- SSM health Care

*You can work in the Traditional Leadership Model **and** you can support a Change Leadership Model at the same time.*

The Power of "AND"

We tend to view life and certainly our workplace from an "either/or" mindset. I can either do things right or do the right things. I'm either a producer or a manager or a leader. I must either please my supervisor or please my customers. In highly effective organizations, the "either/or" is replaced by "and." This new thinking, on the surface, doesn't make sense. For example, I can do things right AND do the right things. I'm a producer *and* a leader. I must please my supervisor *and* my customers. The "ah-ha" is that we must learn to view these and many other workplace realities in new ways. Using the "either/or" approach, we limit our ability to see new opportunities I'm convinced are all around us. I strongly recommend you practice using the word *and* instead of *or* when describing options that on the surface appear direct opposites. Use of the word *and* is freeing and enlightening, and leads you to out-of-the-box thinking. It serves to expand your paradigm, role, and function for the organization in new and positive ways.

The traditional view of leadership, including what I've shared thus far in the book, is forever evolving. The roles in management *and* leadership are continuing to work together at higher and higher levels. The need for meaningful change is increasing at an even faster rate. Here's the related paradigm shift (evolution) that organizations should/could evolve into. *You can work in the Traditional Leadership Model **and** you can support a Change Leadership Model at the same time.* At many points in my career, I was confused as to when I was being a really good manager or when I was being a true leader. My paradigm had an invisible line drawn between management and leadership—and it was wrong. I motivated staff, developed follower-ship, introduced major change, achieved key results for organizations, and achieved success for others and myself. Were my opportunity management instincts, creativity, and risk taking in initiating change a function of my manager role, or was it my role as a manager *and* a leader? Somewhere along the way, I discovered the possibility of operating under *both* the Change Leadership Model *and* the Traditional Leadership Model. This paradigm shift freed me and my staff to work together more as a team, to be more creative, and to bring new thinking into the organization. I challenge you to examine this new paradigm in your leadership role.

One of the ways highly effective leaders and organizations function so well in the midst of change and increased competition is that they have honed their skills in understanding the world of paradox shifts. That is, they're becoming more skilled *and* agile to balance what seems to be conflicting paradigms (*and* rather than *either/or*). Like other tools in your Leadership Toolbox, you must understand the role paradox thinking can play in the workplace culture, and remain open to the power of "AND" thinking. Do not remain locked into "either/or thinking" and actions. Have your paradigms well-grounded and focused on accomplishing the Main Things—the "so what" factor. If you can expand your thinking, it will lead you to new and exciting leadership opportunities.

Big Right Turn in Thinking

Picture in your mind a highly effective organization. What might the management and leadership culture look like? The Traditional Leader concept can and in many cases does thrive there. However, many highly effective organizations will function having both a Traditional Manager *and* Change Leader paradox. You would see the Change Leader role being supported by a highly receptive culture for change and the process for advancing your change ideas would be very flexible and clear. It would function in a way that invites *all* staff to float change idea balloons to be assessed and seriously considered for implementation by *others*. These "other staff" in the organization would also see part of their role as advancing great change ideas, encouraging you and your staff to float the new ideas. The difference is not that a change process exists; rather, it's *who* suggests the change ideas and *how* the change is implemented. You would probably see yourself having the freedom to go outside your role as a manager, being encouraged to offer ideas for change and establishing internal partnerships to bring these changes to fruition.

Now, I want you to hang on; I'm about to make that big right turn in thinking here. Highly effective organizations, like Ritz-Carlton and others, work very hard at taking the art of leadership and change to new levels. The nature and number of revolutionary improvements ("ah-ha changes") are significantly greater than those in a traditional organization, probably to the "power of ten." We are not talking merely continuous improvement or incremental changes here. Rather, the commitment to making significant, meaningful changes would break the planning and policy backs of every gatekeeper in your organization. In most of these organizations, *every* employee would be criticized for not doing her/his job if they *did not* advance change ideas almost monthly, did not actively offer daily input into change ideas being advanced by others, and did not feel empowered to make decisions that delight their customers—on the spot. It's part of their culture, job descriptions, and performance evaluations. These organizations become change machines, and base their success and competitive advantage at the feet of their employees. Guess what, it's working.

I gave Change Leadership its own Chapter in this book because it truly represents a new level of staff empowerment and organizational effectiveness. It's not easy to accomplish but pays rich dividends if it's properly implemented.

So What's Different About It?

The potential impact of the Change Leadership Model goes well beyond the role you might now be playing. The impact of this Model is on the total employee base and on the total organization:

- *This emerging model empowers every employee in the organization to be a leader*—not just those with budget, staff, and position power. Staff are encouraged, invited, and required to be players in creating new change opportunities, for the right reasons and in the right ways.

- It goes beyond senior officials and managers needing to carry the sole burden of identifying and implementing the change process, making the decisions, funding the changes, adjusting existing policies and procedures, and driving home the implementation process. *The entire organization and culture (starting with the senior officials) is focused on identifying and implementing great change ideas* that will move the organization forward—not on egos and turf and chain of command.

- It's an "and" culture; not an "either/or culture." Managers are change leaders *and* employees are change leaders *and* senior officials are engaged in change in new ways. While there is a controlled approval and implementation process for change that involves managers and leaders, *the idea moves the change rather than managers moving the change.* The organization supports the process of change, not just the manager.

- It's a new paradigm. The focus is on creative ways each employee *can do* their job better *and* deliver new products and services to meet current and future customer needs. It begins and ends with the customer being the winner and not the supervisor or employee. Status quo is a bad thing here. **The organization is truly customer-driven.**

Okay, if the listing above describes what's different about the Change Leadership Model, what's *not* different? To start with, managers and senior officials cannot delegate their "responsibility" for how the organization performs. Just because you have new and exciting ideas popping up throughout the organization, no organization can stand total chaos and lack of accountability. Without effective processes and a new set of effective controls and monitoring tools, this model will not work. Secondly, the need for quality data management will be even greater. Finally, the quest for greater efficiency will be strengthened because the entire organization will not only have to continue doing the current workload but will also be engaged in developing and implementing approved change ideas. Efficiency in existing processes and duties will be a must.

The Change Leadership Model will require change within the organization, but what will not change is the common focus on achieving the Main Things and ultimate success of the organization.

Change Leadership in Action

One of the first lessons I learned about the Change Leadership Model actually began with my Administrative Assistant, Donna. Periodically, she would share insightful ideas for change with me. One day, rather than my taking her idea and running with it as a senior official, I encouraged her to advance this change idea to a set of managers and staff outside my unit who were internal customers of the change idea. Imagine an Administrative Assistant floating a test balloon, having an array of (enlightened) managers and staff in the organization looking for creative opportunities, willing to work directly with her on her idea. These staff/managers/leaders met with her and were eager to learn the nature and impact of her change idea. *They* were the customers and quickly became the drivers of the change. This group of staff and managers made the final decision to run with her idea and worked cooperatively with her to implement the change. She remained involved in that decision-making and implementation process. She owned the idea and was encouraged to run with it as far as *she* wanted to. Eventually her idea was implemented, was deemed successful, and served to benefit both the internal and external customers in a significant way.

Who was the true leader in this situation? Was it my Administrative Assistant, was it me as her superior, or was it the broader review team? You could make the case that it was all three, because all were needed to advance the idea and implement it. But other managers and I did not initially recognize this opportunity for change and most likely would never have discovered it. The true change leader in this illustration was my Administrative Assistant.

This example is the Change Leadership Model in action. I can identify other front-line staff that functioned as change leaders, other mid-managers who provided valued leadership outside their departments, and even other organizations (our partners, suppliers, and especially our customers) who served as change leaders.

Do you even *ask* or challenge your Administrative Assistant or front-line staff to share their wild, out-of-the-box thinking, or do you limit the discussion to "how existing goal statements will be addressed" or "what's the next incremental process improvement we can make" or "how can we cut the budget?" Do you ever ask a manager in another department for her/his ideas on how to improve *your* department's operation? Most workplace cultures, unfortunately, tend to stress chain of command and communicating up and down this chain (what terrible words). Worse yet, we tend to overemphasize "control." We create and re-enforce silos between departments and organizational levels. We must be open to viewing leadership as coming bottom-up, side-ways, and outside-in, as well as, top-down. The process for change in this model may be different and on the surface seem chaotic, but the impact is powerful.

Is your organization open to this new thinking and new opportunity? How many incredible test balloons are floating around your team or your organization that nobody ever sees? I see this as "opportunity lost"—for everyone.

For the Change Leadership Model to succeed, it must be well grounded in your organization's culture, value system, management philosophy, reward system, and infrastructure. As I mentioned earlier in this book, organizations are perfectly aligned to achieve what they are currently achieving. You become what you choose to measure and reward. Are your senior officials aligning the organization to generate new change ideas and better ways to serve customers or do they seek control and standardization? Are they recognizing and rewarding those who advance these ideas and see them through to success or do they evaluate employees based solely on their limited job description? In too many organizations, whatever is deemed to be priorities for senior officials become priorities for all staff. In this case, the only good idea is one that's aligned with a priority of senior officials.

Even worse yet are those senior officials and organizations who look for things to going wrong, and unfortunately find them. If they want to find out who's "at fault" or someone to blame for a problem, they'll find it. If they want to discover opportunities for small improvements, they'll find them. If they want to discover out-of-the-box ideas for major leaps in improvement, they can find that too. It's all tied to the attitudes and thinking of managers and leaders. Staff will follow your lead, especially if you choose to unleash their leadership potential through Change Leadership. You have the capacity to tap resources for new leadership right under your nose. It's not *all about you*; it's all about the paradigms you work within and create.

EXERCISE #16: The point of this Exercise is to have you and your team visualize yourselves in the middle of a Change Leadership organization. Within that context, I'm asking you to write your answers as to what this highly effective organization might look like and how it might function. If you were part of one of these nationally recognized, highly effective organizations:

- How would your role as mid-manager be different than what yours is today?
- How would your team's role be different and how would the members react to this change in your role and their roles?
- In this setting, what would be three new change ideas you would consider advancing?
- Is this paradigm even possible in your organization? Why or why not?
- Who might be the strongest opponents of this change? Who might be the strongest supporters? Why?

With all this said, what might be a working definition of Change Leadership? One definition would be:

It's the process of initiating change that brings about meaningful new customer-valued services or direction for the organization by focusing on challenging the status quo. It occurs through a series of change-related decisions originating and flowing from the top down or bottom up or sideways or outside-in, requiring effective listening, facilitating, and coaching skills The leadership goal remains the same: to help move the organization toward achieving the Main Things.

On the surface, the Change Leadership Model runs counter to the easy to understand assumption that position and power make for good leaders. Change Leadership, if pursued, cannot simply be a strategic initiative that's mandated. It's a model that can only be offered to staff if presented with the proper workplace culture and leadership commitment. Once this model is "offered," it must be consistently embraced and supported by staff throughout the organization, especially by senior officials. Staff needs to see that senior officials can back-up their words with actions in support of this new paradigm. *It must reflect a new organizational mindset, infrastructure, and recognition system that serves to create and support new leaders.*

Your role in the future might be to help assess the organization's readiness for this emerging view of leadership. It needs *you* and others to step forward to support *and* lead change. I trust you can see this as an important tool for your Leadership Toolbox, providing you with a better understanding as to how this supplemental role of leadership can emerge within the organization. Be observant and be ready if you see opportunities to pilot and then transition into this Change Leadership Model. If you watch for it and encourage it, you may find it. If not today, then perhaps tomorrow.

What follows are two additional Leadership Tools for your Toolbox that will be strong resources for your leadership journey—whether it's in a Traditional or Change Leadership Model. One has to do with a solid set of 11 *Core Values* that both you and your organization might choose to follow. The second is what I call the *"Three R's for Leading."* I challenge you to discuss these Core Values and the Three R's in some detail with your team and others as you sense the right opportunity. Your leadership role is to help ground others in this new thinking. Use these tools to help prepare your team for change and higher levels of performance. Work to strengthen your personal core values and to link the Three R's for Leading to accomplishment of the Main Things.

Core Values

All of us operate having a set of personal and organizational core values, which are reflected in our daily interactions, decision-making, and actions. Of course, there are different sets of core values. Some are proactive, others are self-serving, and some are informally "acted out." Also, there are core values that individuals *express* but do not *exhibit* each day. Does your organization even have a published set of core values it chooses to live by? If so, does it assess itself to determine if these Core Values are in fact being "lived?" If you're looking for a movement of your organization to the next level, a valid set of core values must exist, be deployed, understood, and lived daily *at all levels*. These cannot be simply words on a paper posted on the wall. They must be reflected in how staff treats each other and how they do their work. These core values must be seen by your external customers. Are your organization's core values an asset that supports movement toward the Main Things, or are they non-existent?

I'll be referencing a set of core values found in a nationally recognized performance excellence system (the Malcolm Baldrige Framework) that I'll address in greater detail in Chapter 11. It presents a proven set of core values that serve to "drive" highly effective organizations. Together, the 11 Core Values, in this Baldrige Framework, create a basis for action, feedback, and performance excellence. They will serve to drive your leadership, strategic planning, policies, staffing patterns and functions, and your communication systems. They will directly support your efforts to accomplish the Main Things your organization has identified.

The listing of core values that follows presents an excellent framework to guide development of your personal leadership legacy over time. After reviewing these 11 Core Values, you'll be asked to rate your organization on how it is "living" each one. This is far more than an exercise I'm giving you—it's an assessment that will reveal a great deal about your ability to "lead" in your current organization.

Review these 11 Core Values carefully within the context of your organization. Are some or all found "living" deep within your organization—at all levels?

- *Visionary Leadership*—provide and effectively communicate clear direction, values, and expectations throughout the organization.

- *Customer-Driven Excellence*—quality and performance as driven and judged by your customers. Customer needs drive change within the organization.

- *Organizational and Personal Learning*—*organizational learning* is continuous and leads to the improvement of existing approaches and instituting meaningful change. *Personal learning* leads to new opportunities for staff to practice new skills.

- *Valuing Employees and Partners*—value diverse backgrounds, knowledge, skills, creativity, and motivation; and building of effective and productive relationships. Understand how your staff and partners define quality and their needs for success.

- *Agility*—the capacity to function in a state of rapid change and flexibility.

- *Focus on the Future*—understanding the short and longer term factors that affect your business and its competitive edge. Plan for the future.

- *Managing for Innovation*—making meaningful change to improve your products, services, processes, and operations to create new value for the organization.

- *Managing by Fact*—dependency on the measurement and analysis of performance to drive business strategy and actions.

- *Public Responsibility and Citizenship*—meeting your responsibilities to the public and the community; as well as, ethical behavior and sound business practices.

- *Focus on Results and Creating Value*—performance measures are established and focus on key result areas (the Main Things). Create value for your key stakeholders (customers, employees, stockholders, suppliers, and partners).

- *Systems Perspective*—view and integrate the organization as a whole, align planning, processes, people, success measures, and actions.

EXERCISE #17: I want you to look at your organization when completing this Exercise and write down your answers.

- Does your organization have a set of Core Values that are communicated and followed?

- Rate and write down how your organization is living *each* of these 11 Core Values on a scale of 1 to 10 (10 being at the "excellent" level)?

- How many ratings were 7 or higher? How many were 5 or lower?

- Write down the three you believe are strengths of your organization? Do your customers see these as strengths as well? Why or why not?

- Write down the three you believe represent the greatest opportunity for improvement?

This assessment based on Core Values will give you a clearer picture of the realities, paradigms, and the workplace culture in which you function. This Exercise will provide insight into some of the causes of organizational dynamics that will either drive or inhibit your organization's growth and success. *It will also provide insight into what helps or hinders your leadership journey.* If, for example, your organization does not Value its Employees, does not Focus on the Future, or is not Managed by Fact, then your opportunities for leadership input are further challenged than if these core values were organizational strengths. However, if there is value placed on Visionary Leadership, Managing for Innovation, and a Systems Perspective, your leadership opportunities are greater and should be reflected in your career planning strategies.

Exercise #18: I now want you to carry this assessment one step further. Write down:

- Which three of the 11 Core Values above represent your personal strengths?

- Which three represent your greatest opportunities for improvement?

- What actions would help improve these opportunities for improvement?

- How would your team answer this question about the values you're living at the workplace?

We all *have* a set of values that drive our thinking and actions, but are they the right values and are they consistently exhibited in your workplace?

One of the primary roles of senior leadership within any organization is to clearly establish, communicate, and model a common set of Core Values, and to place expectations and receive feedback on how *every employee* lives these Core Values. Without an established and followed set of Core Values, you risk a lack of organizational integrity and perhaps even have culture chaos. This state of operation will, sooner or later, bring pain to any organization.

The Three R's for Leading

If an organization is truly customer-driven, what Three R's do you think would be required to achieve success as defined by its customers? No, it's not readin', 'riting, and 'rithmetic. I believe the Three R's are *Relationships, Relevancy, and Responsiveness.* Think of it. If you do not establish exceptionally strong relationships, how will you listen and receive genuine customer input? If you do not deliver value that the customer deems relevant, you will likely lose that customer to your competition. Finally, you must deliver these products and services in a timeframe that's responsive—at the speed of business. Whether the organization is still traditional in its approach to leadership or even if it's open to the Change

Leadership Model, the Three R's are extremely valid and valuable to include in your Leadership Toolbox—learn this lesson well.

You MUST have the Three R's working interdependently, serving to align the efforts of individuals, teams, and the entire organization toward achieving the Main Things. The Three R's are, in my opinion, valid for *any* organization and for *all* employees to follow.

The following is an overview of the Three R's as they apply to the change process:

RELATIONSHIPS

- Understand the needs of internal and external customers throughout the planning and change implementation processes.

- Find a champion within the leadership ranks that will assist in advancing your idea.

- Build partnerships with traditionally conflicting or opposing forces—both internally and externally.

- Build a win-win reputation based on trust, effective communication, follow-through, and a bias for action.

RELEVANCY

- Communicate and prioritize the "Main Things" as well as how success of a proposed change is to be measured by the customer.

- Make sure the person(s) keeping score of the organization's success will find value in the changes you're advancing.

- Communicate the change idea and progress throughout the implementation process in a language and tone that is understood and well received by key decision makers.

- After change is implemented, be accountable for the final impact (the "so what" factor).

RESPONSIVENESS

- Have an accurate sense of timing and urgency in how and when you communicate and act on change.

- Build in a follow-up process to ensure your changes are implemented, working well, supported, and appropriately recognized.

- When documenting and sharing change success, describe your role and how the role of others positively impacted the results. Share the impact of the change in terms that matter to key stakeholders.

- Be timely in your communications, actions, and follow-through.

EXERCISE #19: Write down your answers to the following:

- On a scale of 1 to 10 (with 10 being at the 100% level, consistently), rate your own level of effectiveness in delivering *each* of the 12 bullet points referenced above.

- Next, rate your total organization on *each* of these 12 bullet points using the same 1 to 10 scale.

- Finally, if you wish to live dangerously, share your two sets of ratings with your team and supervisor—let discussion follow. Based on feedback from your team and your supervisor, were your ratings accurate? In which areas did the ratings differ the most?

Without applying all three of the R's effectively, I've seen many creative ideas and great opportunities lost by emerging leaders. These R's are really a reflection of your leadership planning, commitment, competencies, and Main Things. Both those introducing a change idea, as well as, those charged with implementing the change must have the credibility, integrity, and responsibility to succeed. Again, it begins with the *Being* side of leadership, followed by the *Doing* side.

The Change Leader

Today's businesses can no longer talk about the pace of change. Due to rapidly changing technology, the growing competitiveness of the marketplace, and dynamics of the workforce, businesses must deal with the *velocity* of change. Is your organization "agile" enough to change rapidly? Does it have the leadership capacity to recognize and then manage the change process effectively? Is leadership making necessary progress in accomplishing the Main Things? Leadership is needed now more than ever. It needs to be initiated from all levels of the organization—directed down, up, sideways, and from the outside. It's a matter of survival. Highly effective organizations get this new paradigm; ineffective organizations do not.

You, as the Change Leader of tomorrow, must have the ability to recognize change opportunities and have the courage and skills to effectively advance your ideas. This will require great wisdom on your part in assessing and advancing the right change opportunities. Keep in mind that leadership is not limited to advancing only your ideas. Be prepared to support others as they offer their quality change ideas, as well.

In this model, the change process is not tied to hierarchical structures and formal lines of communication up and down the chain of command. *What must follow to support the Change Leadership Model is proper alignment of the organizational culture and infrastructure through its people, plans, paradigms, and processes.* For you and your staff having change ideas, it's like floating that test balloon in an environment that is just *waiting* to hear from you. Any organization that binds the ability of individuals to question the status quo is likely to become an organization watching the competition from behind.

The following chart overviews what Change Leadership IS and what it is NOT:

CHANGE LEADERSHIP "IS"	CHANGE LEADERSHIP "IS NOT"
A process that's triggered by the "right" opportunities.	A role, a position within the organization, or reaction to a mandate.
Challenging the status quo in the thinking, words, and actions of staff for the right reasons (to achieve the Main Things).	Seeking or limiting change ideas to incremental improvements.
Seeing "opportunities" to better the organization by staff at any level within the organization.	A controlled process of who and how change ideas can be considered. It's change that starts at the top.
Encouraging non-managerial staff to advance and influence change from the bottom-up causing senior officials to be willing followers.	Change driven primarily from the top, down through the organization—by senior officials and managers.
Has its own set of processes, approvals, and parameters in which to advance ideas. It has a fluid but controlled process to ensure quality.	Everyone or anyone simply "doing their own thing," creating chaos; thinking every idea is wonderful and should be implemented.
About *"influencing"* change.	About *"managing"* change.
Driven by improving products and services that will please customers—moving the organization forward.	Pleasing staff; making them feel important.

Keep in mind my Administrative Assistant illustration. I challenge you to welcome change ideas coming to you from new parts of the organization. How would you react to an idea for change coming from a business supplier or partner outside your formal organizational structure? Be observant, be agile, be open, and be successful. Change leadership can come from bottom-up, from outside-in, and from side-to-side. Recognize a good change opportunity when you see one.

The Big Picture for Change Leaders

Change leaders are not required to have strong managerial skills. Rather, they must simply have the ability to see opportunities that others might not see and an occasion to share these ideas. Part of what's required is that all staff must see the big picture of where the team and organization needs to move. It requires change ideas that have *context."* You might use the broad term *"opportunity management"* as the new paradigm and management system. This requires organizations to have the ability to first *see* the *right* opportunities. Next, organizations must have a culture and support system that effectively communicates and inspires others to buy into and see the value added from acting on these opportunities.

Change leadership skills are a lot like having creativity skills. Both depend on:

- An ability to see beyond the status quo; beyond *what is* to see *what should be.*
- The ability to have focus and perseverance in spite of gatekeeper barriers.
- The courage to act on those things that challenge the status quo; not merely talking about it.
- A curiosity about how things work (or don't work).
- A thought process that visualizes an opportunity, seeing the big picture and Main Things.
- An ability to connect the conceptual dots.
- A willingness to risk rejection from others.
- A skill for communicating a concept in terms that others can understand and appreciate.
- Being authentic and genuine in expressing ideas.

Traditional Leaders "AND" Change Leaders

In summary, *Change Leaders must be rebels* **with** *a cause.* The Change Leadership Model, like creativity, can only be encouraged and caught within organizations—it cannot be simply mandated. It's a paradigm shift within the organization that must begin with senior officials. It's the concept that will require everyone in the organization, at least several times during the year, to advance a revolutionary idea or vision for the future that's of *significant* value for all. If this door for input is opened, a new set of leadership skills and processes must be learned by many.

While Change Leaders might function differently than Traditional Leaders, they do have many of the same tools in their Leadership Toolbox, such as:

- An acceptable balance and credibility between their competencies and their character.
- The courage to advance quality leadership opportunities even if it rattles the status quo.
- A working understanding of the change process.
- The ability to link change proposals to the "Main Things."
- Insight into the fears and barriers associated with the proposed change.
- Communication skills that will move others to action and follow-through.
- Humility to allow others to say "didn't they have a great idea?"
- Personal credibility that facilitates trust and follow through by others.

I don't believe there is any litmus test to predict whether you can or ever will be a great Change Leader. A great manager will not always make a great Traditional Leader. A great Traditional Leader will not always make a great Change Leader. A great front line employee will not always make a great manager or Change Leader. There is no guarantee that success in one role will translate into a successful leadership role. It's all individual and situational. The best positioning for you is to be ready and to appreciate the informal role you might play at the right time. That fact alone puts you miles ahead of the traditional thinker and traditional employee. Be ready, be observant, and be of value to your team, your organization, and your customers.

Leadership is leadership. The paradigm is that you can lead with followers *and* you can lead by following change leaders. Change Leadership isn't a state of *being;* it's a state of *readiness.* Be ready and be open to new ways to move your organization forward!

Effective Leadership is a team sport. The problem is that we're too often on different teams.

"When you're through with change, you're through."
—Bruce Barton

"People don't resist change. They resist being changed."
—Peter Senge

"Not everything that is faced can be changed,
but nothing can be changed until it is faced."
—James Baldwin

"It is not necessary to change. Survival is not mandatory."
—Edward Deming

"If change is occurring faster outside an organization
than it is within an organization, the end is in sight."
—Jack Welch

"Nothing changes if nothing changes."
—Yogi Berra

CHAPTER 7

THE CRISIS OF CHANGE

Like many of you, I've changed jobs and occupations many times during my career. To some, this is an indication that I've had trouble holding a job. NOT TRUE! Fortunately, each new job seemed to build on the last. While my salary didn't always increase, my learning did. I'd like to believe that each job change was well thought out, well timed, and perfectly placed in my rapidly ascending career ladder. Also, NOT TRUE! Believe it or not, the jobs I really wanted did not always materialize for me. I was not found to be the best candidate in many situations.

For me, there were several "teachable moments" in this job seeking adventure:

- Change may be desirable and sought after but may not match the thinking of others.

- Change in one area has a ripple affect for others. When I was successful in my search for a new job, my change affected every member of my family in new and different ways. It also had serious impact on the staff around me at work.

- In some cases, others brought change to me by offering me a job I didn't even apply for. I've not always been the originator of change—even positive change, but I have tried to examine every change opportunity.

- Several job changes were actually lateral moves, which better positioned me for future promotions. Not all changes thrust you to the next level, but they may be an interim step on the way to the next level. Look beyond your first move—to see the big picture.

The process of change can be positive or negative, desired or opposed, even meaningful or meaningless. The fact is that change is with you every day. Will you cope, capture, or crush it?

Think of the change process as it exists at your workplace. You may have the right motives and your change ideas may be pure but you'll find you're often blocked by others. At the same time, your rationale for passing up change opportunity is logical but others are pushing you to support the change. Other times, the changes are small but serve as step one in a three part change process. Here's a Leadership Tool for you to understand when it comes to change in the work-place: *Pure motives and sound logic are often your weakest argument.* Just because something makes sense to you, that thought may be irrelevant. The change process is very complex and difficult. It need not be a win-lose battle, but it's often a major struggle. That's why I call this Chapter the "Crisis of Change."

Early in my career I reached the startling conclusion that *unless I changed how I thought about change, I was unable to be an effective leader.* I had to broaden my paradigm concerning change and force myself to begin thinking more like a leader rather than a follower. Not only is change coming at you faster each day, but the very nature of change is changing. The velocity of change and the pace at work is making it harder to catch those critical change opportunities. Change is becoming multidimensional and more complex. Tell me again how good it is to be a mid-manager wanting to be more proactive in embracing change. It seems we're past the knowledge part of leadership and are now onto those challenging on-the job lessons in leadership. Remember it's a journey into and *through* your experiences in leadership. Going *into* leadership is the easy part; it's getting *through* that's the tough part.

As a "leader in training" (which is what I think we will always be), you must continuously work to better understand the change process. You must go beyond your "best thinking" to include an "accurate reading" of the dynamics surround-ing the related issues. No one can teach you these things, because most of these dynamics surrounding change are interpersonal and situational. Be sure you're up to the risk-taking and skin-thickening learning experiences you'll have to go *through* in addressing change. This is why so many refer to leadership as a journey rather than a destination. It's because the rules, the players, the agendas, the wins and losses, and the pressures are forever changing. The change process and the multitude of change opportunities will *always* be part of your job. Accept that fact and seek to embrace it. *Change must be addressed with proactive thinking, not defen-sive thinking.* If you think change is difficult but badly needed today, it will be even more critical tomorrow.

Political Capital

Years ago, I worked for the Wisconsin State Legislature as a Fiscal Analyst on the state budgets of several state agencies. Here I was, still a recovering account-ant coming from my jobs in the private sector, thrown into the wild world of government and public-sector politics. Wow, did I experience a learning curve on the change process and on the art of politics. All the experiences were useful but not all were fun to be part of. There is great truth in politics that I found to be alive and well. "There are two things you never want to see being made: sausage and legislation—both are bloody processes." In some ways, this political saying might apply to the process of making change within your organization, as well. It can be a bloody process.

I believe that, in the world of politics, it isn't so much that people opposing a given change don't understand the big picture or the need for change. Rather, for a variety of personal and political reasons, they argue that things are better off if you *do not* change than if you *do* change. Their position on whether to support or oppose change is often based on whose ox will be gored and who is perceived to be the winners and losers as a result of the change. Don't fool yourself by believing that consideration of a given change is an "intellectual exercise." Wrong!! In the workplace, you must understand the dynamics surrounding the process of introducing, debating, deciding, and implementing change because it goes far beyond seeing the big picture issues. *The problem is not the problem; rather, the problem is the* **process** *of introducing, debating, deciding, and implementing change and the perceived* **results** *of the change.* The real problems are too often *self-preservation* **motives,** *lack of* **trust** *in leaders, and* **timing** *pressures.* Understand the dynamics of this three-legged stool—*motives, trust, and timing*—and use this Leadership Tool as one of your first steps in learning to address change.

The following is a reaction illustration any given team member might have to your change idea. "If the change is likely to result in some of my job responsibilities being taken away, or if my job security is at risk, or if my function will change dramatically, or if I'm being transferred to that bad supervisor, guess what—I'll go down dragging and kicking all the way." This person has *motive.* At the same time, your motive as change agent is to make things better for the overall organization. The two of you have far different perceptions as to the impact this change will have and the motives are far different, as well. Let's complicate this illustration further. What if you have the reputation of being *untrustworthy* and generally did not follow through on new initiatives? Add to this the variable, the timing pressures of a busy staff. Even for an effective change process, *time* and timing issues will stir the pot of conflict even more. In every organization, with every change, I guarantee you will experience strong drivers and strong resisters. In short, you will have conflict. Is this the art of politics or is it the course of human nature? It's probably both.

How in the world do you begin to address this change crisis? How do you manage to not take it personally or feel that those attempting to block your proposed change are "bad?" Have you ever felt that your organization functioned like a mini-legislature? Change may be necessary, but it isn't always fun. But then again, having fun is not the primary goal as you're striving toward a greater leadership role. Sometimes, I think I'd rather see sausage being made.

The Seven E's

What are the sources and motivators for change challenges and politics within your organization? Let me offer a starting point. Could the hidden agendas and political strategies have anything to do with what I refer to as the **"Seven E's"** The Seven E's can be found at any level and in any department of the organization. They represent *reasons* why and *strategies* used by individuals and departments presenting stiff opposition to your proposed changes. Look for these Seven E's—I'm sure you'll find them alive and well within your organization.

- *Ego*—I am the center of the universe and I decide what is right for *me*. I know best.

- *Energy*—I will ask questions and raise "red flags" that cause you to waste energy and time answering, clarifying, defending, and fighting the issues I've raised. If I make you use up all your energy on my issues, you won't be able to implement the change.

- *Earnings*—I don't want you to look good to the supervisor so you can receive a raise or promotion. While different than earnings, your change will deflect scarce resources away from *my* earning potential and chance for promotion. I have scarcity thinking.

- *Evolution*—I want change to be slow, deliberate, always under control, and in moderation. Don't talk to me about "revolutionary change;" make it evolutionary.

- *Empowerment*—All I see is the word "power" in em*power*ment, and that's it. I want the power, and will fight you to get it or retain it. We're in a struggle for power.

- *Enlightenment*—You just don't understand how *good* we have it now. Why change this good thing and create chaos for us all?

- *Encampment*—My power base of follower-ship (camp) is bigger and stronger than your camp. I'm not fighting you alone on the field of battle—this is war involving the masses.

It's important that you, as a leader, be aware of these Seven E's and how they represent strong barriers and resisters to change. They in essence are the hidden motives resulting in individual and team positioning on both sides of the change issue. Your biggest challenge will be to get these hidden agendas to the top of the table—into the light of day so they can be squarely addressed. If you don't "confront" the real and hidden issues directly, you're simply deferring an even greater point of conflict down the road of change.

Can you see these forces at work within your organization? There are egos bouncing off each other, human energy being wasted protecting people from the effect of change, fear of earnings/wages being affected negatively, and so on. Each can create political maneuvering and dysfunctional behavior by seemingly good individuals. Skill is required to uncover these forces at work, but even greater skill is required to shift these resisting forces into positive forces that will advance the change. You must not ignore these powerful motivators impacting the change process. Remember that logic is generally your weakest argument when the Seven E's are at work fighting any given change. It's often politics as UNusual within the workplace.

Costs of Change: Time Capital and Human Capital

Costs of Timing

When the need for a change becomes evident and there is great urgency to make the change (similar to someone needing to yell "Fire!"), you will do whatever is necessary to get the change implemented immediately. However, *there is a hidden cost for immediacy or "pushing" the change through*. There is a cost or loss of capital due to your timing. It can cost you loss of trust, commitment, and energy from others the next time you yell "Fire!" or "The sky is falling!" On the other hand, if you intentionally delay making needed change until everyone is comfortable and happy, you will experience another form of cost due to your inaction or delay. You can lose a valued customer, miss a competitive advantage opportunity, continue costly inefficiencies in your production processes, or get your supervisor really, really, really mad at you. This cost can sometimes put you out of business or at least make key officials within your organization very unhappy. This is pressure time for a leader; it's decision time. It's about *time*.

How can you balance the enormous pressures and costs of urgent change versus the enormous costs of unnecessary delay in bringing about needed change? A starting point is to clearly understand and then communicate all facts regarding the nature and impact of this change—on customers, the organization, departments, and individuals. Then, as covered earlier, develop a clear and common understanding of the current realities for yourself and the key stakeholders. If, after this analysis, you must still yell "Fire!," only do so if absolutely required. How do you get others to hear your calls for reason when it's not a fire situation? There isn't one answer. It will be situational and will require your best thinking. This is why leadership is not for the faint of heart.

Human Capital Costs

A second form of hidden cost is tied to your approach to change; that old "what's to gain and what's to lose" decision. At stake is the *loss of human capital*. If your goal is to maintain total control of the change process, regardless of cost, that's what you'll get—total control at the cost of human capital from others. You have change *you* want implemented and want to cut through all the workplace hassle, so you use your position of power to simply make it happen. It's top down, compliance driven, and with a dash of fear thrown in for good measure. This goes with one of my favorite truisms: "Organizations and individuals become what they choose to measure and reward." If the only thing being measured and rewarded is just making that change—that's what you'll get and it will be *all* you'll get. But what are you losing in the process? "Do it because I say so" never worked with my children and that "dog won't hunt" in the workplace either. If building morale, teambuilding, and buy-in are desired long-term goals for your organization, you'd better not use the "total control approach." Seek those new, proactive strategies to achieving your long-term goals while working to minimize the loss of human capital. It will cost you if you don't.

Poor judgment on time pressures and lost human capital will force staff into a perceived lose-win situation or a position where they simply say "I really don't care any more." I believe the worse thing for staff to lose is their "heart" for the change, the job, you, and the organization. Make every effort to avoid having your staff semi-retiring on the job, simply complying (avoiding ownership), or no longer offering suggestions for improvement. It's the kiss of death. This loss of human capital will likely result in a major loss of your ability to "influence" others to accept change next time around. With the loss of influence comes the loss of leadership effectiveness. You're then likely to become a "manager" of change as compared to a "leader" of change.

The power hungry or gung-ho manager may not care about the *cost* of making poor timing decisions and loss of human capital today, but the organization will *pay* for it down the road. Don't kid yourself into thinking the main thing in this change process is to simply get the change made. The analysis of human capital gain or loss must be factored into your strategy decisions. If the only goal is implementation at *all* cost, that's what you may get—*all* cost. *Very few* actions are worth that investment or loss of working capital in human terms.

In my mind I visualize the change process like an iceberg floating in the midst of the workplace dynamic. Everyone sees the actual implementation process as the exposed, top portion of the iceberg, the one-tenth. Out of sight and too often out of mind are the other nine-tenths of the iceberg. This is where the real dynamics are taking place, boiling and setting the stage for action or inaction. *The real political games, human capital, workplace energy, win-lose strategies, and alliances are taking place under the surface. It's pressure to "change" versus the inertia of the "status quo."* Remember this iceberg analogy; *what you **don't** see can destroy your leadership efforts.* A Leadership Tool is to seek a greater understanding of the issues floating beneath the surface on any issue. Once you understand these issues, address them directly.

The Change Challengers

In addition to the challenge of workplace politics, you'll find there are strong (or weak) individuals who will fight you every step in the change process—just because. Don't waste time seeking to "make sense" of this political dance. It's not that they're bad people; rather, it could be due to their personal views on impact of the proposed change or the approach you're using in the change process or the Seven E's. For some, the word "change" strikes fear in their hearts. They will avoid it if at all possible, yet want everyone else to change. They subscribe to the "be reasonable, do it *my* way" approach. Others, however, will fight change (and you as the leader) every step of the way. Any organization that consistently seeks the status quo *stops* moving forward. In fact, over time, they actually begin to move the organization backward.

I've worked with many different types of people with a variety of outlooks on change, but the three types I'm about to list concern me the most. They are *classic examples of those who will challenge most **any** change.* In my opinion, these individuals are extremely dangerous to the health of any organization. I'd rather have staff confront me directly during the change process rather than drag their feet, sabotage, or communicate clueless untruths to others. I've identified three examples of change challengers I've experienced:

- *The Senior Official* who arrogantly believes that tomorrow will be like yesterday plus or minus 5%. Actually, tomorrow will likely be 50% different than yesterday. These people are examples of wanting to see into the future by looking in their rear view mirror. Your greatest danger is to allow people and the organization to believe too deeply that they'll be a success tomorrow because they were a success yesterday. To them, the paradigm is focused solely on what made them a success yesterday, not what is needed to be a success tomorrow—and the next day.

- *The mid-manager* who sees the "customer" as those internal departments or external organizations that impose compliance requirements on your organization. They've lost sight of the real customer you're in business to serve. These people are the hardest to convince to move on issues. They're stuck in the paradigm of control, compliance, and fear of making a mistake. To them, it's all about doing things right. Their measure of success is compliance, not customer satisfaction. Watch for these individuals who exhibit strong "gatekeeper" tendencies.

- *The front line employee* who has been on the job 15 years but in reality has had 1 year of experience 15 times; not 15 years of experience. They're stuck in a time warp and lack the ability to see today's realities, the big picture, and changes needed to be part of the new century. They are generally a combination of being self-centered and fearful of *any* change. To them, it's all about self-preservation, and maintaining the status quo (for themselves) is their only goal. The concepts of customers and competition are not part of their thinking or actions.

Oh please tell me you're not one of these!!!! If you are, stop reading this book immediately and call someone for help. Somewhere there's a 12-Step Program for you. Underneath all three examples is one common theme. *None of them are aligned or in touch with today's realities, the desired vision for the organization, and the growing global competitiveness of business.* Simply stated, they are not in touch with the true needs of your business. Their role, at whatever level and however well meaning, is mis-guided and hurting others in the long run, including themselves. What if some of them are part of your team and are your responsibility? I don't believe the issue is the actual change. It's their inability to comprehend the true reasons to consider the proposed change; it's their perception of reality. It's time to have a very serious talk with them to bring them back to reality and the role you expect them to take regarding organizational change. In extreme cases, outplacement is always an option if they continue being a serious barrier to moving forward with needed change.

I must also note the existence of *flawed thinking often found at the organizational level.* It tends to emerge just before the organization starts its downturn into chaos, including losing key customers, downsizing staff, and turning the leadership focus 100% inward. The two forms of flawed organizational thinking might be summarized as follows:

- The organization firmly believes and acts in a manner as if there is no competition in their business world that can hurt them.

- The organization has a fatal arrogance to believe that their customers need them more than they need their customers. The same attitude exists in how strategic business partnerships are viewed—they act as though their strategic partners need them more than they need the partners.

The types of individual thinking and organizational thinking just referenced represent naive attempts to protect themselves from the impact of change while giving the outward appearance of being proactive. Does the vision of an ostrich come to mind? What do you do with: the senior official who will only risk incremental change, the mid-manager who views success as meeting compliance requirements (the absence of violations), and the front line worker who views her/his responsibility as "what's best for *me?*" How can you get an organization shifted from its island of false security, which ignores its customers, its partners, and the competition? *It's a face-off between internal thinking versus external thinking.* The tidal wave for them is starting to emerge on the horizon. Like it or not, these individuals and organizations will be forced into change or else change will cause them to lose their security in other ways (organizational failure). For the organization that has faulty thinking on change, sometimes all you can do is to let the inevitable happen. That is, to let the pain begin and wait until the proper timing to lead the change process.

Earlier I identified the Seven E's and just presented different "fronts" individuals and organizations present to make-believe they are change advocates, but their actions are really communicating the following:

- The status quo is a comfortable place from which to watch the world go by.

- Organizational change may not be all bad, but they don't want to learn new processes and have to change themselves. They don't mind change but they hate *being forced* to change.

- This too will pass—if they drag their feet long enough, change leaders will move on to another "program of the month."

- Preserving their comfort zone is a daily battle to be fought—it's a war to be won.

How do you move individuals from feeling they're being changed? Better yet, how do you get staff to move off their status quo positions? It's one of the leadership challenges that frustrated me the most. You see, the logic of change will take you only so far. Playing your own game of politics will give you added clout but be aware of the negatives of "playing politics." You can use the power of your position to force change. You can shift people's jobs within the organization and remove them from being an obstacle—today. Or you can *find creative ways to draw key individuals into the dialog and open the door for them to become participants in formulating the change process.* I'm sure there are many other strategies but, to do nothing cannot be one of them. Sometimes you must cause change to happen. The question is, how much human capital can you salvage along the way? In short, you must be a leader in bringing about needed change at the lowest (human capital) cost possible.

On the surface, the word "change" doesn't seem that big a deal. In reality, it's what leadership, organizational growth, and success are all about. You can never remain in a stationary position in business—you're either moving forward or going backward. The crisis of change is real but change is very critical.

The Time/Change Continuum

Let's assume for a moment that your staff has a negative attitude toward a given change initiative. Your job is to influence your negative thinking staff into understanding that the proposed change is valid and needed and that it *must occur.* Part of your advice to those resisting individuals would be that their reaction to this change could very well influence the impact the change will have on them. They have a choice to make as to the role they will play as you move toward change. Do they want to be part of the change process, oppose it, or do nothing? The following are three possible outcomes depending upon the role they choose to play:

- *Change happens FOR you*—This particular change is good for you even though you were not involved in the process of change. You just live right. You benefited from the change but only to the extent that others have decided for you. You're just lucky to be lucky—this time. But those "others" will be back with further change in the not too distant future.

- **Change happens TO you**—The change is bad because you resisted it for too long and now you're a victim of change. In this case, your timing, your judgment, or your attitude toward the change was off. You'd better keep your head down or they'll get you again.

- **Change happens WITH you**—The change may be "different" but it's better than if you had no involvement in the change process. You took the high road; you were a partner in the process to the extent possible. In this case, you had a voice in the change and you likely benefited. You've also positioned yourself better to partner in future changes.

I love this statement: "I cannot promise you that things are necessarily going to get better or worse in the future. I can, however, promise you that things will be *different*. Whether these differences will be better or worse depends on the extent to which you are a full and active participant in the change process." That's the case when change happens *with* you.

It isn't a matter of *if*; it's a matter of *when*. *Your proactive choice is **when** and **how** you will participate in the change process*. You have one of three basic positions to take regarding change:

- You can choose to keep your eyebrows down at the task level only making change when it's at the crisis stage.

- You can keep your eyebrows up taking an early and active role in the process of change.

- You can keep your eyes closed and ask someone to wake you when the change is over.

Are you one who waits for a crisis or are you more proactive in *seeking* change opportunities? Like it or not, the positioning of your eyebrows on this matter can bear a direct impact on your success in leadership (see Chapter 8—Nugget #1). What you see (with your eyebrows up) can affect your role and sense of timing in the change process. If you're a partner in the process, change can often be a good thing for you. If you enter the change process too late, you're seen as a follower or a victim. If you enter too early, you can be seen as a change shopper and hopper; a "chicken little." Hopefully, you're timing and judgment is just right—most of the time.

EXERCISE #20: I'd like you to envision a line or "continuum" that measures your comfort zone or your "preferred approach" as to *when* you enter the change process as a participant (not resister). That is, at what stage of the change process would you normally prefer to become involved? What impact do you believe this timing of involvement would normally have on how this change will affect you?

Recognizing that investment of your time on change initiatives is "situational," write down your answers as to how and when (or if) you would *normally* prefer to invest time and energy in being a participant in the change process.

- *Timeline Preference:* If, for example, the timeline was six months from idea to implementation, would you normally prefer to become involved at the point of the change implementation in month: two, four, or not at all? Why?

- *Timeline Impact:* On a scale of 1 to 10, what impact do you believe your being a full and active participant in the change process near the beginning would affect the outcome (outcome defined as positive for you and most others)? A rating of 1 is no impact; a rating of 10 is a major, positive impact. Provide examples of both good and bad experiences you've had that support the 1 to 10 rating.

- Based on your experiences, are your efforts generally better served attempting to fight change rather than being a participant in the process? Answer: Yes or No.

Each of us has a preferred entry point on this Time/Change Continuum. Some prefer to become involved closer to the implementation date; others earlier in the process. In many cases, being a victim of change is the consequence of your inaction or delayed action. On the other hand, you may believe that you're "selling out" by being an early and active participant in the change process or you may simply be too busy to become involved in most change initiatives. Your preferred positioning and the change dynamics will dictate *when* and *how* you act or react on any given day. Be mindful of this "choice" you have.

This Leadership Tool on the Time/Change Continuum is important for you to understand and model for your team. Generally, the earlier you lean into change the better the impact for you and your team. However, there are times when fighting or simply staying away from proposed change initiatives might be the best course of action. Remember, it's situational.

As you might realize, my preference was to be at the table early, gaining an understanding and offering my input early in the process. Remember, in the long run, change is no longer an option that can be avoided; it's just a matter of when and how change will change you and the organization. Your legacy in leadership will be defined in part by this reality and your response to it. My suggestion; *look for change to happen* **with** *you, not for you or in spite of you.*

Partners In Change

A Leadership Tool I'm now introducing is to seek the right partners in addressing any change (whether you're in favor of the change or not.) I am *not* talking about partners to make you a winner and others losers—that's warfare. I'm suggesting you *seek alliances* with other people, departments, and organizations who share a clear and common understanding of the Main Things and seek mutual success for all parties and for the organization. Then together, you become full and active participants in the change process.

Internal dynamics regarding any change are directly influenced by alliances that are created. This could be termed "office politics," but it is also a way of bringing about required change. Some partnerships or alliances may be formal, but most are informal. You have a choice as to whether you will be that "lone ranger" fighting for or against a given change idea. On your own, you are forced to rely on being that "great communicator" or "great politician" who can share wisdom at the perfect time to enlighten others with clear logic and strong arguments to support your position. That's tough to do! Creating effective partnerships is an alternative way to address change.

The art of building effective partnerships, however, goes beyond building just internal alliances. You may also build support from external partners, as well. Is your team with you, are other departments with you, are senior officials with you, are customers with you, and/or are suppliers with you? Building partners to stand with you, to take the lead when necessary, to cover your backside when necessary, and to communicate on your behalf are all aspects of "advancing" your position on change. One word of caution on partnerships, however. Because most are loosely formed and issue specific, be aware that your partner one day may become an opponent of yours the next. Stay close to your alliances and watch for some to alter their position on the change—on a dime. Avoid standing by yourself on the issue, surprised, alone, and feeling double-crossed.

Change is more than being right. Check your ego at the door, invite meaningful partners, and keep close to them.

Do you recall my earlier comments on the mini-legislature in the workplace? Change is more than being right. Check your ego at the door, invite meaningful partners, and keep close to them. Do not, however, turn this into warfare. You run the risk of alienating others long-term if you make the analyses, related discussions, and actions personal in nature. Your motives, trust level, and judgment as to timing will be greatly enhanced and multiplied if your voice is joined by others. It's not the *number* of partners that will influence others; it's the *quality* of your chosen partners and your collective approach to the process of change. The goal of partnerships should be to achieve win-win solutions to change challenges—not win-lose solutions.

The Three C's of Business

1. *The CUSTOMER is in charge.*

2. *CHANGE is constant.*

3. *COMPETITION is increasing.* "Reengineering the Corporation" —Hammer and Champy

The customer and your competition are the MAJOR forces that should be driving your organization to go beyond simply trying to make periodic incremental, continuous improvement changes. You're being forced to address serious and significant change in order to remain in business. Change *is* becoming a constant. and in many cases is not an option. You'd better be proactive in listening to your customers' as they demand that *everything* you do be *better, quicker, and cheaper for them.* We talk about leadership from two steps behind. You'd better believe that your customers are expecting you to serve them from two steps ahead of their current needs. In addition, your competition is learning all about your strengths and weaknesses from two steps to your side. The competition is benchmarking against what you're doing best and leapfrogging over your weaknesses. *If you're #1 at anything, you will soon become #2 or lower if you don't take the crisis of change seriously.* Then main drivers need to be heavily influenced (driven) by your customers and your competition.

If the Three C's are real (which they are), then how do you consider these C's when you're making decisions regarding change? The following is a listing of several of the "change-related actions" you should consider as a leader working to implement major change.

- *Obtain and communicate an accurate and common understanding of your customers' requirements.* Be agile enough to deliver rapid and relevant change as required.

- *Understand the realities of the internal dynamics resisting change,* and how to be more effective in helping move others outside of their comfort zone (Current Realities).

- *Develop alliances with partners,* both within and outside your organization. How can you work in concert with these partners to move the organization forward?

- *Control the temptation to "rush into change"* in a manner that is generally simple (quick), neat (controllable), and wrong (miss the true target). What are the right changes that will make a significant difference; not simply making change for the sake of change?

- *Learn about and from your competition* by benchmarking against their strengths and weaknesses. Your organization must remain competitive.

As long as we're looking at the organization from a different vantage point (outside-in), let's view what happens to organizations during the change process now that we're up here at 20,000 feet. You'll see that the change process moves slowly through the following three separate phases:

- *Unfreezing people and the organization from what they are currently doing.* You must work to create a supportive environment, culture, and opportunity to examine change alternatives with an open mind (new paradigm). Sometimes you will create this awareness by highlighting the pain if the organization does not change and other times highlighting the passion and reward of moving toward a beneficial change. Keep the ground fertile and the organization agile enough to accept change when the time is right. Change is not an event; it's a process, and part of this process is staff letting go of where they are *today.*

- *Moving (transitioning) staff, partners, and the organization in the new direction.* It's essential that you properly align the plans, people, paradigms, and processes to implement and support this new direction. Leadership involves much more than simply pointing in the direction the organization is to go. The critical three success strategies during this transition period are *communication, communication, and communication.* Do not allow the change process to lose focus or momentum. Provide key stakeholders continuous feedback on progress and the emerging positive impact of change.

- *Re-freezing the people and the organization in the new direction once you've arrived.* A critical strategy is to "re-calibrate" how the organization will support the *new* way of doing business, including proper training and process changes. Seek ways to integrate this new thinking and doing into the daily lives of individuals and the organization. Support this new direction by changes in the infrastructure, procedures, systems, and measures of success. Celebrate your new location on the road to success.

The Pain of Change

Change often occurs only when the pain of actually making the change is less painful than **not** *making the change.* I know there are great halls of knowledge written about change management, yet every organization seems to hear great shrieks of pain in the course of change.

What's important is that you understand *how* the change process will vary by situation, people, and your abilities. The *stress* of change impacts everyone involved. It is real, deeply seeded, and hard on people. A change in one area usually impacts the need for change in several other departments or processes— a domino effect. Do not underestimate the impact of change and the struggle the process represents. For many, stress on the job is already at the breaking point. Now you want to introduce a major change? As I reflect back on my career, I could honestly say that most of the time I wasn't under a lot of stress. But if you'd asked my staff and peers they'd say "Nitschke was a stress carrier." As a leader, you do cause stress, but your job must also include finding those important stress-relievers. Monitor and appreciate the stress levels you add and the stress your staff are undergoing. It will allow you to better understand the reactions you're receiving and to determine the best strategies to move forward *with* support of your staff.

Additional Points to Ponder On Change

- Your organization may be living on borrowed time. It's like trying to pay your MasterCard bill with your Standard Oil Credit Card. It's not a good plan for success and it will catch up with you sooner or later.

- Take time to look at where you are as an organization from the "outside-in;" like a customer would see you. You'll get a different perspective on opportunities to change.

- If you're not concerned or at least somewhat confused about the process of implementing change, you're not thinking clearly.

- Do not underestimate the incredible inertia that the status quo approach to "doing the job" generates. This inertia that's opposed to change will keep on ticking forever unless you can unfreeze it and transform it.

The People Side of Change

Do not try to prepare the organization for where the people are. Do try to prepare the people for where the organization needs to go. All organizations are going to be flawed in some ways; the key is how you respond to these flaws. The root problems relating to change can most often be traced back to internal "relationships" and how staff have been allowed (or even rewarded) to function in the past. Effective organizations have established high expectations for their leaders, managers, teams, and individuals, which are clear, supported, and hold everyone to accountability expectations. Ineffective organizations have a wide variety of accountability measures and systems that are set by individuals and teams rather than by senior officials. Because of this, ineffective organizations usually have very low expectations set for staff, are weak in monitoring progress, and seldom evaluate success in meaningful ways.

As you prepare to introduce a change, how will you involve your staff in the decision-making and implementation process and raise your "expectations" for staff involvement? To what degree are you going to solicit their input and empower them? Of course, the answer is situational, but *you should be leaning toward granting as much delegation and empowerment you feel you can live with.* You want your team to have buy-in toward the change and the opportunity to offer input as decisions are being made. *However,* since you'll remain the person ultimately accountable for effective implementation, how much responsibility are you willing to delegate to your team? Are you willing to accept their decisions even if you don't believe they're the right decisions?

Four Levels of Staff Involvement in Decision-Making

It's your decision as the responsible manager to decide which one of the four levels of staff decision-making you're willing to grant in any change situation. You will create leadership "gold stars" from your team and the organization if you apply the right level or you'll receive a big red "F" if the wrong one is selected. Your decision on this matter is critical—and of course is dependent upon many conditions/situations. A large part of your success is tied to staff believing they've made a significant difference in the change process and that they were true participants in this process. On the other hand, how much of the decision-making process are you comfortable "giving up" to the team?

With all that said, here are *your* four basic options in delegating decision-making:

- *"I'll Share What I've Already Decided You're Going to Do"*—Inform staff that a change is coming and you share an overview of the decision, implementation plan, and their role in the process. There is a narrow range of information communicated without soliciting extensive input. More of a sharing process is followed by a "question and answer" period.

- *"I'll Listen to Your Ideas"*—You share as in #1 above but invite greater staff input as to the implementation plan and staff role. You seek input and may end up making minor modifications to your change plan as a result of this input. However, you reserve the right to make the final decision. Input is received and considered.

- *"We'll Be Together On This Change"*—Staff input occurs earlier in the process and their collective opinions help drive the change-related decisions. Your opinions are matched with theirs and "together" the final decisions are made. Staff has a major impact on decision-making, but you as the leader have weighted voting power. You influence the final decision. This is a consensus-building process with consensus defined as: *Everyone agrees they can "live with the decision;" not that everyone agrees at the 100% level.*

- *"The Team Makes the Final Decision and Runs With It"*—The Team *owns* and *makes* the final decision; you delegate total decision-making authority to the Team. "Here team, you take it and run with it." "I trust you that you will implement the decision well."

EXERCISE #21: Four-Levels of Staff Involvement:

- Which level of staff involvement do you usually operate from?

- Would your team answer the same way? Ask them!

- If you wanted to delegate more empowerment to your team, what changes would you have to make in your communication and accountability requirements?

Four Levels of Staff Commitment To Change

Okay, you've made the change-related decisions and are moving toward implementation. Will all team members (and your peers) be supporting you in this effort? Of course not; it's called "human nature, office politics, payback time, 'I want to retire soon' signals, and 'I'm having a bad day' attitude." You know it intuitively, but there are various forms of support (or non-support) your staff and peers *will* choose to take with you or against you. Watch for those who, on the surface, are your supporters but in reality are seeking to make you a loser. I venture to say that in any large team, on any given change issue, you're likely to find differing forms or levels of buy-in on any decision.

Watch for each of these four levels of staff commitment and actions during the next change process, and be prepared to address each accordingly:

1. *Adversarial Compliance*—"I'll do only what I need to do but you and everyone else will know I'm against the change." "I'm behind you, supervisor, but I'm way behind you." Secretly or perhaps even vocally, this staff member has not bought into the change. In extreme cases, this individual may become a stealth resister in fighting the change behind your back.

2. *Willing Compliance*—"You said this change is to be part of my responsibility, so I'll do it—but no more, no less." You may have to stay close to this individual because she/he may not volunteer improvement opportunities even if needed and justified. Somewhat a "wake me when the change is over" attitude. Seems I have the most difficulty with these individuals.

3. *Sincere Compliance*—"It seems like a good idea supervisor, so tell me what you want and I'll do it, and I'll do more if I can." This person has bought into the change and is willing to follow your leadership *If* you stay close and support him/her. Find ways to involve this individual and others in new and deeper ways.

4. *Full Commitment*—"This change idea is exactly what I can support, and I will do everything in my power to assist you in achieving success in its implementation." "I'll help you find a way to make it happen." This staff member is a champion of the change and can influence others. Just be careful she/he does not carry their enthusiasm beyond their scope of authority or get too far out in front of you.

What's the starting point to evoke this positive level of commitment from others? I believe it begins with YOU having the strength of commitment yourself. Do not try to play-act having a commitment for something because staff will see through you in a minute. Your level of commitment will show more in non-verbal ways than by the words you speak. What do you do if the reality is that you and your team are faced with duties none of you are "fully committed" to do? In this case, the thing to do is simply be honest with your team and have the professionalism to get the job done, do it well and on time, and don't fake your commitment for the activity. At least try to have a Willing Compliance attitude.

EXERCISE #22:

- Which of these four levels of staff commitment have you seen exhibited most frequently by members of your team during the change process? Why?

- What leadership strategies would you employ if you had a group of Adversarial Compliance members consistently "fighting you" on change issues?

- What strategies would you initiate if the majority of your team members, after all your efforts to obtain their buy-in and support, remained in a negative position toward the desired change?

Putting Decision-Making and Involvement Together

On one hand, you have four options as to the level of involvement and decision-making you choose to delegate to staff (see Staff Involvement In Decision-Making). On the other hand, staff has four options as to the level of participation they wish to play in bringing about desired change (see Staff Commitment To Change). *How much authority are you willing to delegate to staff that have varying levels of commitment?* Here is what I've found to be the key. If you have an accurate reading on *the level of commitment* your team is willing to make, it can give you guidance as to *the level of decision-making* you're willing to delegate. For example, if your team or key individuals only have Willing Compliance toward a change, why would you delegate full authority to them to make the final decisions on change?

The Matrix that follows will illustrate how you might wish to match commitment levels with decision-making roles. This is a critical leadership Tool to learn and apply as needed.

MATRIX: THE ROLE OF STAFF IN CHANGE

(Horizontal: Four Levels of Staff Involvement in Decision-Making)

(Vertical: Four Levels of Staff Commitment To Change)

Role In Decisions Level Of Commitment	Only Sharing What You'll Be Doing	Listen to Staff Ideas & Input	Joint Decision— Staff and Leader	Full Staff Authority for the Decision
Adversarial Compliance	Wise	Extreme Caution	Extreme Caution	
Willing Compliance		Wise	Wise	
Sincere Compliance			Wise	Extreme Caution
Full Commitment				Use in limited instances

Remember that *staff **commitment** is different than **compliance** because the level of **commitment** is generated from within rather than imposed from the outside.* A person (or organization), which is committed to something feels compelled to make a "personal investment" to seeing the vision or change become a reality. Their behavior is naturally aligned to and recognized by the strength of their commitment. One tool is to listen carefully to the words and watch the body language of staff to assess their level of commitment:

- **Is the language REACTIVE in nature?** "There's nothing I can do; If I have to; If only; I'll try; He/She makes me so mad; We tried that before and it didn't work." These are examples of staff positioning you for their *compliance and status quo response.* Watch for the ongoing "water cooler meeting" grousing about the change and its impact.

- *Is the language PROACTIVE in nature?* "I will; I'll help you determine the best options; I'll do whatever I can; I'll start here; This time we'll make it work." These are examples of staff positioning you for a *commitment response*. There's a positive "buzz" about the change that's pending.

- *Is the BODY LANGUAGE reactive or proactive in nature?* Watch the eyes, level of eye contact, look for smirks, read the face, are they leaning into the change or backing away?

Pareto's 80/20 Principle—Again

Staff have been made more aware of the need to change, you've appropriately involved them in dialogue regarding key decisions, and you've attempted to coach and support your team more than in the past. You want to avoid mandating this change and you've done everything right—now all staff will embrace the change and give that ol' 110% support. WRONG!!! In the process of introducing almost any change you can predict a pattern as to how any group or team will initially buy-in to your change.

- 20% will immediately be with you, buying into almost any direction you want to take them. You want to recognize and utilize their support fully.

- 60% will "wait and see"—show me first and let *me* decide.

- 20% will fight you any and all ways possible. Ever get the feeling they wake up on the wrong side of the bed?

Your Leadership Tool must be to retain the 20% initially behind you and focus on that 60% "wait and see" crowd. You need to effectively use the strong 20% to gain support from the next grouping of 60%. The first reaction to any change often reflects fear of the unknown and even fear of the known impact. As a leader, you must appreciate this fact and choose strategies that will "draw" those from the 60% group into the change process. A good move would be:

- To learn from the top 20% group, their insights, ideas, and strategies to achieve greater buy-in from the middle 60%.

- A second move would be to "listen" to members of that middle group and seek to understand their expressed concerns and barriers regarding the change. It's important to any of us that our concerns are aired and we're better understood. Perhaps it's only a matter of providing more information and uncovering the unknowns. Seriously consider actions required to remove some of the identified barriers.

- As for the final group of 20%, the resisters, be aware that members of this group could sabotage your efforts either formally or informally. Do not put intense energy into using logic and spending hours attempting to fully address their concerns. On the other hand, it is always important that you communicate fully and listen carefully to the concerns they raise. Some valid issues and perspectives may emerge but many of the real issues will likely remain "under the table." Unfortunately, and most times, the best you can hope for from this group is quiet resistance. Again, these are not "bad" individuals, but simply those having a different position on the matter of this given change.

- If your measure of success is to keep *all* members of your team happy you'll fail every time, but by now I'm sure you've learned that lesson very well.

Remember to apply the Leadership Tools presented earlier in this Chapter regarding political capital, time pressure capital, human capital, and the power of partnerships. Use these and other tools in improving the leadership-minded operating style you've learned over the years—keeping the Main Things the main things.

Is Motivation/Attitude Important?

Think of the last time someone asked you to list your strengths and weaknesses. If you're like me, your list of weaknesses would be much longer than your list of strengths—probably twice as long. It's been stated that *up to 75% of our thinking about ourselves is naturally categorized as negative, with only 25% considered positive thinking*. A similar pattern exists in the general workplace, as well. If this negative thinking pattern exists in your organization, it's no wonder why so many individuals are initially resistant to new ideas and change. You must find ways to shift individuals off their negative attitude to a positive attitude.

I've just shared two useful Leadership Tools I feel you should consider and use to help move your team and organization into change: the Four Levels of Staff Involvement and the Four Levels of Staff Commitment to Change. There are many other tools you will pick up along the way to help lead, shift attitudes, and manage change within your organization. But hear me well; *do not underestimate the impact staff attitude has on change and the impact their attitude toward you has in this entire process.*

You will not change staff attitudes based on your talking louder, threatening more, the academic credentials you might have, by patronizing staff, or the dress for success image you present. The larger question is "what will motivate your staff to change?" Here's a hint: You cannot motivate people to change. It must come from *their* internal motivation, which serves to alter their perspectives or mindsets. *You will seldom motivate someone to **follow** you; they will be more likely to follow your idea based on WIIFM—"what's in it for me."* Therefore, an obvious strategy is to find the critical motivating factors to focus your communication and decision-making efforts. Let's call it the "so what WIIFM factor," which could include:

- The team or individuals or the organization are at a crisis state and everyone knows it. There's no option; it's a matter of survival for all of us.

- The change will improve the workflow and workload.

- The organization supported you during a personal crisis; it's payback time to help out.

- The change opportunity is too obvious to pass up—for example, we can triple our business and we'll all get a $5,000 bonus at year-end.

- We're united against a common "enemy" from outside the organization. We rally around the company flag to fight back collectively—for example, a hostile take-over or buy-out of the company.

Now comes the hard part. What about those employees who don't or won't change even though the "so what WIIFM" motivators are present? In many cases, these individuals will be found to have low motivation, high fear, dislike you intensely, be insecure in their job, or have problems at home. This is the 20% of staff who will generally fight you all the way. If it's a question of information or ability, attempt to coach, support, or mentor these individuals to fill in information gaps. Become personally involved. Address their WIIFM needs if you can, but you can't stop the change process waiting for these individuals to "climb on board."

However, in the process of working with this 20%, do *not* overlook your Main Thing of moving the organization forward. Keep the Main Thing the main thing. If it's a serious matter of staff attitude or lack of motivation, *as a last resort,* you may have to consider these progressive stages of action:

- Seek out the root of their anger, fear, distrust, etc. This requires you to gain meaningful insight into their issues to address their personal and interpersonal barriers in a proactive way. It represents an opportunity for you to grow as well. *Remember to always value your dissenters,* listen and understand their thoughts because it can prove invaluable to you later on. Do not cut this process short; this is the preferred approach.

- Next stage would be to address those areas of fear or correct those barriers identified by staff as appropriate. This would be followed by gradually increasing the pressure to change by exerting a more "directive style" over time—applied gently at first.

- The last resort (and I mean the **last** resort) if individuals remain committed to blocking or undermining the change is the option of moving them toward outplacement services. Several difficult people must not hold the organization hostage, but there is a cost to your leadership if this stage is not done properly and sensitively.

As a manager, you will reach the point of realizing that you must create the **Noah Culture:** *Stop giving reward to those who predict rain; rather, give rewards to those who build arcs!*

Points To Ponder On Attitude:

POINTS TO PONDER ON ATTITUDE:

- "The winner's edge is not a gifted birth, a high I.Q., or talent. The winner's edge is all in the attitude, not aptitude. Attitude is the criterion for success."

—Dennis Waitley

- "A positive attitude may not solve all your problems, but it will annoy enough people to make it worthwhile."

—Herm Albright

- "Whether you think you can or think you can't, you're right."

—Henry Ford

Managing Complex Change

There are a set of eight key drivers for success that must work interdependently as you plan and move to implement the process of change, especially when addressing a complex change. These drivers are Vision, Culture, Incentives, Resources, Processes,

Staff, Action Plan, and *Follow Through.* If effectively supported, coordinated, and implemented, the eight drivers will create an integrated system for individuals and the organization to address the "people and process challenges" associated with change. The result will be having your staff better able to focus on the change process itself, feeling supported, seeing the impact change will have on customers, and discovering opportunities for continuous improvement into the future. In short, staff will have a greater likelihood of buying into the change rather than fighting it. While there is no one formula to ensure successful change, there are essential building blocks to enhancing your likelihood of successful implementation as a leader of change.

It's critical that leaders realize that much of the initial reaction staff have toward change is actually "learned behavior." Is there a reason staff do not dance wildly in favor of major change proposals? How has the organization managed the change process previously? Perhaps you or others have not provided the needed form and level of support as change was implemented in the past. Staff could be anticipating that the needed support will be found lacking yet again. *In many cases, staff behavior or attitude is learned. Look for ways to change the process of change*—to show staff there is a better design for *this* planned change.

Below is a **Matrix For Managing Complex Change** *to illustrate the eight drivers and the negative* **impact** *each could have on staff if you overlook or are unsuccessful in delivering needed support in these eight areas.* For example, the lack of a clear and shared *vision* often results in "Lack of Direction with Confusion" among staff. Likewise, if *incentives* are found lacking, the Impact on Staff would be for them to act in a "Compliance Only or a Resistance" manner. In other words, your lack of support as a leader provides just one more barrier to successful implementation to the change. It's essential that staff:

- Understand and accept a shared **Vision** of the change.

- Work to create and reinforce a **Culture** that is open to change.

- Have **Incentives** that communicate and address "what's in it for me (WIIFM)."

- Receive adequate **Resources** that will allow them to be successful.

- Develop and support new, relevant, and efficient **Processes.**

- Are properly **Trained** to perform new duties.

- Follow a realistic **Action Plan.**

- Receive the needed **Follow Through.**

If all eight drivers are present, properly introduced, and effectively coordinated, the process of successfully implementing complex change is greatly enhanced. The problem is that while many worthy changes are introduced and decided upon by organizations, the failure rate in achieving the desired results is often too high. This isn't because leaders lack having a great change idea or did not care about the effectiveness of implementing the change. Rather, *the level and nature of **support** during the change process is a major predictor of successful implementation.* Even a great idea needs legs to move it forward. The change process is not simply one decision or one-dimensional. It is very complex and involves a series of decisions to be made in a timely manner. It requires both effective management and effective leadership.

The following Matrix shows that the change process (especially complex change) requires an integrated series of drivers and support. Appreciate what to expect if you do not properly support *each and every driver* of the complex change process.

MATRIX FOR MANAGING COMPLEX CHANGE

VISION	CULTURE	INCENTIVES	RESOURCES	PROCESS	SKILLS	ACTION PLAN	FOLLOW THROUGH	IMPACT ON STAFF
Clear, Consistent, & Shared	Open to Change & Risk	WIIFM For Individuals & Organization	Budget, Staff Levels, & Time	New Relevant & Efficient	Training	Coordination	Accountability	If Weak or Missing:
Weak or Missing								Lack Of Direction With Confusion
	Weak or Missing							Lack Of Creativity With High Fear
		Weak or Missing						Compliance Only & Resistance
			Weak or Missing					Frustration, Rebellion, & Burnout
				Weak or Missing				Errors, Lack of Accuracy, Wasted Time
					Weak or Missing			Anxiety, Mistakes & Frustration
						Weak or Missing		Lack Of Focus & Results
							Weak or Missing	False Starts & Gradual Change

Note: There will also be a major *impact* on customers if these drivers are weak or missing.

- **Vision of the Change:** Most people see things as they are, but as a leader, you see things as they might be. Your vision of the future is *pulling you toward action.* If **you** don't transfer this vision effectively and carefully to allow others to buy-into it, they cannot fully share your passion and commitment. This could be termed "vision empowerment;" allowing the team or other departments to share a common direction and outcome. *Without a clear and shared Vision: Staff Lack Direction and are Confused.*

- **Culture of the organization and staff toward Change:** The Culture of the organization will influence staff attitudes toward change. It drives staff thinking as to *why* the change is really required, their perceptions as to *what* the change will do (for them or to them), and their understanding of *how* they can help or hurt the change implementation process. The openness, temperament, approach, risk-taking level, perseverance, and reputation of the organizational culture will help drive positive attitudes and success. Attitude is 80% of the solution. *Without a Culture that is openly supportive of change and willing to take risks: Staff will not be Empowered to be Creative and will function with high levels of Fear during the change process.*

- **Incentives to Motivate and Support Staff:** This might include new systems of recognition and reward, usually based on results rather than pay-offs before the change. Leaders must aggressively seek to understand the barriers staff are experiencing, and step forward to remove these identified barriers. In addition, the organizational incentives must be identified and communicated. As discussed earlier, the key motivators in accepting change are the internal motivators, including WIIFM—take this strategy seriously. *Without Incentives that personalize the impact of change: Staff may be Compliant but many will quietly Resist the change.*

- **Resources:** This would include leadership providing adequate staffing levels, budgets, allocation of time to accomplish the assignments, technology to realize efficiencies, and the necessary access to leaders, information, and support departments. *Without the Resources of budget, staffing levels, time, and access: You will find Frustration, Rebellion, and Staff Burnout.*

- **Processes that are New, Relevant, and Efficient:** In too many cases, great amounts of staff time is wasted in correcting mistakes, preparing reports that no one reads, failures in sharing needed information from/to other departments. Accuracy and timeliness of processes to maximize staff effectiveness is mandatory. *Without efficient and accurate Processes: The result will be Errors, Lack of Accuracy, and Wasted Time*

- **Staff Skills:** In addition to involving staff in the re-design of their "changed" jobs, involve them as you customize the planning and delivery of needed staff training just in time, just enough, just for the staff. Have training results and skill level requirements firmly established. Provide meaningful support in increasing their skill levels to be successful on the job. It's your job to lead them to success; not to blame them for failure. *Without being trained in new Skills required to be successful: Staff will experience Anxiety, Mistakes, and Frustration.*

- **Action Plan:** Have a plan that focuses on the Main Things, divides challenges into doable pieces called goals, break these goals into smaller actionable activities, and prioritize staff time. Establish responsibilities, timelines, resource requirements, and accountability measures. Progress on Action Plans must be carefully monitored, with modification opportunities fully discussed and acted upon when justified. *Without a coordinated Action Plan: You will have Lack of Focus and Desired Results.*

- **Follow Through:** Without leaders supporting and ensuring that the right things are being done and managers making sure that things are being done right, the change process stalls or is marginalized. Follow Through means "working the Action Plan." There are too many variables and too many pressures *against* change to have managers and leaders simply assume the plan will be implemented without difficulty and without unanticipated challenges. Hope for the best but expect major, unexpected difficulties. *Without an accountable process of Follow Through: You will experience False Starts and Gradual Change.*

EXERCISE #23: Based on the Matrix for Managing Complex Change:

- Write down your comments regarding the Matrix. Is it an accurate recap of how to implement complex change? What key drivers might be missing or which of the eight drivers do you feel might be less critical to successful implementation of change?

- On a scale of 1 to 10, how effective have you been as a leader in supporting each of the eight drivers?

- On a scale of 1 to 10, how effective has your organization been in supporting you in each of these eight drivers?

- Write down priority improvements *you* should consider the next time you lead change.

Be aware of the positive impact this Matrix and this process of "supporting" will have on your success factor; it works. While it may not guarantee successful implementation of change, it will lessen or remove many of the reasons for failed change initiatives.

Plan to Plan

Remain close to your staff throughout the change process. Remember there are two basic stages in planning that seem so simple they're often overlooked:

- First, you **develop the plan** with strategies to achieve buy-in, successful implementation, and full accountability.
- Then, you must **work the plan,** including support of the eight drivers.

Some senior officials and managers often forget step two in that they fail to follow through in executing the plan. Without effective monitoring and problem solving *throughout* the implementation process, the entire change initiative can become a disaster. What will often creep into staff thinking will be the good ol' day's mindset: "It was so good back then; why are we changing again?" What will add to this *slippage* is that *these changes are usually being made **on top** of the existing workload.* If leaders do not remain close to and keep their finger on the process of change, why should it be a surprise when staff loses focus over time and revert their energies back onto what has brought them praise earlier. They need *you* to work the plan and to support them.

You must communicate, communicate, communicate and invest heavily in advocating for and supporting staff in prioritizing and assisting them in their daily work. *Keeping the change process focused and remaining a priority over time is often the bigger challenge.* It's called "follow-through" and it will be one of the primary indicators of your leadership effectiveness. You either implement the change to achieve the desired results, or you don't. If you want to leave a leadership legacy, finish what you start. This is why you each earn the big bucks, right?

The Change Failure Factors

You've just reviewed the Matrix For Managing Complex Change with its eight key drivers for effective change. Underneath these drivers are many counter-forces serving to work against your chances for success in introducing and implementing change. The following are but a few:

- *Lack of ongoing senior level commitment and support*—Senior officials sometimes stop acting like leaders, and become absentee leaders. They erroneously call it "delegation" or "empowerment," but the effect can be very negative. They are either off onto a new project or honestly believe the job is done after introducing the need to change. Ongoing monitoring and support of the change process is required.

- *Different departments with different change initiatives*—Did you ever hear of the word sub-optimization? Without cross communication and coordination, the changes *you* are making could very well have a dramatic, negative impact on other departments, and vice versa. Do you know what changes are being initiated in the silo next to you and how those change could affect your operations? Avoid making changes whereby your department wins and another department loses.

- *Lack of a broader framework for change*—Without an overall plan and a common understanding of the organizational vision and required changes, the focus and energy of staff can be splintered and misguided. The organization must have an overall framework and direction as changes are introduced and implemented, leading toward achieving the Main Things. Don't rely on incidental or even incremental change to keep you competitive and on course to achieving the organization's vision.

- *Too many priorities*—You and your team are kept too busy with too many changes. At most, any organization should be addressing two or three major initiatives at any one time. You cannot effectively implement a dozen priorities at once.

- *Everything is an add-on*—No responsibilities are taken away and existing processes are not improved to save time and energy while you're attempting to address the latest priority.

- *No Infrastructure support*—No change in existing processes, budgets, staffing, information, and expectations while moving toward the change.

The Change Success Factors

With all this said, how might you focus on just a few key actions, paradigms, and attitudes that are essential for your success in leading change? Position your thinking and strategies around these Leadership Tools to guide your actions and approaches to change:

- *Decide whether you even WANT to be a change leader.* You're half way through this book; are you still wanting to move forward in this leadership journey? On the other hand, you *will* be involved in change either as a leader or as a follower.

- *Understand what value you bring to the job and to your organization.* Appreciate it fully. Do *not* overestimate your value, but please don't sell yourself short, either. Also, understand the value your team and peers bring, as well as, the value senior officials bring. See the capacity each adds to the workplace and work to align these strengths. Think of it as the workplace glass being three-quarters full.

- *Lead with trust rather than distrust.* Be that role-model who has built solid working relationships with those under, over, and to the sides of you—with integrity.

- *Be committed to the Main Things.* Through your words and actions, others see where your heart is regarding needed change and improvement. Remain committed to leadership and change. *Be* more than a one trick pony when those major change decisions emerge.

- *Believe in and build a team.* Is your first response to a change challenge one that will bring out the *best* in and from others? The days of the Lone Ranger are over. Change must be a team sport, with (hopefully) everyone being on the same team.

- *Share the duties and success.* The roles of communicating, deciding, planning, implementing, and monitoring change must be shared. You need other champions, managers, and leaders. And when it's over, share the success.

- *Be accountable.* Don't wait to be asked. Be prepared to offer an objective and complete assessment of the people, processes, and impact of the change initiative.

Final Thoughts On Change

To wrap up this Chapter on Change, I'd like to recap three high-level leadership strategies that will help you focus on enhancing your organizational (and your team) effectiveness in the Crisis of Change:

1. *Build a "proactive" workplace culture to fight any existing spirit of complacency.* It's been said that there are three kinds of people in this world: those that make things happen, those who watch things happen, and those who have no idea what's just happened. Proactive organizations "make things happen" for the right reasons—to accomplish the Main Things. It's built into the culture and staff attitudes toward change in highly effective organizations. They realize that opportunity for improvement lies all around them if they only look for it. These organizations have staff that "keep their eyebrows up" looking for new change opportunities. Effective leadership keeps the organization prepared for change.

2. *Be agile and nimble enough to change.* Is your organization product-driven or truly customer-driven (in practice, not in name only)? There is a pace and tempo out there in the customer's world, and your competition is watching you keep pace. How are you doing with the challenge of moving at the speed of business? If you're out of step you're likely to find yourself out of business. Build agility and flexibility into your operations and thinking.

3. *Embrace Risk Taking to Achieve the Main Things.* This ties to being proactive and being agile, but it forces you to think and act in ways that get you outside your comfort zone. You can't take foolish risks any more than you can spend money foolishly. Is risk taking built into your organizational culture? Are you willing to "invest" in new risks or are you positioned to "protect" yourself from risks? You have decisions to make; you have leadership to conduct.

EXERCISE #24: The velocity of change (within and outside your organization) brings into question the survival of *any* organization five years from now—perhaps even next year. Please write answers to the questions that follow. In your opinion:

- What key change strategies or proactive initiatives do you feel your organization should undertake immediately that would have the greatest impact on its success (survival) five years from now?

- What markets or products/services delivered by your organization do you think are most vulnerable in terms of its losing competitive advantage to your competition?

- What three areas of continuous improvement should your organization squarely address in the next year to remain highly competitive?

- Ask your supervisor these same questions, and compare your answers. Is there new knowledge that the two of you can agree need to be the source of change?

Although this is just an exercise, it's the level of thinking (at 20,000 feet) that will help you see change and improvement opportunities as they emerge.

Lead the change process by encouraging, supporting, communicating, understanding, and growing with your staff.

Bookshelves are full of material on personal and organizational change, and these resources should be pursued in earnest now and into the future. Your leadership learning curve needs to be a lifelong process; it should never end. It's the nature of leadership and the nature of the challenges being faced. This learning curve, as stated earlier in this book, will require *application* of the knowledge gained through lifelong learning—applying this knowledge in the day-to-day leadership experiences on-the-job, gaining proficiency in using new Leadership Tools, and growing in "wisdom" through the lessons learned.

Clearly, the change process would be easier if you simply waited for top management to initiate the change in more of a top down manner. But you can't always wait (nor should you wait) for that to occur. Leadership is not always about permission. It's about commitment to success for the organization and your team. Of course top management plays a critical role in setting overall direction and outcome expectations, but you'd be amazed at the power that's held by a well-led team and collection of well-led teams. Leadership is the critical connecting link between front-line staff, other departments, and top management. Sometimes you're the connecting rod; other times you're the lightening rod. It's often like prodding that wild herd of cats in the right direction. You're leading others into the unknown, the world of uncertainty and new learning, and into new areas of responsibility. Lead the change process by encouraging, supporting, communicating, understanding, and growing with your staff. You will have to work twice as hard as they will, but the ultimate rewards for all involved will be great. Enjoy the journey.

"To improve is to change; to be perfect is to change often."
—WINSTON CHURCHILL

*"I consider my ability to arouse enthusiasm among men
the greatest asset I possess. The way to develop the best
that is in a man is by appreciation and encouragement."*
—CHARLES SCHWAB

"People are lonely because they build walls instead of bridges."
—JOSEPH F. NEWTON

"Wallowing in the past may be good literature. As wisdom, it's hopeless."
—ALDOUS HUXLEY

*"A business has to be involving, it has to be fun,
and it has to exercise your creative instincts."*
—RICHARD BRANSON

"When you come to that fork in the road…take it."
—YOGI BERRA

CHAPTER 8

20 WORKPLACE SUCCESS NUGGETS (TOOLS)

Attitude, Competency, Character, Focus and Will are "key" leadership attributes, but how do you "live" these attributes in everyday work life? You've been given a large number of tools for your Leadership Toolbox in earlier Chapters to give you a head start. Now use them. It's about the *Being* and *Doing* of leadership; not just the knowing. In this Chapter, I'm sharing 20 additional tools to: create greater *Awareness* of how duties can be performed more effectively; change your thinking on how to *Improve* what and how you lead; help you *Motivate* others to accept change ideas; and encourage the building of strong people-to-people *Relationships*.

I refer to these additional leadership applications I've learned and used along the way as "Workplace Success Nuggets." They're nuggets or tools with an unusual twist. Some of these tools are common sense, others humorous, and others relate to the tougher aspects of doing your job and simply surviving. I hope you'll find them as valuable as I have. I urge you to try several of them over the next few months, and learn first hand whether or not they're effective for you. Consider them useful tools for your Leadership Toolbox. Try them; you may just like them.

AWARENESS

1. *Watch the Eyebrows.*
2. *Whether Vane Test.*
3. *Job Depression.*
4. *The Four Decisions in Decision-Making.*
5. *Just "Sit On It."*

IMPROVEMENT

6. *Slight Edge Principle.*
7. *Nurf Ball Behavior Modification.*

8. *The Chess Match Challenge.*

9. *The Five "Why's."*

10. *The Three-3's.*

MOTIVATION:

11. *Two Questions Every Employee Wants Answered—Every Day.*

12. *The Two Great Motivators in Life.*

13. *Individuals and Organizations Become What They Choose To Measure and Reward.*

14. *The Mirror Test*

15. *Just Mean What You Say.*

RELATIONSHIPS

16. *Think Like A Customer.*

17. *Customer-Driven "Utility" Value.*

18. *Tyranny of Time.*

19. *The Three "R's"*

20. *The Sponge-Bobbing People.*

Awareness

Lesson #1: Watch the Eyebrows

Have you ever noticed that some of your co-workers are more forward thinking and generally more optimistic than others. Others are more tactical in their thinking and are extremely cautious in addressing change. Over the years I've observed that you can often tell where staff fall into these two categories by simply watching the eyebrows. This may sound weird but I've learned to watch the eyebrows of staff when certain issues are discussed or situations arise. There are two main types—those with their eyebrows up and those with their eyebrows down. When you discuss strategic planning or budget or opportunities for improvement next time, watch the eyebrows of those sitting around the table. Do you see a parallel between eyebrows and personalities?

*Let's start with those walking around your organization with their **"eyebrows up."*** I've learned that many of these individuals tend to see the glass as being ¾ full and are often light-hearted, much more willing to take risks, and are highly creative. They tend to be strong leaders, leaning into new opportunities and in fact are often seeking these opportunities daily. Could you identify three individuals in your organization who have their eyebrows up and meet this description?

Next, look for those walking around with their **eyebrows down**—what are they like? More often than not, they tend to be strong managers, like the details, be more conservative in nature, and are more analytical. In many cases, they place great value on meeting compliance and policies parameters first and *then* are open to new ideas. On the whole, they are far more cautious about taking risks or jumping into change. Could you identify three "eyebrows down" people in your organization?

There's a third set of eyebrows I'll simply mention, but be aware that these eyebrows send a signal of their own. Look for those walking around with their **eyebrows bent.** By that I mean their eyebrows bend up and then down, and their eyelids remain half shut—making them look sad. These individuals often see themselves as the victims of certain workplace issues that you see in their lack of enthusiasm and unwillingness to become involved. These individuals need your assistance to straighten out their eyebrows (and their attitude). But for purposes of this Workplace Nugget, I want you to focus only on the eyebrows up and eyebrows down individuals—those who are actively engaged in balancing the organization's approach to change and to the Main Things. Eyebrows bent folks need your guidance, but are not a model for leadership.

Eyebrows Up

Those with their **eyebrows up** tend to serve the organization as "opportunity scouts." That is, their eyes are wide open to see creative opportunities available to the organization long before it hits others in the face. They tend to be free thinkers or perhaps change leaders. While any given change opportunity may have a positive impact on the organization, these folks may often overlook the serious change implementation challenges this opportunity might present. They simply see this change being good for the organization and will lean into it. However, if these "upper" people were not out there encouraging the organization to capture the critical and necessary changes, the status quo might not be adequately challenged on a regular basis. Believe me, your competition is looking for these same opportunities; waiting to gain your customers. Be grateful for these "eyebrows up" individuals keeping the organization agile and aware of needed changes.

I've coined the term "opportunity lost cost" as being the hidden cost to an organization for *not* seeing a significant, positive opportunity on the horizon and therefore never making the necessary change. There is a cost for inaction or for missing needed change opportunities. While your accounting department has no way to record the impact of this opportunity lost cost on an Income Statement, it *will* eventually hit your bottom line—for both the organization and you as a leader. This "lost cost" is not a conscious decision by the organization; it's the absence of having enough *opportunity scouts*. The major opportunity was never even seen, much less captured.

Eyebrows up people, in addition to seeing emerging business and change opportunities, may also be more sensitive to the non-verbal communications being sent by their co-workers. With their eyes wide open and eyebrows up, they tend to be better observers of staff, watching others as to the lift of their shoulders, the bounce in their step, and the smile on their face (or lack thereof). Seeing and responding effectively to non-verbal communication is an important tool (skill) for your Leadership Toolbox. What you don't see can hurt you.

Eyebrows Down

The **eyebrows down** folks see realities of the workplace clearly and have their feet placed firmly on the ground. They are not blue sky thinkers; they are doers. In addition, they keep the workplace in balance and get things done well and on time. Without their guidance, the organization could easily spend (waste) all its time assessing and attempting to implement 30 new opportunities at the same time, with perhaps only 10% of these ideas being successful. Organizations can't keep moving forward by chasing a "change of the month" mode of operation. Meanwhile, the rest of the work required to maintain operations would take a downturn, creating problems with quality, budgets, maintaining partnerships, internal moral, energy level of staff, and meeting compliance requirements.

The organization isn't always ready for change and not every change is right for the organization. The "eyebrows down" people help keep us radical risk takers in check and force us to keep our feet on the ground. They are actually our "reality checks." What would we do without them? Be grateful for these eyebrows down individuals throughout the organization.

The challenge is to keep both the "uppers" and "downers" in perspective and to improve the thinking of the **eyebrows bent** individuals. Keep all three in balance. The following are a set of questions for you to consider as you begin to watch the eyebrows of your co-workers:

- What is the extent (percentage) of eyebrows up people in your organization? Do you have enough of them or too many? Do you have enough eyebrows down people?

- Are you watching the subtleties of non-verbal communications closely enough? You can learn a lot by watching these communications.

- *What are you—an upper or a downer?* Please don't be an eyebrows bent person.

Just as I've tried to present management and leadership as being joined at the hip, the same holds true for those with upper or downer eyebrows. We need both, and each has a critical role to play. The objective of this Leadership Tool is for you to realize there are ways to predict how different staff might react to different workplace situations—and that may include watching the eyebrows of your co-workers. Remember, one is not good and the other bad—*you need both.*

Have more fun along the way and watch more eyebrows—both your own and those of your co-workers.

Lesson #2: The Whether Vane Test

Do you ever have days when you come into work and you're not sure "whether" or not to introduce a change or a new idea? I've learned a tool to help assess the "weather" of an organization as to whether or not I should venture into change leadership that day. I guarantee this will not be found in other books and I'm sure it's not very scientific, but if you're interested in effective leadership, please consider this Leadership Tool. As with all tools, you must be selective as to when, how, and with whom you apply it.

While you want effectiveness in change leadership to be based on pure logic, you know better. In fact, sometimes logic can be your weakest argument. When I worked as a legislative lobbyist in Wisconsin I quickly learned that even the best idea introduced at the wrong time is most often a dead idea. Even more startling is that a mediocre idea introduced at the right time often turned out to be a new law. *Timing is everything in most instances, and the readiness of an organization for change is a driving factor in determining whether or not a change idea is accepted.*

My **Whether Vane Test** is simply this. Every day when I came into work, I would keep my senses very focused to assess the **Tone, Tempo,** and **Timing** of the culture surrounding key decision-makers I needed to be in contact with that day. I'd keep my eyebrows up. As soon as possible, I would conduct my Whether Vane Test on the organization's readiness for change. I would assess each of the *3 T's (Tone,*

*The organization and individuals must be **ready to receive** your change ideas— introduced at the right time, to the right individuals, in the right way.*

Tempo, and Timing) on a scale of 1 to 10, with a rating of 1 meaning: keep your head down, go home, or hide in your office immediately. A rating of 10 meant the organization was ripe for their idea and the supervisors were just waiting to give everyone a bonus for a great idea.

The Test involves asking and then rating the 3 questions that follow. Based on the cumulative score, you *then* decide how assertive or how passive to be in introducing a change *that day*. It's your Whether (or not) Test.

- What's the **Tone** of key staff and the culture today—positive or negative?

- What is the **Tempo** of activity and momentum? Is it a good pace or is it dragging?

- What is the sense of **Timing** to introduce new ideas, improvement, change, or "honest" feedback? Are eyebrows down with people too busy on crisis management issues?

This assessment and awareness of the tone, tempo, and timing should serve to guide what you say, when you say it, and how you say it. As a consultant often working in multiple organizations during the same week, it's incredibly helpful to gain a rapid assessment of how hard to push for or to introduce change on one given day. The *tone* or mood swings can range from incredible anger to joyous squealing. The *tempo* can range from staff skipping in the hallways to them lying on the floor asleep. The *timing* can range from receptivity to change due to an external customer opportunity to having crisis budgeting issues where major cuts are required but yet unknown.

This isn't rocket science. *It's simply awareness of the factors that impact your ability to introduce and succeed in implementing change.* Having an accurate sense of the workplace dynamics, the ebb and flow of emotions, and politics are important Leadership Tools to acquire and use. I do, however, suggest you avoid sharing your daily assessment of tone, tempo, and timing with others. If you share your assessment, it may be interpreted as attempting to manipulate decision-making. Instead, share the basics of this tool and encourage others to make their own assessment daily. It's not always what you know or how good your change idea is. The organization and individuals must be *ready to receive* your wisdom in the form of your change ideas—introduced at the right time, to the right individuals, in the right way.

Lesson #3: Job Depression

The subject of job burn-out strikes fear in the hearts of workers everywhere and I believe is a word that's often over-generalized and over-used. You talk to some people and they say "man, am I ever over-worked and I'm burned-out." If you'd watch some of these individuals for a while, however, you'd find half of the highly vocal ones border on being lazy or highly unorganized. The ones I'm more concerned about are the quiet ones who simply keep plodding along but you can see the joy in their lives and the bounce in their step depleting. These are the ones to watch. Don't let them just drift away from you.

Have you ever experienced job burn-out? I have, and it's no fun. You believe your work is drudgery and your job is empty; you feel drained and all used up. What's wrong ? Your motivation and enthusiasm have gone dry, but you still have the same skills and knowledge, and the same responsibilities. Burn-out could be termed job depression, or deep bum-out.

The good news is that if the fire in your belly for work has gone out, at least it was lit once. And it's possible you can get that fire restarted. As a mid-manager, you're faced with some significant decisions, often involving someone else's career or the survival of the organization. You're working under very demanding time schedules, a good portion of your work involves detailed, repetitive duties, you attend too many meetings that waste time, and you function in a world of workplace politics. What's worse is that you may have hit that wall of believing you're adding no value to the organization. You've lost your motivation, your balance, and your center of focus. "I don't like this anymore—but I can't just go home to bed and pull the covers up over my head."

In my world, I experienced burn-out on the job, but my breaking-point came when my supervisors and peers consistently blocked me from pursuing change I was highly passionate about making. It drained me, and I eventually gave up. I saw opportunity but was forced to stay with the routine. I wanted to take risks but was forced to be compliant. I knew change was needed but I had to retain the status quo. For me, I had lost my passion; that fire in my belly. On the job, this generally happy guy turned into a grouch, a rumor monger, and a supervisor hater. It was as if I was seeing someone else turning mad and bad. I saw little humor in things and saw even less future in my career path. It was a black hole in front of me. Worse yet, I lost my "heart" for managing well, and my team saw it. Not only had I changed but I was affecting the workplace culture around me.

Let me share how I dealt with this critical situation. My solution was to seek a new focal point to regain a balance in life. I discovered I was seeking to receive *too much value and personal worth from my work* and job, and it was no longer there. Thankfully, I was able to shift my paradigm and found worth in the *real* things in life—outside of work. I discovered a new philosophy: "I no longer lived to work, I worked to live." This shift sounds too simple but can be most difficult. For me it was a life saver. I had a wonderful support system. Fortunately, I had my family and my faith. Life is too short. Check with anyone lying on their death bed and ask them if they wished they'd spent more time at work in their life. Get Real, Get a Life, Keep a Balance, and See the Big Picture. I did one thing more. I decided to add "choice" to my career, and I chose to begin looking for another job. While I didn't change jobs at that time, I gained new breath and once again saw that I had choices in my life—and that gave me new hope and a new vision.

The job that's supposed to add value to your life can turn out to be the blood-sucker of your joy. It's up to you to manage and learn to cope better with the workplace circumstances in which you find yourself. It's not necessarily do or die—but it can be. The goal should not be "survival." Rather, it's about being whole and a success. Discover again the fun parts of your job *and* life.

Lesson #4: The Four Decisions in Decision-Making

There's a marketing theory I learned long ago that breaks the decision-making process your customers go through into four separate decisions. It's not just a simple yes or no, one-dimensional decision. I found I could transfer this marketing concept into a Leadership Tool to apply when introducing change into the workplace. Your strategies and actions must be directed at moving the customer or staff through all four levels of decision-making. Over the years, I've learned to apply this tool widely to customize my approaches to introducing change. The four levels or stages of decision-making in my marketing-based model are:

1. *Awareness*
2. *Comprehension*
3. *Conviction*
4. *Commitment*

Let me illustrate each of these four stages by reviewing the process of two individuals moving from dating to marriage. First, there is an *awareness* that the "other person" even exists—you notice them and think, "Okay!!!!!" Secondly, there is *comprehension* by both parties that it would really be great if we got to know one another better. Thirdly, you transition to the *conviction* stage and ask for a date, and the other party agrees. Now you're both at the "convicted" stage. You have this date and had a wonderful time, and the conviction stage repeats itself in the form of "Can I see you again?" The dating continues until and if *both* parties make the decision to move to the *commitment* stage, which involves the question "Will you marry me?" Each decision stage becomes a more personal form of communication and commitment. Just as in this illustration, *you cannot advance a change idea on the job by just making others "aware" of your idea or begin by asking others for their "commitment" to the change.* Obviously, there's a flow of understanding, communication, buy-in, and decision-making that must occur naturally.

When introducing change, the first step is to *create the proper awareness* that will first inform staff that this change idea exists and why. How and when you introduce this change idea will influence how others initially react to the idea. After Awareness, the Comprehension Stage involves *communicating effective messages about the change* that will create greater interest in understanding the change and its intended impact. Create an openness to your change idea and a desire in others to learn more about it. You've then achieved the second level of buy-in, and the invitation to take communication to the next level. The Conviction Stage can be a lengthy one because it requires others to *plunge into deeper learning and acceptance* about the idea and its implications on themselves. This is the stage of analysis and assessment. The process of moving through Conviction can involve identification of barriers or adding incentives to keep the focus and interest advancing. Resisters to change will revile themselves in this stage, so strategize carefully. Once others become convicted to act, the Commitment Stage must be experienced, with the decision made to buy into the change—*supporting the change* with budget, time, and "commitment." The decision-making process is complete. You must customize your communication and approaches in each of the four decision-making stages with your supervisor, other departments (their managers) and perhaps with external partners. The process of working through the four decisions of change is not an easy one—but that's the role of leadership.

*The key point of this tool is that communication and the process of change is **not** one-size-fits-all and it is **not** just one decision to be made.* It's the process of achieving buy-in through a phased-in set of decisions. In addition, each stakeholder must be given the opportunity to work through each of the four stages; otherwise it becomes change by fear or resistance.

Lesson #5: JUST "SIT ON IT"

I don't care how hard I tried, but I would form that terrible "first impression" of job applicants (or staff) who greeted me with that wimpy, cold, wet handshake. Has that ever happened to you and, be honest now. Didn't it form a negative initial impression of that person? I would look at that person during the interview and remember the handshake experience. I'm not proud of my forming that first impression, and I really felt sorry for the applicant. In some instances, the interview process went so well I could move past that first impression. The applicant was that good, and I could picture her/him performing at a high, functional level on the job. However, she/he would first have to overcome that "negative" in my mind. This illustration doesn't stop with the interview setting.

Have you ever thought about that first impression you make when meeting with the big supervisor in the corner office or meeting customers when you had to give a critical presentation? Nerves will do that you know—give you that cold and wet handshake. I'll explain later how you can begin working on that wet hand problem. As for the wimpy handshake, it's in your technique. Remember, do not just grab the fingertips when handshaking; grab the area around the other person's thumb but don't squeeze the fingers too tight. A firm handshake is good, but remember that a handshake is not a macho event. Control your grip; don't break fingers.

As for the wet and cold situation, here's a tool I've used. I warn you, it may sound goofy but I challenge you to tell me of a better way to avoid showing nerves when shaking hands with someone you deem important. The tool is to "just sit on it." That is, while you're waiting for that important meeting, take your right hand, palm up, and slip it under your right leg or if you prefer, your right cheek. Warm your hand up and keep it dry. Then, I want you to fully appreciate how silly you look doing this little exercise while waiting for the interview—grin to yourself. You're getting away with a strategy to improve your interpersonal relations right in front of others. You're good!!!! It's okay to lighten up and smile a little; it helps the nerves.

Okay, you're now more relaxed because you know your hand will be warm and dry when you meet and greet that important person. In addition, you now have that goofy grin so your face looks relaxed too. When you rise to meet that person, thrust that warm and dry hand out assertively because you *know* that first impression will be a favorable one. In the course of your meeting or interview, you may want to consider placing your right hand under your right leg again— if it's not too obvious to others. Use this technique to relax you and keep you loose. When the meeting is concluded, again, thrust that hand outward with confidence. If nothing else, you will not have a wimpy, wet and cold handshake to overcome. Whether or not the interview or presentation went well is up to you, not your handshake.

Don't scoff at this until you've tried it. It sounds odd but I guarantee it *can* make a difference and will serve to keep you from delivering that negative first (and sometimes lasting) impression. It's troublesome that, despite my best efforts when interviewing or dealing with staff, those physical experiences affect my initial reaction and thinking. I only trust that my integrity and focus went beyond those first impressions, but I know some other interviewers who are so affected by a wet and cold handshake that they noted that very fact on their interview recap sheet for those applicants.

Why take the chance? When you have an important meeting and your nerves are popping a bit, try this approach and remember to "just sit on it." If nothing else, it will help take your mind off the meeting pressures for a minute and cause a smile to form on your face—and that's a good thing. Keep your hand dry, your greeting warm, and make that good first impression.

Improvement

Lesson #6: The Slight Edge Principle

For many years, my Dad and I would have a "Christmas Fudge Cook-Off" to see who could make the best fudge as judged by the other family members. I would buy the ingredients and follow different recipes to the letter but somehow, almost every year, my Dad would win the contest. His fudge would be nice and smooth and creamy while mine was good but dryer. Finally he shared his secret—he "cheated" by adding more butter to the recipe. I was amazed at what a difference a little extra butter made. As great chefs know, a slight difference, that added pinch of something extra, will make all the difference in taste quality. And guess what, those chefs become famous.

It isn't just improvement in one area that will make the slight edge difference, it requires slight improvements in multiple areas.

Another "ah-ha" is if you look at the average salary of a professional baseball player having a respectable 250 batting average. He is getting one hit every four times at bat on average, or 25 hits every 100 times at bat. What happens if that player could improve just a little to have an *extra five hits every 100 times at bat?* That 250 batting average jumps to a 300 average. Can you say: "Double his annual salary and on his way to the Baseball Hall of Fame?" Just five extra hits every 100 times at bat, that slight edge, makes a huge difference in his value to the team. But to achieve this goal of five extra hits, he must take extra batting practice, lift more weights, work on his running speed, and listen to the batting coach more. It isn't just improvement in one area that will make the slight edge difference, it requires slight improvements in multiple areas.

I've mentioned the importance of attitude, competency, character, focus, and will many times throughout this book. What makes someone a good leader or manager and others an "average" leader? It's tied to their ability to perform slightly better than others—consistently, and in many areas of the job. They have a slightly better attitude when things turn negative. Their competencies are practiced more with their skill shown in critical on-field situations. Their strength of character is exhibited in new ways. Their ability to focus is honed, and their will shows they will not give up. Chances are they're slightly stronger in each of these attributes because they are committed to adding even more value to their work. *We too often look for the "Big Quick Fix" when the meaningful answers are found in doing many things just a little better than average—consistently.*

Here's a philosophy one CEO shared with me. "If you want to get noticed, volunteer to do the tasks nobody else wants to do." While some of you may disagree with this, there is a good deal of truth to this statement. Isn't your volunteering for a task nobody else wants a matter of positive attitude, character, focus and will? In addition, wouldn't you gain competencies and skills from this new experience? Besides, it doesn't hurt to show off a little for the supervisor. The cost is, like that baseball player, more time, carrying added responsibility, making yourself more efficient, and listening to wise counsel of others along the way. Most of us were not born athletes or leaders, we had to work hard to achieve success at whatever level. There are always those who *want* success more than others—and they achieve it. *They are the ones who take advantage of this "slight edge principle." They add to their value by doing and practicing improvement in areas others were unwilling (or unable) to do.* To them, "opportunity comes disguised as hard work."

It's doing the right things a little better than others that will open new doors and opportunities for you as a manager and a leader. You do it because you're committed to excellence. *It's not always the big things that separate the good from the great, it's the culmination of the many little things in life that make the real difference.*

I learned from my fudge-making days that I must commit to investing more in doing the little things a little better to improve my value—in life and in my work world. Just invest a little more to deliver that slight edge difference for others.

Lesson #7: Nurf Ball Behavior Modification

I don't know why it is but every organization has some stinkin' thinkin' people that believe every new idea is a bad idea. Sometimes these are other managers or even your supervisor. Every time you advance a new idea for improvement or change, they immediately block it with classic defenses like "we've tried that before and it didn't work" or "we don't have enough time or budget" or "it will never work." The idea balloon is floated and immediately shot down before getting two feet off the floor. How do you deal with that manner of thinking and negative attitude? While I don't have any magic pill, I've found one fun Leadership Tool that worked very well in changing the attitude of my team of senior managers. I used nurf balls.

I had a team of seven managers reporting directly to me that I called the Magnificent Seven. Wonderful people but when I first arrived on the job it was a challenge to bring these divergent functional roles and leadership styles into focus—as a team. When one would bring up an idea for change, another would give a blocking statement that immediately cut off discussion. The problem was, we needed to listen better to understand what each of us considered valid ideas for change. We weren't giving ourselves time to have adequate discussion and never thought outside-the-box. I saw the faces of individuals feeling they were "cut off at the knees" with a good idea. I knew I had to change this team dynamic and culture, but how?

What I did was to bring some fun into these team meetings by modifying our approach to the organization's change challenges. One team meeting, I brought in a basket of brightly colored nurf balls, the ones about six inches in diameter. Each team member was asked to take one and guess why I was doing this. Obviously no one guessed why. I informed them of the nurf ball rules. Each was empowered to throw their nurf ball at *anyone* in the room when they heard someone make a blocking statement—that included me. They were directed to throw it immediately, as hard as they wanted, and to retrieve their ball immediately.

I have to admit it was distracting to conduct a meeting with most of the seven managers bouncing their nurf ball on the table just waiting to throw it. As the team leader, however, I never held the attention of my team like I did then. The listening was intense, all eyes were wide open, and they were having fun. Without fail, somewhere, sometime, one of us would make a comment that was "perceived" to be a blocking statement to a new idea or thought. All the balls would be thrown at that person followed by two minutes of people running around the room to pick up their respective nurf ball. They'd return to their seats and continue bouncing the nurf balls on the table. What followed was discussion and positive feedback on what the person making the blocking statement meant and how it was interpreted by the others. We then brought the new idea back for a full discussion and consideration. It wasn't about what was said, it was about what others perceived to be said. We needed to change our thinking, then our words, and finally become more open to new ideas and thoughts. And we grew as a team.

I did this for six monthly meetings of the Magnificent Seven and by that time, there was a noticeable difference in how we responded to each other and how much more open we were to new ideas. Any of us can fall into a pattern of speaking and reacting negatively to ideas, not realizing how many good ideas are left on the table. The objective of behavior modification by using nurf balls was accomplished but I kept that basket of nurf balls in my office. You'd be amazed at the times my managers (and others) would talk about that behavior modification experience. I could have tried to use a hard line approach on this poor listening and understanding problem, but I lucked out and found a fun way to accomplish the same thing. Is this a useful tool for your Leadership Toolbox? If so, keep a set of nurf balls handy.

Lesson #8: The Chess Match Challenge

I'm actually more of a checkers man than a chess player, but I know enough about both games to plan several moves in advance if I expect to win. In chess, every piece has a different move—some diagonally across the board, others straight vertical or horizontal, others in an "L" move, and others one space at a time. In the workplace, there are many aspects of leadership and there are many different players, each with their own rules as to how they act, react, and move. Every key player in the workplace can have a different agenda, strategy, role, and set of allies. While you only make one move at a time in chess, you must actually plan at least three moves in advance. Your strategies will vary based on who you're playing. This is also required in the workplace.

I often use the term "scenario thinking" when positioning for change, or advancing a new idea. I use tools such as the *Three T's of tone, tempo,* and *timing,* changing the stinkin' thinkin' staff who immediately block any new idea, and seek to better understand the nature and source of workplace politics. In addition, I seek to understand those who are my resisters in any workplace issue, the policy barriers, and strategies to gain as many supporters as possible. What moves do I make, when, and what play will my challengers make next? Then what counter move would I make, will they make, and so the game continues. For those having been in the heat of workplace change, you understand this mental game and scenario thinking. It isn't evil or wrong; it's being proactive. The game of chess and the workplace games are all about your ability to "position yourself" for the next move(s). You must plan ahead for the expected, as well as, the unexpected. *The error is if you take actions of others personally and make it a war against people when it's really a war against change.*

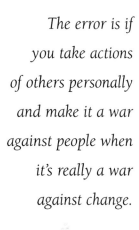

The error is if you take actions of others personally and make it a war against people when it's really a war against change.

When I first entered the role of management, I naively thought change would occur because I had a great idea. I was shocked to learn that others would oppose me publicly and was overwhelmed that some would even badmouth my ideas behind my back with others. Hello??? Over time, I learned to think more strategically about how and when to introduce change, how to achieve buy-in earlier in the process, how to outmaneuver those public and private attacks, and how to make winners out of many of my resisters. This sounds like wartime tactics but it's a reality of organizational change. I would make every effort to use logic and strength of character to win others over. But I would also be prepared to use timing and emotion to my advantage and attempt to gain support from those with my power of position and influence "just in case" it came down to a power game. Just like in my Boy Scout days, I would "be prepared."

I would build scenarios as to my chess piece moves, the likely moves of others and how I could position myself today to make counter moves to block or remove barriers tomorrow. I would make my moves in a timely manner and keep my reputation intact. A major difference I see in this workplace comparison is that, unlike chess, I attempted to build my change scenario to achieve a win-win outcome. While I needed to be fully prepared to play the game to its conclusion and to give it my best effort, I clearly understood that I could not achieve a win-win on my own. I would use my Mirror Test (Nugget #14) to check my integrity and lose my workplace ego. I would *set the dialogue and agenda at a high level to keep the focus on the Main Things for the organization rather than making it a personal agenda.* Know that this is difficult at times, but it is a *must* if you want to survive to play this workplace game another day.

Perhaps I'm being too dramatic in this chess match analogy, but those of you having been in workplace battles understand exactly what I'm saying. *It isn't simply logic that will carry the day, you don't make moves in a linear fashion, and the moves must be varied based on moves of others.* Finally, be prepared for the unexpected by building scenarios to plan your alternate strategies. Some say life is like a box of chocolates; I say workplace change is like a chess match.

Lesson #9: The Five Whys

The five Why's is a useful decision-making tool popularized by Taucki Ohno, and has application in both personal and workplace situations. *It will assist you in discovering the root cause of problems or assessing why a change is needed.* The concept is that you *ask the question "why" up to five times to peel your problem or change onion to a deeper level.* Imagine someone asking you as the leader, "Why do you want to implement this change?" If you don't have an immediate answer that is rock solid, then perhaps you're not ready for that change. If, on the other hand, you can give an instant, solid, common-sense answer to the question "Why do you really want to do that?" you are a giant step closer to implementation.

Why change? What must you communicate to others regarding change? These seem like such logical questions, but you'd be surprised at what you and others can discover by first asking the simple question "Why?" Seek to uncover the root reasons the change is required and the root impact. *The Five Whys are a powerful tool to determine whether change is being advanced for the right reasons.* The process is simple; *ask and answer the question "Why" five times.* Dig deeper each time. If you get past three times, you're doing well.

Let me give you several illustrations. First is when I wanted to buy a new car. *Why,* because my current one had 90,000 miles on it and was five years old. *Why,* because I wanted reliable transportation at a reasonable cost. *Why,* because I had to drive 45 miles each way to work and we were thinking of a family trip to Disney World. *Why,* because I wanted to ride in comfort and have the family proud of me as being a good provider. *Why,* because it made me feel good. You see, I wanted to spend $25,000 on a new car because the root of my need was that it made me feel good and my family would be proud of me. I knew I could spend $950 upgrading my current car for reliability and safety, and it would go another 40,000 miles at least. I could even rent a car for the Disney trip if I wanted.

A second illustration is based on a real work situation involving a dispute between two of my managers. They were fighting over everything and even their staffs were fighting. It took me a while, but after the fourth level of asking "why" I discovered the root problem. The previous manager had re-written one of their job descriptions to mirror the other manager's job description. They were stepping all over each other's written job duties and were, of course, in conflict. It wasn't an issue to be mediated, it wasn't a personality clash; it was a matter of clarifying job duties. Discovering "why" saved me from firing one or both of my managers.

Answers to the series of *The Five Whys* are often very revealing, even to yourself. Why do you want to change the organizational structure in your unit? Is the fifth "Why" because you don't like the job one manager is doing and this is the easiest way to shuffle him around? Why is this person a difficult employee? Why do I want this new software? I'll bet you'll discover some interesting answers. It can be done as self-discovery by yourself or, better yet, as a team.

It's not hard to see how the process of asking *Why* five times will help get you to the root of your problem. *The process of digging for deeper, more basic answers and solutions is a powerful part of the process of change.* By making The Five Whys a part of your analysis process and your team discussion, you will create a tool for identifying basic, fundamental, comprehensive changes in your attitudes and actions that can have a wide-ranging benefit. As a leader, you're also sending signals to others that it's okay to ask the tough, probing questions—and to discuss openly the tough answers. Guess what? You're communicating at deeper levels as a team.

The starting point in any change opportunity or planning process is to develop a clear and common understanding of the current realities. The Five Whys will help get you there.

Lesson #10: The Three 3's

Isn't it amazing how complicated we make things like strategic planning, personnel evaluation, conflict resolution between staff, and continuous improvement in general? While it's obvious to everyone that these communication and direction setting processes are essential, you simply don't have time to invest at the level these processes often require. How do I know I'm doing the Main Things as others see the Main Things?

This is one Leadership Tool I've probably used most over the years. Even if you don't use or apply this tool in a formal manner, let it influence your thinking, as well as your actions. It's simple, objective, low risk, and highly effective in communicating real improvement opportunities. The tool simply asks three questions, seeking the top three answers for each question. I call it the Three 3's, and I ask the following questions:

1. What are the three things being done "so well" that you **must continue** doing them?

2. What are the three things that create serious problems or are of concern to others that you should **stop** doing them?

3. What are the three most important things you should **start** doing to increase your value to others and to the organization?

What must you **continue** doing because it's adding so much value to others that it would be a significant loss if you (or your team) stopped? *It's a pat on the back* and opens the door for continuous improvement in that area. What adds little value to others or is actually hurting the effectiveness of others that you should probably **stop** doing that activity or behavior? You want your work to make a positive difference, so awareness of opportunities to make life better for others can only be a good thing. What things do you need to **start** doing because it will add even more value to the organization and to others? How can your *talents have an even greater positive impact?* We all have opportunities to add value for others; let's do it. **The Three 3's** *will give you or others that needed pat on the back, a kick in the pants, and an opportunity to be of even more value to the organization.*

By allowing others to offer constructive input on the Three 3's, you have opened the doors to serious feedback and honest dialog. If you're serious and secure enough, this can be a valuable exercise. It also serves as a vehicle to document and prioritize what activities should be continued, stopped, and started. Finally, it creates a document to encourage follow-through.

I've used this as an informal evaluation tool for staff, for pastors (at their request), and for feedback on my own performance. This was followed by action planning to determine what forms of support would be most helpful in carrying out *The Three 3's*. It served as a personal action plan. I've even used The Three 3's in several organizations to begin the strategic planning process. It aided in establishing a clear and common understanding of the current realities facing the organization and opened thinking beyond what "new" initiatives they must address. As a consultant, I used this process to address conflict resolution issues between major units of an organization. I even used The Three 3's with my own retirement planning in terms of identifying and facing the new and challenging changes this new lifestyle would present.

It's a tool that will force communication and direction setting, generally with input from a group of individuals. The Three 3's is also a way of thinking about the many workplace issues, including: "How do I prioritize my work today to get the major projects done?" What do I continue, start, and stop doing to add greater value? Enjoy using this simple but effective tool.

Motivation

Lesson #11: The Two Questions Every Employee Wants Answered—Every Day.

This tool may sound a little soft for some of those "macho managers" who think it's a great strategy to remain aloof and separated from their employees, but I disagree. Every manager and leader must choose his or her own motivational techniques, and I subscribe to that old saying "I don't care how much you know until I know how much you care." For me, I'm convinced that *every* one of us secretly wants to know the answer to these two questions *every* day:

1. Am I still important to you? Do you care about my personal and professional success?

2. How am I doing? Keep me informed of the good and the bad, with integrity.

"Am I still important to you?" This is the first question. You want to establish a positive work culture, one built upon respect, professionalism, commitment, trust, and personal loyalty? At least I did. Before others will buy into this preferred culture and receive your leadership and correction (when required), they first need to know you have a sincere interest in their success and future. You don't do this simply with words "I really, really care about your success," or "Wow, are you ever a wonderful person doing such a super job." Let's be serious now. You let others know you care by the nature and frequency of your communication and with your daily decisions and actions. Your staff expects you to walk the talk. To walk alongside of them, not hover above them.

If you're a mid-manager, every day is filled with meetings, phone calls, reports, personnel issues, and the next crisis. How do you find time to connect effectively with staff? I found several approaches that worked for me. First, I made a commitment to come into work early each day before the daily routine and commitments to meet with staff on a more casual, personal level. I'd grab a cup of coffee and do the manager's walk around. I'd meander through several departments just shooting the breeze, taking time to "chat," sometimes about business topics other times about their kids or their last vacation.

Get to know your staff personally in a relaxed atmosphere and on their turf. I know some managers who don't even know the names of their staff, but by golly they expect these people to bow down before them and jump through their hoops. Secondly, I loved to celebrate with staff—birthdays, employment anniversaries, births, retirements, and so on. Be real; have a little fun along the way. If you sincerely want their respect, you must first give it in a personal but professional way. Thirdly, I'd find excuses to be invited to departmental meetings and placed on the agenda to share a relevant topic with the team. While there, I'd listen to other team meeting topics and contribute (not dominate) as appropriate. Fourthly, I'd communicate this culture approach to other managers. I wanted to deploy this "connecting" style throughout the organization. Remember, your staff is your greatest asset—treat them as such.

You're working to create a new workplace culture and team environment. With this culture shift and focus on staff, you will gain greater insight into key issues, as well as, "little things" going on right under your nose. These folks are on the front line, and they know what's working well and what isn't. This isn't just a goodwill walking tour you do each day or a happy face you're presenting. It's a reflection of your commitment to connect with and learning from staff by drawing closer to them in real time. Let me assure you that your staff knows whether this is an act or manipulation tool you're giving them. In a hundred ways each day, they will see, based on your decisions and actions, whether you're the real deal. Decide whether or not this approach is worth the effort and fits your style. You must be real in communicating the message that you having a caring attitude toward staff and you're committed to living it.

"How am I doing?" This is the second question. If someone is honestly doing a good job, tell him/her. If they're messing up—let them know that too. I believe staff desire to be dealt with honestly, directly, and in a timely manner. Don't waffle on the truth but tell your staff how they're doing in a constructive way. I believe that 98% of employees truly want to do the best job possible and *will be open to correction and improvement if **first** they understand where their manager is coming from—that **you care** about their future.* Correction is not hollering and shouting because they made you, the manager, angry. It's not because you got in trouble with your boss, because of their mistake and now you're going to inflict pain or want to make an example out of them. It's also not because you think they're too dumb to improve based on your light, subtle suggestions. We've all seen these styles acted out and probably experienced each along the way. "How am I doing?" is not an invitation to inflict pain. On the contrary, give individuals and teams constructive feedback in a timely manner—don't wait until annual performance review of employees.

You are in the people improvement business; don't forget that primary role and the critical impact it will have on the organization.

The Leadership Tool here is to be consistent in your correction and praise of staff. If they know what you expect and do it well—tell them, "Good job." If they know what not to do and they do it anyway—you must tell them. Do not let them guess as to how they're doing or where you are in your thinking. Throughout this book I've stressed that you're in the people improvement business to make a significant difference for your team and for the organization. Understand that this Tool of answering these two questions for staff every day has a genuine return on investment for all parties concerned. You're building an improved culture, affecting staff retention, correcting problems at the cause, creating meaningful two-way communication, and creating an improved environment for accepting needed change in the future. Show your respect for staff by respecting their professionalism and desire to make a positive difference for the organization.

This lesson is as simple as "treat others as you would like to be treated." I believe we all want to know that our supervisor "likes" us and shows it in appropriate ways. We want to know and see that our supervisor has an interest in seeing each of us succeed, and is willing to invest in both the softer side of the relationship, as well as, the tougher side. We want to have meaningful discussions with our supervisor knowing that we're being heard and being recognized when we perform well. When we do mess up, we usually know it but value a gentle, honest correction along with appropriate support from those in authority. How else are we to grow and how will our supervisor know we're growing? Don't treat your staff like mushrooms, keeping them in the dark and simply expecting them to grow and pop up suddenly as a valued resource for you. You are in the people improvement business; don't forget that primary role and the critical impact it will have on the organization.

"Am I still important to you?" and *"How am I doing?"* are reflections of your personal character and attitude toward your job and other humans. Come to think about it, these aren't bad strategies to incorporate into raising children or for building solid relationships of any kind.

Here's a bonus lesson: *The absolute worst thing you can do to someone is to show her/him* **indifference.** *People want to be told, honestly, that they're doing a good job or a bad job. Whatever you do, don't leave people in isolation or in a state of wondering.*

Lesson #12: The Two Great Motivators in Life

Think back to a significant voluntary change in your life. What really motivated you to change? There were probably two factors involved: The timing was right and your motivation for change was real and internally driven. Think about times when you knew you should probably change voluntarily but didn't. Why not? Well, here's my take on the two great motivators for change. For (voluntary) change to occur, you must be either:

- (1) *"pulled with the passion"* or (2) *"pushed with the pain"*;

- *In between the zones of high passion and high pain is what I call the "apathy gap"* where you **will not** *voluntarily change. It's your comfort zone, and most of us rest here—sometimes longer than we should.*

Using the real life example of my needing to go on a diet, why haven't I changed my eating habits so I *will* lose the weight? If my doctor told me I'd have a heart attack in less than one year if I didn't lose 40 pounds, fear of a heart attack *would* motivate me to change. Fear of a heart attack creates the pain which is greater than the pain of losing weight. On the other hand, I love playing baseball and I've been asked to join a senior league. My extra 40 pounds is hurting my knees so badly that I can't play ball any more. The passion of wanting to play should be motivating me to lose weight, but it hasn't generated enough passion. I've spent the last 20 years trying to diet my way to health by "wanting" to look better for my class reunion or hating these bulges on my sides because they are no longer useful love handles. I diet, fall off, diet, fall off, diet, and gain more. My "apathy gap," as I call it, doesn't stop me from wanting to lose weight; it merely isn't providing me with a sufficient level of passion or pain to get the job done.

As a leader, you must motivate individuals to change as you deal with personnel problems, modify policies and procedures, or introduce a major change idea. Change, as you know, *isn't just a matter of logic or an intellectual exercise; you need to create the necessary internal motivation to move individuals and teams out of their "apathy gap."* How do you generate this internal motivation? You have the option of using the power of your position to exert subtle pressure on staff to accept the change or you can mandate the change, forcing staff to comply. While undesirable, it's sometimes necessary to have staff be compliant in making the change but you lose the multiple advantages of having full buy-in from your team. You have two other options. You can either *create a higher level of passion among staff* or *wait for a higher level of pain* to materialize. For you it's situational. To achieve buy-in, you may start by assessing the current level of staff passion *for* the change and assess whether you can build on that internal motivation. Or, you can assess the level of *pain* with current conditions and build on that. Your ability to judge the current realities on which to build support for change is essential. Which of the three options will be the best motivator for change: (1) Raise the level of passion; (2) Raise the level of pain; or (3) Accept staff compliance through forced change? Don't overlook this Tool as a key strategy to motivate staff buy-in for a given change. Motivate them to be open to change.

With this said, you might want to follow these steps in applying this Tool to workplace issues:

- Do not always try to protect staff *from* the pain of status quo.

- Seek first those opportunities to create or re-inforce the passion *to* change.

- If apathy persists and you *must* act immediately, accept the resistance or at least compliance attitude among staff. Sometimes the change simply must be implemented.

- In every case, try to communicate how making this change will serve to reduce the level of pain or bring about positive results that will benefit staff (the passion) in the future.

Lesson #13: Individuals and Organizations Become What They Choose to Measure and Reward

We read about the "carrot and the stick" approach whereby some animal is being blindly led around in pursuit of a prize or carrot. It doesn't say much for the animal does it, and what does it say for the individual using this motivation strategy? This may be one step above managing by forced compliance—both are manipulating staff. It places all the responsibility on the animal to work while all you have to do is hold the stick. While there is some logic to this approach if all you want is short-term results, I would urge you to remove the Carrot and Stick tool from your Leadership Toolbox if the goal is long-term success in leadership.

Effective motivation is not about the carrot; it's about what adds the most value to individuals, your team, and the organization. The preferred tool is about **establishing success measures** that matter and move others toward achieving the Main Things. Its application goes beyond simply communicating these measures. Relate these measures to the Main Things, set your expectations high for staff, and then effectively define, motivate, and support staff in moving toward these measures. The "home run" is when you hold others accountable for achieving the results, the results are achieved, and you properly recognize individuals and teams for their efforts.

Some managers measure and reward the meeting of compliance requirements (status quo) more than meeting the rapidly changing needs of their customers. That's bad. Some managers only value meeting the true needs of customers and pooh-pooh any compliance requirements. That's bad, as well. While you can't hyper-focus on compliance requirements, you can't avoid these requirements either. Perhaps you should focus on measuring and rewarding the right things, the things that make a significant difference in achieving the organization's Main Things? The Leadership Tool is that you, your staff, and your organization will become what is seriously measured and rewarded. The two key measures must be: 1. How you're meeting what your customer's value most and 2. Are you achieving the Main Things?

What are the Main Things that will make a significant difference in how your organization defines success (the carrot)? It's mandatory that you and your team know these Main Things, communicate the importance of driving decisions and actions toward these Main Things, and support staff as they move forward. Meet with individuals and teams to learn their thoughts on barriers and needed improvements; gain their understanding and buy-in along the way. Keep in mind, this is not a carrot and stick approach. As you work to monitor progress toward the Main Things, do everything possible to remove ineffective policies, procedures, processes, or people under your control. By doing so, you're creating incentives and reflecting your buy-in to the role of your staff. You're making their jobs easier and more focused, not dangling a carrot. Finally, work to change the support system of supervision and celebration. The employee evaluation process must measure, evaluate, and recognize the right things that make a significant difference in their jobs. If they are in fact making progress toward helping the organization achieve the Main Things, give an honest "thank you" to staff and recognize their efforts.

If you measure employee attendance and recognize it with an attendance pin, you'll get good attendance. If you want others to be more productive by being creative, then recognize the impact of these creative efforts. If you strive to be a better manager, then you should be recognized for your efforts to elevate the role of your team as they move toward increasing market share for the organization. *You become motivated toward achieving those things that are deemed important and actually measured by the organization.* What gets measured gets done. You can manage things but you must lead people. What is being measured and rewarded under *your* leadership? Is it meaningful; is it moving staff and the organization forward?

Lesson #14: The Mirror Test

Have you ever had to make those tough "people decisions" that stretch your comfort zone, like firing someone because they were unable to perform at a satisfactory level? I'm not talking about someone who just punched you in the nose or stole from the organization. That's an easy decision. The hard one is when it's a performance issue that has not improved over time. Wow, that was definitely the hardest part of my job and one that I liked least. Your actions not only affect that individual but also her/his family and the work team. That action can also send negative signals within the organization. Make sure you're able to address that decision and action *with integrity and courage, being able to live with the consequences that will follow.*

Over the years I developed this idea of doing a Mirror Test as my "integrity check" before taking such action. I needed to *have my motives in alignment with that of the organization, the team, and the individual* being fired. I would find the courage and the words better if I could keep "myself" out of this decision. You know how there's a tendency to blame either that person or yourself for not doing enough? Blaming will not make the actual firing process go any better. Rather, be in the position of knowing you're doing the right thing. If you do, the meeting to fire that person will go better than if you have hidden doubts or agendas concerning your actions.

I would conduct the Mirror Test two times. The first was when I had to make the final decision to fire someone and the second time was the morning the actual meeting was to take place. I would look at my aging face in the mirror; then stare right into the reflection of my eyes. I would ask myself a series of related questions that I had to answer honestly and seriously. "Have I removed any and all personal motives for the action concerning this individual?" "What positive impact could this action have on the team and on the organization?" "Is there anything I could do to benefit or help this individual in light of my decision?" "If I were that individual, what support might I need from my manager and the organization to move forward?" *My focus was on attempting to remove my emotion and ego from this decision and action.* This wasn't about me; it was all about the team, the organization, and that individual. Sometimes, my words and actions tended to be about protecting me and my actions—not about the greater good.

My approach in the actual meeting to dismiss the individual was to follow all human resource policies, keep it short, have the key points documented, getting to the points quickly and surgically. Immediately after the meeting, I would share this action with his/her team and appropriate staff—no details, just the actions taken. I would request their support during the transition of rehiring or reassigning job duties. The shock of being fired is a significant emotional event for anyone and you should expect this shock to be followed by anger and defensive comments about the firing—both from the individual and some team members. It's for this reason that you, as the manager, need to keep your emotions clear, your integrity level high, and your communication skills fully utilized—it might get tense and even ugly.

There is no easy way to make these tough decisions and there's no easy way to conduct these meetings. You must find your own sense of courage, timing, style, and words. I encourage you to use the Mirror Test and remove yourself from the middle of these and other difficult situations. Remember, it's not about you and the results of this firing action have many ripple affects.

How honest can you be with yourself in those moments of truth, stress, or hard decision-making? Look at yourself squarely in the eyes (the windows to your soul) reflecting in that mirror and check your ego at the door **before** the meeting. Your ego is a terrible thing to keep. Place focus on a higher agenda that matters (to the individual and the team). Let your integrity show in all that you say, do, and communicate during this difficult situation—use the Mirror Test.

Lesson #15: Just Mean What You Say

When you ask almost anyone in any organization what the three greatest problems areas are, at the 100% level, one of these three will be "communication." Of course there are many aspects of communication, but I'm focusing on how you communicate with your team, your peers, and your supervisor. Are your words, tone, and commitment the same for all three of these groups, or are they different? I'm certain there are style differences, but I hope the basic message is the same.

Two Leadership Tools to remember when addressing these communication issues are to simply "say what you mean" and to then "mean what you say." The content of your communication should of course be accurate, concise enough to be understood, personal, and open-ended for questions to be asked. Communication should not flow just from the top down when addressing staff issues or when communicating with your supervisor. It needs to be two-way. But what I find to be almost amusing is the side-to-side communication, mind games, and word games often played between peer managers. Why do some peers use this communication process for power positioning or wear that politicians' hat by being vague or trying to get more information out of you? Often it represents a win-lose contest of words. What a waste of good breath trying to talk around these word games or attempting to return the verbal volley. Oh, the games people play!

When dealing with staff, the great lesson I learned is that "informing is not the same as communicating." Out of habit or circumstances, we tend to cut communications short with staff by informing them what *we* feel is important. In fact, it should be more two-way. I'm not talking about discussing the kids or the last fishing trip, but rather communicating effectively so staff will have at least a general understanding as to "why" the decision was made and have enough knowledge to avoid making preventable mistakes. *Place value on not wasting time, but seek ways to communicate more clearly.* Likewise, when you have to correct staff for a "teachable moment," don't dance around the issue. Be more direct in what the issue is, discuss the resolution, communicate to make sure the error or issue will not reappear, and then move on.

Have you ever noticed how communications change when there's a meeting of peers with their supervisor? Communication gets more formal and crisp, but is it effective communication? As for your one-on-one meetings with your supervisor, it's too easy to simply have one-way, top-down dialog, rather than true communication. When you do speak, don't be fearful of couching your words too carefully so the supervisor misses your real points or simply waiting for the supervisor to talk. Say what you mean. Do not let protocol become the driver, bringing you to the point of being a "yes person." If you don't understand what your supervisor is saying, ask for clarification. If you have something of value to add, share it. If you need more time to communicate a matter in greater depth, request more time in the future. Treat your supervisor as you would expect to be treated. Strive to make the communication two-way and clear. Along the way, apply this same communication process with your staff.

Some hints. Nodding your head up and down means "yes", sideways is "no." Right is right and wrong is wrong. Eye contact is good. Listening is as much a part of communication as speaking. Too often we are thinking about what to say next or how to answer instead of truly listening.

There's too much miscommunication with everyone blaming the "communication system." Fact is, it's a people-to-people issue and only individuals can improve the communication. It's a matter of awareness, attitude, and commitment. I'll bet there's a 20% cost to a business in terms of lost efficiency due to poor communication at the person-to-person level. Savings in personnel time, energy, and frustration will result in improved profits, accomplishments, and workplace culture. Begin with *you* saying what you mean, and mean it.

Relationships

There's a significant difference between acting with Producer Logic versus Customer Logic, and there's a significant difference for your organization.

Lesson #16: Think Like a Customer

In light of workplace pressures and politics, it's too often the case that customer quality is being defined by the organization rather than by the customer. Why is this? While organizational culture can be the primary reason, part of the problem lies with how each of us defines quality on the job. For most of my career, I defined success on the job in three ways. First, I needed to survive on the job by producing what I was hired to produce with quality as defined by my supervisor. I was able to survive. When I got a chance to breathe, the second level of attention was on the obvious incremental improvements in processes and communications. This improved the quality of my performance. Thirdly, when all was going well, I finally took time to ask my customers how I could increase their satisfaction with our products and services. Time and internal needs defined quality and success for me; not the customers. I put the customer last in my priorities for most of my career.

If this describes your work priority system, I urge you to change because it will not advance your organization or carry your leadership journey to the next level of success. Highly effective organizations have almost a reverse priority order. *They first think from the customer's point of view, not like a producer.* They understand and are driven by the Main Things; that is, what serves customers, what improvements are critical, and then the busy work. *This is a paradigm shift: Stop thinking like a "producer" and start thinking like a "customer."* There's a significant *difference between acting with Producer Logic versus Customer Logic,* and there's a significant difference for your organization. See how the following questions contrast these two paradigms.

What Is It We Do Again?

Producer Logic believes that your purpose is to develop and deliver products and services. The focus of your work is on obtaining the established internal approvals and the selling of your products. It's an internal focus and all about the making and moving of products and delivering services.

Customer Logic recognizes that customers will not be "sold" anything, they only buy "use value" (what your products and services do for them) and that this use value is ever changing based on their needs, not yours. The focus is customer-driven and is external.

The organization must provide the capacity for customers to meet *their* needs, not yours. The organizational focus is on the customers' "end-use" of what it delivers. Real value begins with understanding what the customer is seeking and ends with what the customer actually receives. What you must do is "deliver use-value," not produce and deliver products and services.

What is Being a Manager?

Producer Logic believes you manage assets and describes what managers do in terms of numbers (staff, budget, equipment, facilities, etc) they control. The focus is on growing assets and then "utilizing this capacity" to maximize efficiency for the organization. Managers own, maintain, and control assets that can build power, status, and hierarchy.

Customer Logic recognizes that customers don't care what we "own" but they do care about what resources are brought to bear on meeting *their* needs. The focus is on managers *coordinating* a variety of resources to generate the capacity to deliver, rather than concern over owning the resources. The operative question is what "access" do you have to needed resources?

Your focus is on making sure the customer's goals and needs are met, by whatever means. Partners and suppliers are part of the process of bringing capacity to serving your customers. Strengthen your networking and access to assets; not on owning them.

How Does Your Organization Measure Success?

Producer Logic has the organization focusing on averages, numbers, revenue, growth, etc. How are you doing as an organization at the aggregate-level—as viewed at 20,000 feet above the front-line?

Customer Logic is driven by "customer satisfaction" (and dissatisfaction) and "customer goal attainment." This customer success is balanced with your organization's success—the pursuit of numbers and growth. You provide and measure value one customer at a time (it's a market of one). *Every* customer is critical to your success. Monitor at 20,000 feet but deliver quality at ground zero—as defined by the customer.

It's your ability to modify the traditional processes by moving toward customized product and service quality so "it's right for the individual customer." You cannot, however, be all things to all people, so there must be an orderly means by which to prioritize customer markets and services—it's not solely a volume business. You grow business by retaining and growing good customers. Do not take them for granted.

How Do We Manage What We Do?

Producer Logic is organized around standardization, predictability, and procedures—keeping everything under control and running smoothly. The focus is on doing things right.

Customer Logic wants range, variation, and agility to meet changing customer needs—to offer value and return on investment (of time, money, and energy). Customize the opportunities; don't standardize them. Transition your focus to doing both: *things right* and the *right things*.

It's cheaper to keep current customers than to find new ones. Those leaving for other providers can tell you a lot about what you *don't* do well. Remember to learn from *all* customers.

How Do We Handle Mistakes?

Producer Logic focuses on *visible* mistakes and departures from the procedures that have been standardized. The focus is internal and tends to find fault, punish, and create a culture of "gotcha" management. There is little opportunity for risk-taking and a strong fear of failure.

Customer Logic understands that it's okay to experience mistakes, provided you learn from them and can afford to live through them. It's not whether you made a mistake or not, it's whether you're so committed to meeting customer needs that you're willing to move outside your comfort zone to serve them. Risk taking is a requirement—not something to fear.

Your focus should be on *new* ways to provide value by seeking fresh ideas and solutions. Don't let accuracy prevent you from being creative. It's okay to make mistakes that are *invisible* to your customers.

- Think like customers; it's all about "use value" for them.
- Encourage all staff to be reliable and accountable for desired results.
- Allow for mistakes in being creative and innovative. Learn and grow from them.
- Build customer loyalty by meeting their unexpected/unrealized needs.
- Do the right things, and make things better for the customer.
- **Your *Customer* is a process unique to that customer—customize your services.**
- ***Customer* perception is all there is.**

Lesson #17: Customer-Driven "Utility" Value

Peter Drucker has noted that "What a customer buys is never a product. It's always utility value—what the product or service does for them." To retain your customer base, *you must be driven toward what customers value most.* It's not about your selling—it's about their buying.

The customer defines utility value as *the value your product or service will provide for them.* For example, student customers invest in higher education for the knowledge and a degree that will have utility value in the job market, either for that immediate job or promotion in the future. You buy certain foods at the grocery store because of how it will look and taste at the dinner table. You're willing to pay that little extra for a car with a great low maintenance reputation.

There are different aspects of "utility value" to examine—the value the product quality offers and the value service quality offers. Examples of service value would include the time, place, and availability of customized products. In some ways, service quality can compensate for a lower product quality. The "home run" is when both product and service quality are met.

- **Time Utility—**   Product: *When* the customer needs the product.

                              Service: *Access* to assistance in buying it ***now.***

- **Place Utility—**   Product: *Where* the customer wants to buy or have the product delivered.

                              Service: *Convenience* of buying location.

- **Form Utility—**   Product: *Customized features* and options.

                              Service: *Customer focused* processes (user friendly).

- **Quality Utility—**   Product: *Reliability and durability* that adds value.

                              Service: *Reputation with integrity* that adds confidence.

High performance organizations stress all four of these Utility Value Factors. These factors are built into the Main Things that drive organizational decision-making and change.

Below are five levels or types of Values organizations can produce and deliver for their customers. Which one of these Value Levels does your organization strive to deliver?

1. Deliver Value based primarily on **low cost and compliance**—prioritize doing things right.

2. Value great products—value based on **product-driven** production and marketing.

3. Value being "customer-focused"—**listen to customers** on needs that drive minor changes.

4. Value being "customer-driven"—personal **relationship with customers;** actually driving major changes in products, processes, and services based on customer input.

5. Value dynamic leadership—**empower front line employees** to meet directly with customers and suppliers, changing customer requirements with support from agile processes.

This Tool is intended to challenge your thinking to identify the specific **value positioning** used by your organization. It's embedded in your organizational structure, its culture, its focus on change, and its level of perceived competition. *It's the responsibility of leadership to set the value focus as one of the Main Things—and for you to set for your team as a mid-manager.*

It's all about delivering what customers want and value. You cannot effectively market a product that doesn't deliver use value, and you only get one chance to deliver great service. With that in mind, understand and position the utility value you want to deliver to the customer at the right price and with the right conditions. It's all about serving "a customer of one," with individual needs and wants being met consistently and with a passion to serve them well.

Lesson #18: The Tyranny of Time

Have you ever worked with people who whenever you asked: "How are you doing" they'd answer "I'm so busy I can't turn around" or "The work just keeps piling up and piling up?" Some of them are using that old Peter Principle technique of "paperofeelia," They say how busy they are in order to cover-up their incompetence. For the most part, *I think many of us allow processes, paper, and people to control us.* At one point in my career, I was working an *average* of 65 to 70 hours each week and couldn't seem to get a handle on why or how to change. It reached the point where I told my supervisor that if I couldn't do my job, on average, in 55 hours per week, either he'd have to fire me or I was going to look for a different job. I was becoming frustrated and physically exhausted. I made myself examine what I was spending time doing and actually found ways to delegate better, communicate more efficiently, and to stop doing some things. Result was, I reduced my hours by at least 10 hours per week *and* I was doing what I was doing better.

Working harder after a while becomes counterproductive. We all know that but why do we keep trying harder and working longer? I'm convinced my problem was "me." I basically wanted to please people because this was one of my first big administrative jobs—"look how strong I am carrying all this weight on my shoulders." Secondly, I was taking too much personal value and self worth based on my workload. I was getting out of balance with my personal life. Thirdly, I was not managing the people issues well enough. I wanted to remain "available" to my staff but "being available" didn't necessarily mean *any* time for any length of time on any issue. Why was I spending that extra half-hour talking about someone else's kids when it was keeping me from spending an extra half-hour that night with my own kids? I had to establish priorities and then manage them better.

I've stressed the point many times that you must keep the Main Things the main thing. Not everything is urgent; not everything is a crisis. The tyranny of the urgent does not mean you can avoid those genuine crisis issues—*deal with them immediately and effectively, but don't make everything a crisis.* Establish priorities to accomplish the Main Things, and find time around those priorities to fit in the personal discussions about someone's kids, or that extra meeting, or that favor someone has asked of you. Also, be prepared to **stop doing work that should be delegated.** Identify the key work *that must* be done—not everything is a "must."

Here are some related tools I've learned along the way:

- Everyone sets one hour meetings, so *why not make them 45 minutes instead.* Prioritize your meeting agendas to complete the most important things first and then reschedule for the rest. Take that extra 15 minutes to listen to phone messages, return one or two, gather your thoughts and material for the next meeting, and show up at that meeting on time.

- Look seriously at the paper flow, approval processes, and activity-based reporting requirements—change them. *Change the processes to delegate more and do less* review and approval of things with lesser importance, because it's simply micro-management.

- Find times (often early in the day) to do that management walk around with staff. *Have fun dialoging with them **before** you begin that daily marathon* with meetings and crises.

- *Meeting management training is a must.* Know how to plan meetings better, distribute general communication handouts before the meetings, have meeting outcomes identified, establish timelines for discussion, and invite only those who need to be there. Run all meetings effectively and efficiently—save time.

Take control of your workload, priorities, and time requirements. It begins with awareness of time busters and time wasters. Manage time wisely, and have a bias for action in your investment of time on the true priorities you've established. Otherwise, tyranny of time will prevail.

Lesson #19: The Three R's

Yes, we all need to apply the traditional Three R's on the job but your role in leadership requires an additional set of Three R's. In Chapter 6 I shared a set of The Three R's for effective leadership: **Relationships, Relevancy, and Responsiveness.** Think of it. How long would you remain an effective leader if you could not develop and grow effective Relationships with staff and customers? How long would your organization remain in business if it didn't provide Relevant products and services (providing use value to customers)? How long would your supervisor put up with your delays in providing that major report if you turn it in two months late—you must be Responsive to established timelines. Effectiveness begins with effective relationships, it grows by your being responsive to requests for services, and those services (and products) must be relevant. The Three R's have many applications in the workplace and in life.

You may be saying, "Yes I like these Three R's as a critical Leadership Tool but are there other 'practical' applications of The Three R's at the workplace? Well I'm glad you asked. Here are two applications of this Tool that I've used many times over the years.

1. *Giving a Speech on Short Notice.*

   If you ever find yourself needing to give an impromptu speech, I suggest you frame your speech around The Three R's. First present the importance of building and sustaining effective *relationships* in whatever your speech topic involves and how it forms the basis for trust, action, and growth in the future. Provide examples of how effective relationships have carried you through difficult situations. Secondly, describe how you are assuring and delivering *relevancy* based on what adds value to your customers. This also serves to enhance established relationships with these customers. Finally, explain how you deliver these relevant services in a *responsive* manner—timing and conditions—and how that impacts customer satisfaction and serves to strengthen your relationship with that customer. In two minutes, you have an outline for your speech—then wing it.

2. *Strategic Planning Outline.*

   What must your organization do to survive in this competitive, worldwide marketplace? In Chapter 5, I outlined a Business Survival Course 101 that explains requirements for survival in business: *Providing excellent products and services that add value to your customers, with prices and conditions that beat the competition.* With these survival requirements as "Main Things," I've led strategic planning sessions where my starting point was simply "How do you improve *relationships* with key customers and stakeholders, how do you change internal operations to be even more *responsive,* and how do you **know** at the 100% level that products and services are most *relevant* (provide added value) to customers?" Then I ask planning participants to prioritize strategic actions based on these Three R's. Why couldn't this outline of The Three R's be part of the planning process for taking your team or organization to the next level?

What are The Three R's all about? They represent a leadership strategy to help develop new thinking and action planning to achieve the Main Things. They're also a simple Leadership Tool for you to use in advancing your change ideas. There is no guaranteed formula; it's all situational. But *The Three R's represent the critical communication and strategy points I've found universal for every organization in which I've worked.* Try it, you may like it. If you invite others in the organization to join you in the processes of relationship development, meeting the key relevancy requirements, and tightening the responsiveness parameters, you're providing needed leadership.

Lesson #20: The Sponge-Bobbing People

Remember when, as a kid, your parents would tell you to clean up your room, or do your homework, or something else you really didn't want to do? Some of us (be honest now) would nod okay and then intentionally go on doing what we were doing until Mom or Dad showed up again—to remind us to "do it or else." Can you relate this to the workplace? It's one thing to say "yes I'll do it" and another thing to actually do it. It's called follow-through.

I'd rather have someone push back (in my face) when asked to do something if they know they really won't follow through. However, these individuals tend to nod their head, say okay, and even take notes on what I'm asking them to do, and then conveniently get distracted and not follow through. I refer to these individuals as the "Sponge-Bobbing People." They bob their heads up and down, you push in on them like a sponge hoping they'll be filled with a commitment to follow-through, and when you leave, they pop back to their original shape doing what they've always been doing. Yes, they retained what you've told them (like a sponge holds water) but they just lie there—useless and filled with themselves. What a waste of time, ideas, good breath, and trust. They are one of those change resisters who keep chopping your knees out from under you, undermining your effectiveness. My role as a manager turned out to be that of a parent and then these same people complained when I sometimes turned into a micro-manager.

I would offer incentives and create positive recognition opportunities for those exhibiting great follow-through. On the other hand, I learned to inflict pain on those I found repeatedly lacking in follow-through. One thing for sure, I would never recommend those Sponge-Bobbing People for a salary increase, much less a promotion. It was very frustrating for me and others around them wanting to move forward and focus on the Main Things. While follow-through will not get you that career advancement, it's most certainly a blocker if you're found lacking in this area. Just do what you say you'll do, do it on time, and do it well. *If you want a powerful Leadership Tool for your own career growth, do what you say you'll do, do it ahead of time if possible, and always follow through with excellence.*

Sponge-Bobbing People need to be addressed directly. Watch them as you introduce your ideas for change. They will nod, smile at you, say okay, take notes, and then never follow-through. You know who they are. What I've found useful is to go around the room after they've assumed their "sponge position," and ask everyone to state their opinion on the discussion and to verbalize their support or opposition to the change idea. I'd even have them individually verbalize their commitment in following through on the assignments we collectively agreed upon. I would then ask each what they needed from me to be successful in completing their assignments. It's okay to discuss positive consequences if everyone pulls together and follows through as agreed upon, as well as, negative consequences if the group or individuals fall short. *Set the stage for **your** follow-through on **their** lack of follow through.* It sounds like a waste of valuable meeting and management time, but I believe, with those change resisters, you must drag them out into the light of day and force them to commit publicly. Nail their feet to the floor. Then, if they play Sponge-Bobbing People again, nail them, including a written warning in their personnel file.

Is this too hard a line? I think not. Sometimes a select few are allowed to continue blocking the masses from moving forward toward the Main Things for years and years, and no one stops them or holds them accountable. It's like being that parent again. If you have children that challenge you often and long enough and want to have a confrontation, oblige them. Follow-through is as much a character issue as it is a focus issue. Help staff and the team succeed and stop the Sponge-Bobbing People from hindering the success of your team.

Recap of Chapter 8

My goal in sharing these 20 Workplace Success Nuggets is to provide you with an expanded set of Leadership Tools I have used frequently over the years. My philosophy has always been that leadership cannot be experienced using a cook-book formula or approach. Each day has its own set of opportunities, as well as, challenges and these are your golden moments for growth. Your objective is to "respond" (not react) to these opportunities and challenges and to apply the best tools you have in your toolbox. Increase your skill levels in using each tool and throw out the ones that do not work for you. A few well applied tools can take you to one level, but you need to continue adding and applying an expanded set. If you possess many Leadership Tools but have a limited skill level in their application, you're on the edge. *Knowledge without wisdom is dangerous.* My goal is for you to seriously expand your set of tools and to learn their application well. You will be better positioned for tomorrow's unforeseen opportunities and challenges.

Perhaps you don't fully agree with or understand all of the 20 Workplace Success Nuggets in this Chapter—that's okay. I do hope, however, that you had a grin or two and could relate with most of what I presented as being real and practical. Your best teacher is on-the-job application of leadership; it requires nothing but good judgment, creative thinking, good timing, and effective communications. *Awareness, Improvement, Motivation,* and *Relationships* are areas of growth we all need, so you'd better acquire more tools and enter tomorrow's workplace realities prepared to succeed. Oh, and along the way, try to have some fun built in.

The role of mid-manager and your growth into and through leadership requires drill and practice. Some of these Workplace Nuggets are admittedly wild and out of the ordinary, possibly even difficult for you to embrace. I challenge you to create your *own* "nuggets" and pin your own creative titles to them. It's fun and it's valuable to you and others. I found titles such as Sponge-Bobbing People, The Whether Vane Test, Just Sit On It, Watch the Eyebrows, and the Nurf Ball Behavior Modification just fun to say, plus fun to do. In light of what you go through each day on the job, it's okay to have your own warped form of amusement and identity.

PERSONAL EXERCISE (Voluntary)

As you continue advancing deeper into leadership, you will find yourself applying many of the Leadership Tools learned from this book. In addition, and perhaps even more importantly, *you will learn and apply your own new Leadership Tools that you find effective on the job.* Would you consider sharing your new tools (and titles) you develop over time with others—including me? Many of us would enjoy learning from **you.**

This Personal Exercise involves the new and unique "nuggets" you've identified. Would you communicate these new and different Leadership Tools so I can add it to my Leadership Toolbox? If you do, perhaps a future Action Step for me will take the form of writing another book; this time capturing the Workplace Success Nuggets from **you** and other emerging leaders. We could and would grow through your leadership experiences and I'm sure chuckle at your many unique titles and experiences. Seriously now, I challenge you to share these Nuggets. Contact me by writing to my address in this book or looking me up on the internet. Leadership may be a journey and a continuous learning curve, but it doesn't have to be experienced alone or with your eyebrows down. Let's have some fun along the way and grow together; shall we? If you do not share your new Leadership Tools, I may be forced to write a second book on my own and entitle it *"How to Whine (not wine) Your Way To Victory."* I need your help to keep this focus on applied leadership moving forward—not writing about whining.

"One of the things that may get in the way of people being lifelong learners is that they're not in touch with their passion. If you're passionate about what it is you do, then you're going to be looking for everything you can to get better at it."
—JACK CANFIELD

"Giving people a little more than they expect is a good way to get more back than you'd expect."
—ROBERT HALF

"Leadership is not so much about technique and methods as it is opening the heart. Leadership is about inspiration—of oneself and of others. Great leadership is about human experiences, not processes. Leadership is not a formula or a program; it is a human activity that comes from the heart and considers the hearts of others. It's an attitude; not a routine."
—LANCE SECRETAN

"One quality of leaders and high achievers in every area seems to be a commitment to ongoing personal and professional development."
—BRIAN TRACY

CHAPTER 9

SEEK A LEADER; BE A LEADER

(The Mentorship Model)

Remember that childhood game of "Follow the Leader?" Most of the time the leader would blindfold you as she/he would lead you in a variety of fun activities. Invariably there'd be some jokester leader who would lead you into a tree, cause others to run into you, or find some way to make fun of you. A leader isn't just someone you follow blindly or one who simply gives you directions. She/he must be someone you trust; someone you want to emulate and learn from. Be careful who you follow and trust to give you true wisdom and counsel; be careful who you call "leader."

In Chapter 8, I offered a set of 20 Workplace Success Nuggets for consideration and use in your journey into and through leadership. You can do much on your own with these and the other 40 or more tools advanced in this book, along with self-study, trial and error, hard work, and some good luck. But along the way, we all need some personalized guidance, support, and deeper wisdom from leaders you can easily access, lean on, trust completely, and learn from. We all need someone to mentor us. In sports you have a coach, after surgery you have a physical therapist, for investing you have a broker, and in skilled trade occupations you have apprenticeships. Hard work alone is not the only path to success; there are too many variables. Through your mentor, you have more than a teacher. You have a "partner" and "guide" to help apply the tools in your Leadership Toolbox and to aid you in learning the leadership two-step. *This* is your new learning place. While this book and other resources can provide some knowledge, the best learning takes place on the front lines of leadership. You need a quality mentor providing applied wisdom as you move "through" the wild up and down experiences of leadership. This is your true opportunity to grow.

I've noted several times that: "Whatever business you're in, your role in leadership will always be in the people improvement business that results in organizational improvement." To some, the idea of dedicating a full Chapter to mentoring is a waste of good paper; it's too soft and fluffy. It doesn't drive home the hardness

Mentorship is about learning from the best.

it takes to be a leader in this tough work world. To them I say, "Get over it already." Whether these hard-hitting people realize it or not, they had their own mentors along the way. Do not believe those who try to claim they were "born leaders" and did it all on their own. If they're successful today it's because they too had a learning curve. Their issue with mentorships is probably how much time is being invested and the thought that "if it's not producing profits this quarter it's not worth the time today." As you know, not everything of value in business or in life can be framed in a three-month timeline. I believe the growing and nurturing of quality leaders in an organization is one of them. *Included in the measures of organizational success must be the development of skilled mid-managers and the building of overall leadership capacity for tomorrow.* The support and guidance, provided through mentorships, are essential for professional leadership growth and for building a highly effective and competitive organization.

Of course, the Mentorship Model requires a focused investment of time, expertise, and energy. There's a cost to anything worthwhile. However, there must also be documented return on this investment. In my experience, a well designed and functioning Mentorship Model will pay a wide array of dividends in personal and organizational growth. This is far more than a warm and fuzzy connecting experience. It's a serious Leadership Tool and a vital growth strategy for highly effective organizations. What does your organization think about supporting you in leadership growth through a Mentorship Program?

The mentor is, in a way, leaving her/his leadership legacy through the mentee. As a mentee, you're preparing for your future in leadership, learning from the experiences of others, being guided in the application of new Leadership Tools, and being supported in producing results that make a difference to the organization. There are no losers in this effort. Are you ready to invest in an age-old process of being mentored and willing to become a mentor for others sometime in your future? As I suggested earlier, *we're all leaders in training.* Mentorship is about learning from the best—and then structuring this learning so others can learn from *your* best. Consider yourself a leadership trainee today who will someday become the trainer for others. This is the legacy for you and a solid leadership building strategy for any organization.

It's Like Riding A Bike

In some ways, an effective mentorship program parallels parents teaching their children how to ride a two-wheeler after taking the training wheels off. As a parent, you want so badly to keep them from harm but you know the time is right to simply let go. You train them, get them started moving forward, run next to them holding on for balance, then stop running next to them, and trust that okay things will happen. You've given them wings, freedom, and confidence as you open up a whole new world for them. That's all well and good but as a parent it sometimes gives you worry, fear, and the occasional need to provide them with medical attention. There will be bumps and bruises, but eventually they learn to ride safely.

This parallels the Mentorship Model. Think of a key mentor in your career; you've probably had several already. Of course, you learned a lot by simply observing him/her function in different situations, but a true mentor will add great value in other ways. They connect with you in meaningful ways, when and where you need them most. They encourage you to keep moving forward, correct in gentle but direct ways, and provide you with tactics, strategies, and insights that provide those critical wisdom lessons. They run next to you holding on so you can retain balance, stop pushing you after awhile so you can solo, and encourage you in creating your own leadership momentum. Finally, they trust you as you roll ahead from one leadership project to the next. You took your leadership training wheels off and went solo thanks to a little help from your mentor guide. Now what can you do to help pass along this leadership legacy through you onto others? The Mentorship Model is a circle that you must complete. *You need to seek a mentor **and** you need to be a mentor for others.*

Advancing Into Leadership

Every manager wanting to be a leader is right for leadership—do you agree? Of course not! The fact is, I've seen some pretty "weak" managers pop up with really great change ideas and, because of the power of their idea or some other reason, they've been dubbed "leaders." The organization buys into their idea and these "pop-up leaders" receive a promotion or are put in charge of implementing the change. You know what's coming next, don't you? These people were so inept at managing change and leading people that the great idea was never fully implemented and failed to achieve meaningful results. In addition, teams and other staff were damaged along the way. These "pop-up leaders should have had a serious mentorship program to support them.

Leadership is not *all* about ideas. You must factor in the ability to transform the ideas into reality, as envisioned—to achieve the Main Things. You might become a great leader by chance, or you can learn from "true leaders" and lean on them to grow straighter and taller in your leadership career. The best approach is to learn as your grow.

I'm offering *three leadership effectiveness attributes* I've found essential as mentors and other leaders attempt to build and support leadership growth within organizations. These attributes are: **caring, connecting,** and **mentoring** of others. I believe so strongly about these three attributes that I've outlined a major portion of this Chapter around the topics of Caring, Connecting, and Mentoring. I'm asking you, as you read this Chapter, to reflect on these personal attributes that can add so much to the overall effectiveness of your various roles as manager, leader, and mentor. Individually, not one of these three attributes will guarantee success in your future growth and success. But, collectively, they address the *Human Side* (the *Being* side) of leadership. I've learned to place great value in these attributes, and have found them absent in most pop-up leaders. You will be a better leader if you consistently and effectively exhibit the ability to care, connect, and mentor others in ways that grow individuals and the organization.

Caring

LEADERS WHO CARE—To The Power of 3

Simply put, leaders must "care" about their responsibilities, their staff, and their organization. The entire theme of this book has been that leadership is all about others; it's not all about the leaders. In this section I'll share some of the personal traits and qualities I value personally and have attempted to emulate over the years with the help of my peers and various mentors. This is a simplified listing of C-A-R-E to the power of 3—meaning the three C's, A's, R's, and E's. In my opinion, these 12 traits are vital for leaders, managers, front-line employees, for marriage partners, for friends, and so on. But our focus here is to give you suggestions to help you *Be* the leader you need to be. If you "care" about being an effective leader, then *Care* enough about *Who* you are.

Many of these 12 traits have been referenced other times throughout the book, but I've chosen to list them again because of their importance to your effectiveness. I urge you to take them seriously and reflect on whether you agree with them or not. If not, why? If you do, were there specific mentors, leaders, or situations that taught you these traits? This is about growing as a "person." It's about your ability to be effective in all that you do that serves to "turn on" the tools you now have in your Leadership Toolbox. These are *not theories to be learned;* they are *traits to be applied.*

The "C" in CARE

- (Who Are You? What is the core of who you really are; your foundation?)

Character

- Integrity in everything you do.
- Strong set of personal core values, which you live daily.
- Passion for a purpose that matters and makes a positive difference.

Communication

- Listen actively (to verbal and non-verbal messages); communicate early and often.
- Know, communicate, and act on the "Main Things" things, not just the urgent things.
- Respect your co-workers and understand their spoken and unspoken needs.

Courage

- Act when action is required, not just when you feel like it.
- Confront others when required. Confrontation can be an important tool for effectiveness.
- Balance in achieving the required results, but remain mindful and aware of the needs of others.

The "A" in CARE

- (What's driving you? What do others see in you?)

Attitude

- Abundance thinking, not scarcity thinking. Leadership and change are not zero-sum games.
- Opportunity management, find new opportunities every day if you look for them.
- Win/win goals, strategies, and *results.*

Ability

- Continuous learning of competencies and growth through application of what you've learned.

- Skills in building a plan of action and then working the plan— through others.

- Solution-oriented actions directed at achieving the Main Things.

Accountability

- Value and exhibit follow-through, *consistently.*

- Achieve desired results/outcomes as measured by meaningful criteria.

- Accept consequences for actions/inaction and/or failed efforts.

The "R" in CARE

- (How you do your work? How to grow in leadership?)

Relationships

- Build common agendas and trust with others (character and focus).

- Servant's heart, attitude of understanding and meeting the needs of others.

- Capacity to deliver what's promised (competence), when it is promised (trust).

Responsiveness

- Ability to be agile and flexible in meeting customer needs.

- Sense of urgency and *a bias for action.*

- Ongoing communications (connectedness, avoid false starts).

Relevancy

- Outcomes that are driven by customers (which add value). Be customer-driven.

- Outcomes that are delivered on time and exceed customer expectations.

- Effective partnership building with suppliers, customers, and other businesses.

The "E" in CARE

- (How you balance life and work? Do your efforts make a difference?)

End

- Sense of moving forward in your "life *and* work priorities;" achieving the Main Things.

- See those around you succeed; making a meaningful difference in the lives of others.

- Be excited about tomorrow, but enjoy today.

Experiences

- Learn from the "teachable moments" as they come (grow continuously).

- Learn to act with a "purpose" and with a passion.

- Be a mentor who shares learned experiences.

Enjoyment

- Be balanced in your life and work, remembering there are seasons in life.

- Take satisfaction (have peace) in who and where you are.

- Laugh a lot and smell the roses around you.

EXCERCISE #25: Write down the 12 traits of C-A-R-E.

- Rate yourself on the same 1 to 10 scale on how well you're "living" each trait.

- Identify your strengths and weaknesses based on these traits and note what areas you believe you should focus your improvement efforts. Don't be afraid to celebrate those traits which you consider as strengths.

I believe these 12 traits must be balanced and exhibited consistently. Some days we all get too up tight for our own good. We need some higher ground to look at for survival. *Although leadership is not a destination, true leaders accept it as destiny.* They commit to leadership daily because they CARE about the role they play in moving the organization, others, and themselves forward.

Connecting:
Skills to Lead the Performance of Others

Leadership is accomplished **Through** others, it's done **For** others, and your success in leadership is measured **By** others. What do these "others" need and look for in effective leaders? What do they find in you? How can you "connect" with staff in meaningful ways to better implement successful change more effectively? You must find the proper balance in connecting effectively to *Be that leader worthy of* voluntary follower-ship.

Consider these Leadership Tools I've found extremely useful in helping to connect in meaningful ways with individuals and teams:

- Invest the necessary time and effort to allow others to *catch your vision* of a new opportunity.

- Share your commitment to the challenge and your willingness to take measured risk. *Have courage with wisdom, and don't be afraid to let your passion for the change show.*

- Be sensitive but remain committed to a spirit of *"de-constructive improvement."* Understand that the process of change must disassemble the current conditions before it can begin rebuilding in a new way. Help your staff "unlearn" some of those things they currently hold on to and do that brought praise in the past, but are not part of **this** change and their new future.

- Demonstrate a willingness to *take responsibility* **and** *be accountable.* Don't blame others, play the victim role, or shy away from being fully accountable and responsible for the successes or failures of change initiatives. Some managers and leaders side-step responsibility and blame their peers or their team for failure.

- Maintain a *competitive spirit* that draws you and others toward the challenge, creating wins for as many as possible. It's not an "I win, you lose" contest, but the change is a prize for the organization to obtain. Create the bigger "we" in achieving success.

- *Model a mental focus and toughness* that will persevere and follow-through in difficult times with difficult individuals.

- *Have respect for your peers and teams* because you value their roles, support, and success. Build a history of trust and mutual respect. Be easy to follow and a user-friendly partner with staff during the good times and bad times.

- Function with a *communication style* that consistently makes it easy for others to understand and follow your leadership. Help others understand that the need for effective and ongoing communication will increase (not decrease) throughout the change process.

EXERCISE #26: Leadership is about connecting with individuals in ways that truly help them succeed in making a significant difference. This Exercise is a tough self-assessment but be honest in looking at your ability to "connect" with others and how it affects your ability to lead.

- Do others see you as a "connector" that makes a positive difference for staff during the change process? In what ways?

- On a scale of 1 to 10, rate yourself on *each* of the eight points just listed?

- How would your team rate you? Ask them and write down their responses.

- In what specific areas and ways must you improve?

Mentoring:
The True Mentors I've Known

For me personally, the most influential people in my career weren't always the top dogs, the smartest, or even the people closest to me. Instead, they were those three or four key individuals in my life (besides my wonderful wife) who made the commitment to mentor me in my thinking, *BEing,* and *DOing.* The only "agenda" for truly effective mentors is that they want *Your* success for no reason other than they are committed to advancing "leadership" in the organization. In addition to your supervisor, of course, mentors should seek to develop you. My idea of a Mentorship Model is that *You* select the mentor. Sometimes we all need private guidance that's honest and confidential to get us through those challenging leadership (and life) experiences.

Influential mentors in your life will come in all shapes and sizes and from all parts of the organization.

Influential mentors in your life will come in all shapes and sizes and from all parts of the organization. I've had administrative assistants who have taught me more about leadership than my CEO's. I've had very young people teach this old dog many new tools of leadership. Do not stereotype those vital few who will vault you forward in leadership thinking and acting, but do choose these people well. **Caution:** There are many false prophets in the workplace who will offer you well-meaning counsel but give misguided advice and direction. How do you know what to look for in a mentor? Some of it's luck and some of it's wisdom. In this case, wisdom means accurately judging a mentor for his/her willingness and ability to mentor you successfully. That's why *you* must select the mentor who's right for you.

Seven Areas of Strength

These individuals will be your *personal teachers, your professional guides, and your leadership trainers.* But what "strengths" should I look for in a mentor? The following is an overview of the personal and professional strengths I've found embedded within the most effective mentors in my life. They were qualified to formally and informally help me grow. As you seek your next mentor, look for the following qualities or traits.

1. *A strong commitment to achieving the Main Things that becomes a focus; a destiny.*

   Leaders (and mentors) must have a strong sense of purpose. They must also be highly focused on achieving the Main Things and have a balanced measure of confidence. We all need *context in which to manage and lead,* and a strong Vision is essential. Understand the difference between what you *can* do versus what you *must* do, and why this distinction must be made. *Be driven toward a destiny **for** the organization **through** others.*

2. *Perseverance—refusal to accept failure, never give up, run with endurance.*

   Effective leaders are just ordinary leaders who didn't quit when they got poked in the eye or kicked in the shin. Believe me, it requires mental, emotional, and physical toughness to be a leader. Along the way, be prepared to openly admit mistakes and re-direct your efforts as necessary. *These mistakes must become your wisdom-points and teachable moments.* Gain new skills and perspectives based on your past mistakes, and have these lessons carry your leadership journey to the next level.

   I learned far more by going *through* the tough times than I did going through the good times (Guess which one was more fun?). Those tough times forged character and gave me a foundation on which to grow. Remember, you will never fail until you admit to failure. Do not accept failure easily. It's not how you start; it's how you prepare and pace yourself to finish the race. So run this leadership journey well, with courage and perseverance. Remember you're running a leadership marathon, not a 100-yard dash. Finishing well is rare, but most rewarding.

3. *Be Self-less—humility is good so long as it's balanced.*

It's tough to take a joke on yourself. It's tough to admit mistakes. It's tough to learn on the run, having others correct or even criticize you publicly. *Your ego is a terrible thing to trash.* Perhaps the journey into leadership should begin with "Boot Camp." Here you get torn down and then rebuilt into a newer, stronger, and more valuable asset for your team and organization. You will quickly learn that in leadership, success has many partners. But in failure, you tend to stand alone. Sometimes it's necessary to accept that blow to your ego and perhaps even your reputation.

A balanced degree of humility is part of your preparation for future success. What I've found is that a person without the right degree of humility is often viewed as being arrogant. A person too humble, on the other hand, is seen as a wimp. Humble pie can be food to help nurture your growth but retain that passion to grow and succeed in leadership—for all the right reasons. The key is that you don't lose sight of your focus and you don't fall away from your "will" to succeed.

4. *Know Yourself—be open, be real, and be honest about who you are.*

Many leaders are very talented and bold in visualizing what individuals and organizations need to do in order to move forward. *This quality of boldness, however, can also create "blind spots" as to areas of weakness in style, ego, paradigm, or knowledge base.* How do you know whether you're too bold or too soft as a leader?

One approach is to request honest and direct feedback from your peers, staff, and customers on the "effectiveness" of your own leadership style. Don't live in ignorance or denial about your strengths and weaknesses. *It's not humble to remain unaware of what you do well or what are not doing well.* Actually, it's false humility and a different form of pride. Don't be fearful of obtaining honest input from a select few—your mentor, supervisor, trusted team members, and valued peers. Even your mentors need ongoing feedback if they want to help you lead.

5. *Not afraid to Fail/Risk Takers*

If you're bound by the fear of failing, you'll never take risks. Wes Roberts said: "I would rather try and fail than be mediocre. For in failure, there are lessons to be learned, but mediocrity breeds false satisfaction." There is a big difference in how we view failure and how others view it. There are many roads to failure and I've found most of them over the years. Do not be afraid of failure. Do not be afraid to take risks with wisdom and do so with a minimum of fear.

- **Redefine failure.** Failure isn't falling short of the goal; it's not having a goal. Real failure is when you do not learn from your mistakes and are not being willing to try again. As Babe Ruth said: "Never let the fear of a strike keep you from taking a swing."

- **Refuse to compare yourself to others.** If you think you're doing better than others, you become proud. If you think you're not as good as others, you become discouraged and perhaps even paranoid. Simply *be* and *do* the best you can with what you have.

You can be a Risk Taker, or a Care Taker, or an Under Taker. You can't walk in leadership without risk and, in turn, experience some failures. However, it's not necessarily those who take the biggest risks who win. Be willing to take *smart* risks, move off dead center, make mistakes, learn, and ultimately succeed. Some of you are too committed to safety; you must have things all figured out and be able to predict what will happen before stepping out. Without taking calculated risks, you reinforce the status quo and become a "care taker." If you have a serious fear of failure, you will become an "under taker" for your team.

Be willing to learn as you forge ahead into the unknown. Courage with wisdom is easy to say and frightening to do. Wisdom will come with experience; risk always involves the unknown.

6. *Perpetual Learners—be Teachable*

Openness to being teachable requires that you take personal responsibility for your own development. Leaders must take initiative to learn the breadth and depth of their role, profession, organization, competition, and team. They listen to tapes, read books, attend seminars and conferences, further their formal education, learn from other leaders, they ask a lot of questions, and they learn from teaching others. They want to be teachable.

Teachable leaders are ones who never act like "they've arrived," know it all, or have heard it all before. They're submissive, eager, and willing to learn from experiences placed in their path. You must *want* to grow, learn continuously, and remain open to honest feedback. *It's not the learning or knowing that's important, it's applying what you've learned to improve continuously.*

7. *Leaders are Ultimately Followers.*

The very term "leader" should mean you're leading, right? *But,* effective leaders must also be effective followers in appropriate ways. First of all, you must incorporate into your leadership strategies what you've learned from your team as to their culture, needs, career objectives, and motivational "hot buttons." In essence, you are considering the needs of your team when customizing your decisions to achieve the Main Things. Along the way you're building the level of trust, respect, and success for them and the organization. Secondly, you must be observant and *follow* the big picture direction from your supervisors and pursue the Main Things for your team and the organization. You must also *follow-up* on the multitude of change opportunities that *will* present themselves every day. Finally, you must *follow* the policies and rules that govern your organization. Like it or not, you too are a follower. *If a leader turns around and no one is following, they are merely taking a walk. Do you have followers or are you just taking a walk?*

EXERCISE #27: Based on the Seven Areas of Strength for Mentors:

- Write the names of two or three individuals who have served as mentors for you during your career; who have you looked up to and attempted to emulate?

- Behind each name, identify which of the Seven Areas of Strength they clearly exhibited. Which of these Strengths meant the *most* to *you*?

- On a scale of 1 to 10, how would you rate yourself today in each of the Seven Strengths?

Most of us are grateful for the help we received "on the way up" and *want* to give back to individuals and to the organization. Look at it as part of your responsibility as a leader. Your role includes building leadership capacity in your organization through others. Effective leaders must also think ahead as to who can replace them when (not if) they're promoted to the next level or if they should leave the organization. You must hire, train-up, and retain the best managers and leaders possible. Be that mentor you had or you wish you had, and train up that handful of staff *you* would like to see grow on the job.

Mentorship; it's a form of legacy building. It's a process to help strengthen the core values you carry forward into effective leadership. Your legacy, your "preferred" legacy, should leave people better off than when you found them and better positioned for success. Remember, whatever positions you hold throughout your career, a true leader will always be in the people improvement business. The real winners (when you serve as a mentor) will be the mentees, the organization, and then yourself—in that order.

Maximize Your Investment

Your organization has made a substantial investment in you over the years and most certainly wants you to continue growing in value, career, and satisfaction. Flat out, if you're considered a valued employee, they want to keep you. Do you know what it costs an organization to replace a valued employee? It's *at least* one year's salary, probably more. Every organization needs an effective employee retention strategy to keep valued employees and a succession plan as valued employees leave or retire. Turnover rate is one of those Key Result Areas that is closely monitored by highly effective organizations. It's obvious that a high turnover rate is an indication that something is not right within the organization—and there's a cost for turnover. The logical question is, if employee turnover is deemed bad and mentorships/succession planning are good strategies for the organization, why aren't more organizations supporting a formal Employee Mentorship Program? It appears to fit well into an overall, proactive strategy to grow and retain good employees, doesn't it?

If your organization doesn't have an established mentorship program, you might have a large task in front of you to get one started. Some businesses feel they're much too busy moving forward to worry about a new "soft" activity. It's possible that all you can do, at this time, is research highly effective organizations and successful mentorship programs to document the "so what factor." Would it be worth the cost? Is this something your competition is doing? Is it something your key customers are doing? Define the intended outcome and measures of success, and work the communication upward as opportunities arise. When the timing is right for a mentorship program, you'll be ready to help lead the organization into this initiative. In the meantime, why not seek an "informal" mentorship with someone you're close to and you know would like to help you grow. *Leader or Not; Here I Come!*

Your Action Planning for Becoming a Mentee

Assuming your organization already has a mentorship program and you wish to become part of it, I'd make the following suggestions to prepare you for a successful experience:

- *Choose your mentor wisely.* Is he/she a willing participant, having the time and talent to guide your growth—when you need the help? Be aware of their character and leadership vision for you that will undoubtedly "come out" during the mentorship journey.

- *Commit to a plan.* Define what you want to accomplish through this mentorship. Make a set of major growth goals you're seeking, establish the frequency of meetings, and understand the expectations from both sides. Then be prepared to "work your mentorship plan."

- *Commit the time.* If you say you will meet for one hour weekly, schedule it and follow-through with the meetings—even if it lasts only 30 minutes. It's too easy for either of you to simply "get too busy."

- *Grow in your "big picture" exposure and knowledge.* Have your mentor open doors for you to meet and learn from leaders in other departments, organizational officials, specific project teams, and external groups and partners.

- *Be prepared to discuss the emotional challenges of leadership, as well as, the skills of Doing leadership.* Share your struggles and failures candidly. Egos must be left at the door but confidentiality of what's said between the two of you is a must.

- *Be there for each other.* Both of you should be available for calls at home and at unscheduled times because you cannot schedule every mentee "teachable moment" or your mentor wisdom moments.

- *Document progress.* What are the Key Result Areas you've identified as defining the success of this leadership growth experience (mentorship)? Monitor your progress and celebrate achievements with your mentor.

- *Have fun along the way.* Don't be afraid to laugh and create a lasting friendship, because that's what the two of you will establish over time.

Mentorship At Its Best

My experiences of being mentored and being a mentor have been some of the most rewarding activities in my career. You develop a valued, trusting relationship with committed individuals, and you share a common commitment to growth and success. I've formally mentored ten individuals during my career. In addition, at my last place of employment before semi-retirement, I informally identified and mentored five individuals to help grow and advance them within the organization. They were all very qualified and had a burning heart desire to grow. This informal mentoring process occurred over a period of three years. The potential in each mentee was obvious to me and I made the commitment to help these five individuals achieve that desired promotion and advancement in their careers. From a selfish standpoint, it was part of the legacy I quietly left when I retired. These individuals remained and reflected the *Being* and *Doing* approach to leadership that I helped instill within each of them. The organization is better off because five individuals are now better leaders. It worked!

Parenting, Little League coaching, classroom teaching, Boy Scouts/Girl Scouts, Big Brothers/Big Sisters, and countless other life enriching experiences rely upon the concept of mentoring. I would go so far as saying *"you won't truly be an effective leader unless you've been mentored and have served as a mentor."* Be your best; share your best; be a mentor. Seek it and commit to it. As a mentor, you are preparing others to be effective leaders, expanding the organization's capacity for the future, and you're learning more about yourself and leadership than you ever thought possible. I've discovered that the greatest learning in the classroom occurs within the teacher. The greatest learning in mentorship's often occurs within the mentor.

Be that leader and manager who cares, connects, and then mentors others. This is a pure form of leadership. When asked why the team and other managers should listen to your leadership ideas, it's because you CARE about the success of the organization and its individuals, you're willing and able to CONNECT with them and involve them in meaningful ways, and you're a proven MENTOR who is willing to walk alongside of them during this change journey. Set new leaders up for success *and* mentor them into and through new assignments. It's a journey for them—and it's a responsibility for you.

Caring, connecting, and *mentoring* are three tools to include in your Leadership Toolbox. Be prepared to grow in application of each because each is intertwined with so many other Leadership Tools. It goes back to the concept of *Be* before you *Do*—it's the personal and interpersonal side of leadership.

- *CARE about others and for their success.*
- *CONNECT with others at both the professional and personal level.*
- *MENTOR others in their thinking, being, and doing.*

"You cannot lead where you do not go."

—DON WARD

—✥—

"We cannot become what we want to be
by remaining what we are."

—MAX DUPREE

—✥—

"The very essence of leadership is [that] you have a vision.
It's got to be a vision you articulate clearly and forcefully
on every occasion. You can't blow an uncertain trumpet."

—THEODORE HESBURGH

—✥—

"Strategy is not the consequence of planning,
but the opposite: it's the starting point."

—HENRY MINTZBERG

—✥—

"You cannot build a reputation on what you're "going" to do."

—HENRY FORD

—✥—

"Planning is an unnatural process; it is much more fun
to do something. The nicest thing about not planning is
that failure comes as a complete surprise, rather than
being preceded by a period of worry and depression."

—SIR JOHN HARVEY-JONES

CHAPTER 10

STRATEGIC PLANNING IN LEADERSHIP

Are you one of those who are directionally challenged while driving? Isn't it frustrating that when you finally get up the nerve to ask someone for directions, you get one of those old timers who says "go down the road a yonder, turn north for a piece, turn west and then make a quick northwest turn, and there you are—it's by that big tree." You're not only directionally challenged but directionally lost as well!!! That's what happens in too many organizations. They're full of directionally challenged staff wanting to follow directions but not knowing north from south. In addition, their senior officials provide directions like that old timer. These senior officials have taken a vacation from effective leadership, conducting planning as an "event" without teeth or serious direction. Is it any wonder why staff remain confused as to the Main Things and priorities?

I've attended several Stephen Covey workshops when he asked everyone in his audience to close their eyes and point to "true north." Hands would go up, pointing in *all* directions. It's amazing how many norths there are in the minds of well-meaning staff—in so many different directions. Watch those successful organizations (and leaders)—they have everyone in the organization perfectly aligned, all heading in the *same* true north direction. Unfortunately, too many organizations spend more time having staff work harder and not enough time setting and communicating a common direction. *One of your primary jobs as a leader is to set and then effectively deploy what true north is for your organization.* This function is more important than many staff realize.

Highly effective organizations require that daily decision-making and actions of *all* staff be done having a common focus and direction. These organizations then ensure sufficient and timely support to staff to make certain that the right things happen. *By aligning staff to act on matters and to achieve desired results in areas that truly matter, you're positioning the organization to move forward in ways that "make a difference."* You do not accomplish these results by telling staff to "try harder" or with simple slogans or by making current processes more efficient through incremental changes. **Significant results require significant change,** and this change process requires significant planning and follow-through during implementation.

211

The key to successful and meaningful change is to:

- Position your organization to be truly customer-driven—listen and deliver.
- Develop a focus and passion for planned change that points *Everyone* in the same direction to accomplish the Main Things.
- Support an aligned infrastructure to drive *Everyone* true north.
- Identify and monitor Key Result Areas that make a significant difference in moving the organization forward (beyond the compliance measures).

Having a solid framework for developing a Strategic Plan requires the right set of processes and tools, as well as, having the proper mindset for new thinking. Clearly, this is one leadership function that must be delivered with excellence if you are to become a *Great Leader* who is leading from the front, not from two steps behind. Become that leader *you* would choose to follow. Envision yourself in that key role as you read and work through Chapters 10 and 11. How will you apply these Leadership Tools when you are in that position of senior leadership, and what can you begin to apply today?

Up until this point of the book, I've presented material on leadership, the Leadership Tools, and a set of Exercises you can begin to apply immediately. *In this Chapter and the next, I'm presenting new information as if you are NOW a senior leader needing to move your organization to the next level of performance and competition.* What new tools and leadership concepts might assist you in this task of moving an organization through change—with you as a senior leader? As I present information on "Strategic Planning" (Chapter 10) and "Leadership From 20,000 Feet" (Chapter 11), I want you to understand that having a basic, working knowledge of both planning and a big picture view of the organization is vital for you, both today and tomorrow. This knowledge will position you well to move your organization forward in the future and make you more valuable in your mid-manager role today. You must move beyond tactical thinking and actions to the more strategic levels.

Changed Thinking About Planning

Many individuals and organizations do not fully understand the short- and-long-term value of "action-oriented" strategic planning. *The term "strategic" in strategic planning should mean something significant and required for your organization. It must be seen by all employees and stakeholders as a process that moves the organization forward.*

Clearly the term "strategic" should not be confused with "operational" or "incremental" planning and change. Strategic Planning does not represent an opportunity for you to "tell the world" all that's on your work platter and how important you are to the organization. But you know what, that's the mindset I've seen many managers and senior officials begin with as they approach strategic planning. Their planning process is problematic in four ways:

- It's either watered down because it strives to be all inclusive with too many thoughts and directions or, in the other extreme, its completion is directed by a handful of senior executives in the boardroom with almost "no input." Nothing in between.

- It's a required annual event or task for the organization, like a financial audit. It's completed, approved, and then placed on a shelf.

- It's a document that identifies needed changes in key processes rather than key "repositioning" initiatives for the total organization.

- It's an example of management-level thinking that is void of leadership-thinking.

Effective strategic planning must be framed by the question: *"How do we define success for our organization and what three to five Main Things **must** be achieved to get us there?"* You don't begin by jumping prematurely into deciding who should be doing what and when. Rather, you begin by (and spend adequate time) developing a common vision and a common understanding of what defines ultimate success for the organization. *Then* you can begin to prioritize what must be done to get you there. It requires new thinking and new planning processes. It requires true actions and desired outcomes that are truly "strategic" in nature. It cannot and must not reflect "business as usual." *If the status quo is not seriously challenged and moved, your planning is not at the strategic level.*

The "traditional" view of strategic planning that many organizations subscribe to is:

- Creation of a longer range outlook for the organization; a look into the future.

- Providing the organization with a set of agreed upon priority action goals and a lengthy set of objectives.

Review your

Strategic Plan

and ask the

"so what" question.

- An opportunity to prepare a document for sharing direction and accountability information with boards and external stakeholders.

- The prospect of actively involving staff from throughout the organization in this process.

- Facilitating communications and developing a sense of institutional commitment.

All of these points are good, aren't they? But the focus for many of these points appears to be at the "input" level—not the "results" level. Will the traditional approach actually move the organization forward to true north, to deliver quality as defined by customers, build new business, position the organization to survive three years from today?

The question I often ask regarding this traditional approach to planning is "so what?" If all you are is proud of or are satisfied with this planning document, you're in for serious status quo business. *It should be a document that opens the eyes of anyone reading it and gets their hands sweaty. It should lay out the need for serious changes in a handful of targeted initiatives that, if accomplished, will move the organization forward in measurable ways.* You must seek to *create passion, not pride* from this planning product. If you review your Strategic Plan and ask the "so what" question, I hope you can answer it by listing a series of significant outcomes resulting from moving a small set of "big rocks."

Proactive Strategic Planning

I'd like to offer a more "proactive" alternative to the "traditional view" of strategic planning. The processes and paradigms surrounding Proactive Strategic Planning are significant. The differences are real and my hope is that, after this comparison, you'll be better able to assess the kind of strategic planning your organization conducts. The following compares the differences between the *Traditional View of Planning* versus the *Proactive View of Planning:*

Comparison of Approaches to Strategic Planning

THE <u>TRADITIONAL</u> PLANNING APPROACH IS:	THE <u>PROACTIVE</u> PLANNING APPROACH IS:
Action to be taken in the future.	Actions and decisions to be made **today.**
The development of a Strategic Plan document that provides **direction.**	The process of planning **significant change** (at the strategic level) to move the critical few "big rocks—causing significant outcomes."
Running of the organization—bordering on an Operational Plan.	**Moving** the organization forward in three to five "major" areas. A hyperfocus on changes that will make the significant differences.
A document for staff to take pride in their hard work and what **process-oriented improvements** they will be undertaking.	Staff developing an understanding of and having a passion for a **new level of performance** for the organization.
Conducting the planning process with extensive **staff input.**	Staff having a clear, common understanding and extensive **"buy-in"** to the new direction.
Success as measured by **completion of actions** (objectives).	Success as measured by movement toward **organizational measures of success—results.**
Focus is on planning **"input."**	Focus is on planning **"significant results."**
The Plan does not drive significant changes in the organization's budget plan—they tend to be **independent processes.**	The Plan **drives and is supported by** the organization's budget plan, staffing plan, and continuous improvement plan.
The Plan is bound and reviewed semi-annually, with **action on objectives recorded.**	The Plan is a **living document,** updated continuously, with progress closely monitored.

EXERCISE #28: Obtain a copy of your organization's Strategic Plan and review it carefully. Write down which view your organization has on strategic planning—traditional or proactive?

- Are "significant results" clearly identified? How many are there?

- How often during the year do *you* reference the Strategic Plan when making decisions?

- On a scale of 1 to 10, to what extent does the Strategic Plan "drive" changes in your next Budget Plan?

It's obvious that effective leaders having proactive Strategic Plans will cause meaningful strategic change to occur—beginning immediately. That's the one common trait I've found in effective planning, in that decisions and actions begin occurring *today* rather than in a year or two. Staff are expected and motivated to seek opportunities to make *current decisions in light of the preferred future as presented in the Strategic Plan.* For this to occur, your Strategic Plan *must* give clear guidance and direction as to *what should be done now to make the desired things happen tomorrow.* Strategic Plans should serve to pull the organization into its preferred future—it should not be a wish list or a set of generic listing of the desirable, nicely worded goals we want to achieve. Define, in clear terms, exactly where you want the organization to move and identify key measures (outcomes) that will validate this movement has occurred.

Strategic Plans are too often passive rather than passionate. "Planning for meaningful results" and then achieving those results is required if your organization is to survive in the future. Is survival a fervently-discussed topic during your planning meetings? If not, it should be. Do you have a planning agenda item that evaluates your competition? If not, it should be. Planning must not be soft and philosophical. It must be highly focused and hard hitting. Specifically, it must define and chart a clear direction based on what the "next level of performance" must be and the key actions required to get the entire organization to that level.

Barriers to Effective Strategic Planning

- *Time Pressures: "I'm too busy to plan!"* The urgent pressures of your workplace are forcing you and your team to take one day at a time, causing everyone to be more reactionary and short-sighted than they should be. Without a plan and a vision, you tend to address each problem and challenge in isolation—without a broader context. In this way, the *urgent matters keep you from doing the truly important things. You're managing the day-to-day in lieu of leading for tomorrow.* The symptoms to look for are:

Too many initiatives, with too much activity producing little or no meaningful results.

Improvement initiatives are unrelated, with each department doing their own thing.

When allocating resources, it is unclear how much money (and staff) to give to whom and what is the most important work to support. Worse yet, you may have an "incremental" budgeting process not being "driven" by the Strategic Plan.

It is hard to tell when you are successful—no roadmap exists to chart your movement.

It's not apparent whether planned activities will take the organization to where you need to go because there's no clear vision of success. How do you measure success?

Your organization spends most of its time reacting to crisis; little time innovating.

- **Attitude:** "I've been successful in the past as a manager—*why would I need to change?*" The same mindset holds true for the entire organization. Remember the PDCA Cycle introduced earlier in the book? If you don't plan well, you'll generate a lot of "do, do." There's flawed thinking about the planning function because past experiences have not been at the strategic level, may have proven negative, have caused nothing but more work for you, which produced no meaningful results. If the attitude is that all is okay, then the traditional approach to strategic planning is just fine. "Planning is no big deal" is the prevailing attitude.

- **Approach:** The process of planning ends up being a mini-negotiating session with various internal factions arguing why or why not a given initiative should be included. The approach relies too heavily on emotion and not enough on facts. Current realities are not examined in enough depth and the preferred vision ends up being more of a "hope to achieve floating target" rather than a set of clearly defined results (Main Things) that *must* be achieved.

    One approach is to first establish organizational success measures by benchmarking against the best-of-the-best organizations for performance excellence criteria. *Think bigger, better, and from outside of your organization*—recognize and learn from your customers and your competition.

A second approach is to *deploy the plan throughout the organization* and place accountability expectations on successful implementation of the targeted performance enhancement measures linked directly to the strategic goals.

A third approach is to implement the revised, focused Strategic Plan with new, proactive thinking and actions. *Make the plan strategic, highly focused, and integrated* into the budgeting, staffing, improvement, and monitoring processes.

The problem with strategic planning is that for many organizations and individuals, it has become an annual exercise or event. Strategic planning needs context in which to define specific measurable goals and objectives to be accomplished within a given time period. Will achieving these goals and objectives result in movement toward the Main Things? How will you measure your progress? What is the significant "so what" factor resulting from your planning? It's all about the "so what" factor *after* the plan has been thoroughly implemented—what's changed!

The Leadership Side of Strategic Planning

Effective strategic planning places the organization as the center of focus—not *me* or my departments or maintaining the status quo. The entire organization must be actively engaged and challenged in deciding where and how it *must* move to remain competitive. Strategic planning, as in leadership, is about others and the organization. It doesn't begin with the individual or you.

How do I determine whether a strategic plan is effective or not? One way is to monitor whether staff actually *use* the plan in their decision-making throughout the year. Do they assess the impact each of their key decisions and actions have on the plan's goals, objectives, and outcomes? At the organizational level, another indicator is whether the plan is *aligned with and drives other organizational plans*. Integrated planning and proper alignment make the Strategic Plan "real and significant." Your Plan should directly influence and drive the following:

- **Annual Budget Planning**—to align budgets with priorities and strategic initiatives. Reprioritize current operations as to impact and importance to success of the organization.

- *Human Resources Planning*—to provide (or reallocate) staffing at the necessary levels and the training to prepare staff to accomplish the priorities and strategic initiatives.

- *Process Improvement Planning*—continuous improvement to streamline processes, reduce waste, ensure customer satisfaction, improve information systems, and maximize resources.

- *Staff Evaluation Process*—set expectations for staff going into the year, support staff in their priority performance expectations during the year, and hold them accountable at year-end.

The essence of an effective, proactive strategic planning process is that it affects and drives changes vertically and horizontally within the organization to achieve meaningful results—and this includes budgets, staffing, processes, and staff accountability.

Summary of Planning Elements

The critical elements that I believe should be addressed in any Strategic Plan would include:

- A re-visitation of the current organizational Vision and Mission. Ensure that the organization's Vision is clear, accurate, and sufficiently bold. It must be so clear and concise that it readily creates a picture of the "desired state" for the organization in every employee. It must serve to link people, processes, paradigms, and related plans. How do *you* know that what *you* do will positively affect the organization into realizing its Vision?

- The Vision drives data, discussions, and decisions as to the Main Things that must be accomplished to achieve this "desired state." How the organization will accomplish the Main Things must be categorized into a series of measurable action steps and outcomes.

- The Strategic Plan must reflect the organization's:

  Mission

  Core Values

  Strengths, Weaknesses, Opportunities, and Threats

  The Major (big picture) Challenges Facing the Organization

  Key Customer Requirements for your products and services

Process and Continuous Improvement Priorities

Key Measures of Success

- The Strategic Plan links where the organization "must move" (desired state—Vision) with how the organization will "get there" (strategic goals and objectives).

- The Plan succeeds in generating a focus, passion, and support from staff in accomplishing the strategic goals and objectives.

- The Plan is linked to other key plans and the monitoring/accountability systems.

I've prepared the following matrix that addresses the critical elements listed above. It serves as a guide that illustrates the interrelationship between these critical elements of planning. Most Strategic Plans are limited to a series of goals and objectives, which are obviously critical components of the Plan. Your Strategic Plan **must** support leadership and complement the collective role of all staff in achieving the Main Things for the organization. Therefore, the challenge is to link the Goals with other key organizational elements:

- Incorporating your organization's Core Values to be followed and strengthened during the Plan's implementation process.

- Identifying key customer segments and making sure the Plan moves the organization toward meeting their quality standards and Success Indicators.

- Critical areas of process improvement that *must* be addressed as part of moving the organization to the next level.

The following Matrix for Effective Strategic Planning links these key elements to the desired key result areas for the organization. The plan should direct, align, support, and place expectations that make a difference.

MATRIX FOR EFFECTIVE STRATEGIC PLANNING
ELEMENTS AND RESULTS OF STRATEGIC-LEVEL LEADERSHIP

ELEMENTS OF STRATEGIC PLAN	Provides Clear Direction, Roles, & Focus	Enhances Our Passion to Serve and Succeed—Self & Team	Creates Alignment of Priorities and Resources	Receives Support from Senior Leadership & Key Partners	Drives Decisions, Raises Expectations, & Invites Accountability
Principles that Guide our Work & Team Culture—**CORE VALUES**		X	X	X	X
Clear & Common Understanding of who we serve, why we serve them, and how—**MISSION**	X	X	X	X	X
Clear & Compelling Statement (image) of our preferred future—**VISION**	X	X	X	X	X
Commitment to a set of Success Indicators—**KEY RESULT AREAS**	X	X	X	X	X
Identify Key Customer Segments & their primary requirements—**VALUE-ADDS**	X		X		X
Analysis of Strengths, Opportunities, Weaknesses, & Threats—**CHALLENGES & CURRENT REALITIES**			X	X	X
Identify key Process improvements that will drive Change NOW—**PROCESS IMPROVEMENTS**	X	X	X		X
GOALS—Strategic Action Plans for individuals, teams, & the organization.	X		X	X	X

As a leader, your role is to make the planning process meaningful, eventful, and accountable.

EXERCISE #29: Write down your answers based on the above Matrix.

- How effective do you believe your organization's strategic planning process is in addressing and strengthening each of the eight Elements listed in the left hand column?

- On a scale of 1 to 10, how would you rate the impact of your organization's strategic planning process on you and your team?

- Review the Strategic Goals listed in your Strategic Plan. Are they the "big rocks" that are absolutely essential in moving the organization to the next level—or not?

- Does your Strategic Plan "drive" your organization's annual budget?

These are not "gotcha" questions. Strategic planning is a critical process (not event) that brings about needed change and improvements in the organization. As a leader, your role is to make the planning process meaningful, eventful, and accountable. Without a meaningful and clear plan, staff is directionally challenged—and often lost.

Strategic Leadership for Strategic Planning

As you view strategic planning for your organization from your current chair at the mid-management level, the question you must ask is "how would I approach this process if I were in charge?" In answering that question I suggest you begin by *focusing on the process of planning rather than the Plan itself.* The key is how you "plan to plan" and how valuable and influential you truly want this Strategic Planning process to be on your organization. Examine what actions or changes in thinking will facilitate your planning process and ultimately the organization's success. Will you take the traditional approach to planning or do you want a proactive approach?

The following are *seven strategic leadership requirements* that, if implemented with excellence, will lead you in planning for a more effective, proactive strategic planning process:

Leadership Strategy #1. **Context for Change**—what are the motivating forces driving your organization to "move" and "change?" It's the "so what" factor.

Answers to this question *must* not only be motivating to others but must also be based on accurate facts. They must be widely understood within the organization. This will require a valid assessment of current realities and make a strong case for a new, desired state (vision).

Leadership Strategy #2. **Mission Review.** Seriously review the current Mission to make certain it's still valid, clear enough, and is fully understood by staff throughout the organization. Make your reason for existence and focus (your Mission) real and understandable.

Leadership #3. **Vision Review.** With assurance that your Mission (reason for existence) is accurate, what picture do you want to create as to the desired future state for your organization? The Vision must be clear, widely understood, and serve to motivate staff to change in a planned manner. Better yet, the Vision should guide staff in making current decisions based on their passion to see the desired future state for the organization actually realized. The Vision must be more than a nicely worded statement that's hung on the wall. Rather, it must be a clear picture of your desired future state that instills a passion that's alive in the minds and hearts of all staff.

Leadership Strategy #4. **Identify and then Move the Main Things.** Focus your planning and action on which "Main Things" must be achieved to move the organization forward at a meaningful pace. Staff should only be asked to address two, or at most, three major initiatives (Main Things) over a three year planning period. Select these initiatives very carefully. Make sure these are strategic, highly impacting, and measurable—that, if accomplished, will proactively move the organization toward success.

Leadership Strategy #5. **Organizational Planning (not Management Planning).** *How* you plan and *Who* you involve in the process will have a direct impact on the success of your Strategic Plan. This must not be a Plan developed in the back room by a Good Ol' Boys Club of Managers. Rather, *it must be a Plan for the organization to be accomplished by the organization.* Input from and appropriate buy-in by staff and other key stakeholders both within and outside the organization is essential for success. The danger is that you can compromise or water down a good plan without someone or group process to prioritize and make the final decisions. Be aggressive in receiving input but be strong in keeping the Plan meaningful.

Leadership Strategy #6. **To Move Forward—Change.** View the big picture—organizational challenges from a 20,000 feet vantage point. See them objectively and clearly. At the same time, fully understand the operational framework for running a highly effective organization and the interdependent parts of this framework (Note: See Chapter 11—Leadership From 20,000 Feet). You must be fearless in determining focused Strategic Goals and actionable Objectives based on these challenges, the operational framework, and the organization's desired results. Minimize the impact of internal politics, the tendency to seek "compromise," and the strong resistance from "status quo forces." Focus on meaningful change, with a bias for measurable action.

Leadership Strategy #7. **Manage After The Plan** *(Support, Follow-through, and Monitoring).* In Chapter 7, I presented a Matrix For Managing Complex Change. The strategic planning process is one of the most important leadership activities you will face and it presents your organization with a serious set of complex changes. Base your follow-through actions and strategies on the eight drivers in the Matrix. At all costs, follow-through and monitor what you've begun in this Strategic Plan and encourage and support staff in utilizing this Plan in their day-to-day decision-making and actions. Hint: If you want to make sure they will use the Plan, include strategic planning updates as an agenda item periodically in your team meetings and performance reviews. If you measure their usage of the plan for decision-making, they'll use it. Use it (the Plan) or lose it is an appropriate caution to offer to you as a new leader.

The Strategic Planning Process

While there are a common set of key elements to every strategic planning process, there can be a significant difference in how organizations act on each of these elements. Effectiveness in leading your organization through these five elements will drive your success and your legacy.

- *Senior Leadership Review and Recommitment.* Thoughtfully, consider any needed modifications to the following organizational guideposts:

    Mission—make sure it clearly identifies, in 30 words or less,

    Who are your customers?

    Why are you serving these customers?

    How are you serving them?

    Vision—that clearly describes your preferred future (in 30 words or less).

    Core Values—how you want to behave and what you value as an organization.

- *Situational Analysis.* Assess the "Current State" and "Desired Future State." Conduct a SWOT Analysis (Strengths—Weaknesses—Opportunities—Threats)

  Current Internal Strengths and Weaknesses and Current External Strengths and Weaknesses.

  What internal and external strengths should you capitalize on and continue to grow?

  What should be done to address the major weaknesses you've identified?

  What are the three to five major challenges your organization is facing currently?

  Conduct a SWOT Analysis based on the Desired Future State/Vision. Future Internal and External Opportunities and Threats.

  What are the exciting opportunities (internal and external) that should be included in your planning to make sure they materialize?

  What are the real and emerging threats for which you need to build defensive strategies so they do *not* materialize or are at least minimized?

  Identify your competition and the competitive advantages they have over your organization. What must you do to beat the competition in the future?

  Evaluate Results. Identify and prioritize the key challenges facing your organization now and into the future. Brainstorm a set of key strategies to address these challenges.

- *Three-Year Strategic Plan.* Describe the "Desired Future State" in detail and identify the vital few "Main Things" that *must* be accomplished in the next three years to achieve the "Desired State."

  Based on your critical review of the Vision, Mission, Core Values and your Situational Analysis, where *must* your organization be in three years? Set meaningful targets and measures for these targets. What must you look like, be doing, and achieving?

  What are the three to five major Goals (Main Things) that, if achieved or completed, will move your organization to this Desired State?

What measurable actions (beginning immediately, not in three years) will be required to achieve each Goal? These objectives must ensure that accountability and responsibility are assigned appropriately, along with timelines established, required support resources provided, and proper monitoring of progress being made.

Critical Success Measures are identified. How will you monitor and measure success?

Deploy the final Plan throughout the organization, creating a common understanding of the three to five Goals and what it will take (by individuals and the organization) to achieve the Desired State. Communicate how "success" is defined and what that means for staff and the organization.

- *Short-Term Focused Strategies.* Break the Three-Year Plan into *Priority Goals for the First Year—A One-Year Plan.*

  Communicate first things first—what are the priorities for Year One. Help staff understand what must be done (and what existing job duties might have to be reprioritized)

  Allocate budget and staff resources to support these priority actions.

  Develop Critical Success Measures for Year One. What results are expected?

- *Monitor Progress.* Continuously

  Movement toward the Three-Year Goals during Year One.

  Staff—focus on accomplishing and measuring Year One actions.

  Prepare to address related challenges of empowerment and accountability.

To visualize how these planning elements work together, see the chart below entitled "Flow of the Strategic Planning Process."

FLOW OF THE STRATEGIC PLANNING PROCESS

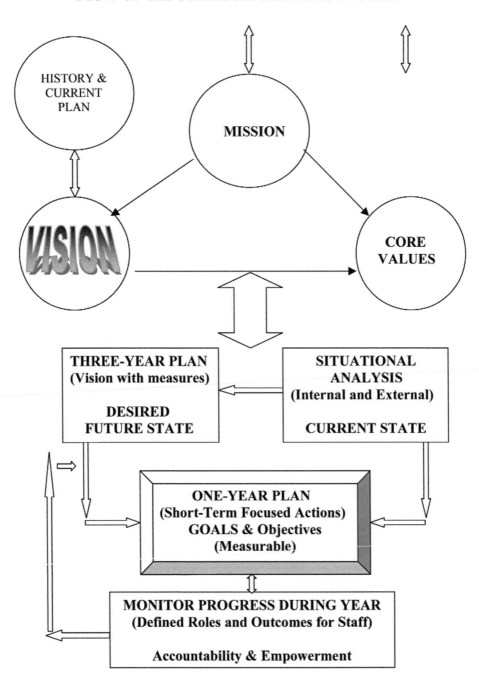

EXERCISE #30: One of the critical roles for senior leaders in this planning process is reviewing the organization's Vision, Mission, and Core Values. Effective organizations will *never* gloss over the importance of these drivers to short-term and long-term success.

- Without looking at the formal statements for your organization, write down how *you* would define the Vision, Mission, and Core Values.

- Compare what you've just written with the organization's formal Vision, Mission, and Core Values. How close were you to capturing the essentials of these formal statements?

- In your own words, write the Vision, Mission, and Core Values for your team. Share these statements with your team members for feedback and possible revision. Then, finalize these three documents and share them with your team and supervisor. Over time, analyze how your team is doing "living" these documents.

Common Understanding of Staff

You've reviewed key Elements and Flow of the Strategic Planning Process and completed an Exercise to express the organizational and team Vision, Mission, and Core Values in your own words. Now, there's one additional dimension of planning to share, because it's critical to your success. It's about *the role "people/staff" play in the planning process and their degree of "buy-in" to the Plan.* What strategies could you utilize to maximize staff understanding, involvement, and buy-in? Plan and implement these strategies carefully. Each strategy is situational so I can't guide you on what to do, simply do it. To the extent possible, engage staff in meaningful ways as you:

- Develop a *common understanding* of the **Current Realities**—Situational Analysis, Environmental Scan, Focus Groups, Competitive Analysis, or other activities.

- Develop a *common understanding* of the **Desired Future**—The next level of performance, new positioning within the market, a different way of operating internally, a revised vision, or other "organizational movement."

- **Plan and Act On** these *common understandings* of the current realities and future state in ways that communicate answers to these questions:

    Where we are going?

    Why we are going there?

How we're going to get there?

How you will **Measure** the journey?

Please note use of the words "common understanding" in the summary just detailed. The Strategic Plan is simply a nice document unless the entire organization knows and understands the key goals and are committed to moving in that direction. How and whether this common understanding dimension is achieved serves to separate great leaders from average leaders. Along your leadership path, *learn this skill of obtaining a common understanding* of the current state, the Main Things, the future state, and measuring progress along the way.

The process of developing and monitoring a meaningful planning process is hard work. Do not underestimate the importance of staff in the planning process, as well as, the implementation process. Remember, you must "work the plan," not just prepare one. In some ways, *the "plan" is relatively unimportant, but the process of planning and implementation is essential.* If staff sees and understands the direction and are involved in ways that allow them to "buy into" this new direction, you are a long way to successful implementation of your Strategic Plan. You must move individuals as you create and implement the plan. Then, the organization is prepared to move forward.

The lesson here is that strategic planning is a key Leadership Tool for you to understand, apply, and deliver with excellence. It's not a "nice to know" tool—it's a *Must Know.* Strategic planning falls within the definition of leadership because:

- The planning process recognizes that you're in a **people business.** People (staff) ultimately determine the "worth" of the Strategic Plan and people are required to effectively implement the Plan.

- The Strategic Plan has a focus on the (vital few) **Main Things** that make a significant difference to the organization—today and tomorrow.

- The Plan provides a **common understanding** among staff and allows all staff to make decisions around the "right things."

- The focus is on **moving individuals and the organization forward**—on the path to success **as the organization defines success.**

EXERCISE #31: Compare what you've learned about Strategic Planning from this Chapter with your organization's latest Strategic Plan. Identify and list what you believe to be five opportunities for improving the strategic planning process or product for your organization. Be specific and explain why this improvement is needed. (Caution: Be careful to make this a "personal exercise" and not one you

Do not underestimate the importance of staff in the planning process, as well as, the implementation process.

share widely with others. While it's to your advantage to have these thoughts on improvement, it's best to wait until you're in the position of influencing the planning process by virtue of your position or invited role in the process.)

Plans, like annual budgets, are meant to be living documents that ebb and flow with opportunities and changing conditions. The real question to ask when preparing a strategic plan is: "Are you thinking big enough, deep enough, and far enough into the future?" You will become what you choose to measure and reward. How successful do you want your organization to become based on your plan? Plan it, implement it, and become it.

"The greatest danger for most of us is not that our aim is too high and we miss it, but that it is too low and we reach it."

—MICHELANGELO

❧

"Unless there is a sincere commitment to successful leadership over the long run, the whole exercise becomes. . . . . Value Subtracting."

—AUTHOR UNKNOWN

❧

"Knowledge without action is simply a pipe dream. It increases expectations, gets you nowhere, costs time and money, and irritates the staff."

—DENNIS NITSCHKE

❧

"Execution is the ability to mesh strategy with reality, align people with goals, and achieve the promised results."

—LARRY BOSSIDY

❧

"The best vision is insight."

—MALCOLM FORBES

CHAPTER 11

LEADERSHIP FROM 20,000 FEET

(FRAMEWORK FOR HIGH PERFORMANCE)

The title of this Chapter, "Leadership From 20,000 Feet," indicates that we're about to look at leadership, change, and performance excellence from a very high vantage point. This is absolutely essential for leaders in highly effective organizations and is found missing in far too many "average" organizations. I believe part of the problem relates to that old saying: "...Can't see the forest through the trees." Organizations are very complex and it's difficult to understand the dynamics of what s causing wrong things (or the right things) to be happening. How do you determine the high-level change priorities that will ensure organizational survival or, on the other hand, move the organization to the next level of performance?

Why do some organizations and senior officials fail to see these priorities? Perhaps it's due to one of the following:

- Just as in strategic planning, many senior officials feel they're too busy to spend time trying to identify those long-range and big picture issues and strategies. The focus is on crisis management. This is why these individuals should be referred to as senior managers, not senior leaders.

- Senior officials have tried to take that high-level approach but their past experiences have not proven successful. In some ways, their experiences ran parallel to this story about the mating of two elephants.

  all the work was done at very high levels;

  the work was often done in the dark;

  the work was accomplished in the midst of dust, kicking, grunting, and much trumpeting;

  great amounts of grass and sometimes people were trampled in the process; and it took two years to see if all that work was successful. Most often it was not.

Excellence requires the positioning of your leadership so the key people, plans, processes, and paradigms are properly aligned.

Why is there a fear of heights and the benefits this vantage point can provide to the long-range success of any organization? If you don't have a plan for accomplishing the Main Things and you don't understand what "excellence" looks like, how can you be the leader your organization requires? If all you do is view the organization at ground zero or from only 500 feet, how do you know what your competition is doing, which may be beating your efforts? How do you make sure the organization's infrastructure is able to properly support your leadership efforts? How do you monitor and define success of your efforts in terms that are meaningful to the organization? Leadership must judge today's decisions within the context of your competition, alignment of and coordination with other organizational priorities, the availability of budget and staff support, and knowing the right measures of success. Leadership cannot function in a vacuum without knowing answers to the questions just asked. You need that vantage point from 20,000 feet to see and then direct change, the support for change, and the outcomes of your efforts.

Strategic Planning (Chapter 10) is critical to moving your organization forward, but this planning and change process must be conducted within a broader, defined context of "excellence." Excellence goes beyond change initiatives just being "good enough," or at the "continuous improvement" level, or from the perspective that "my department is the best." *You must define and recognize excellence at the organizational level.* It requires the positioning of your leadership so the key people, plans, processes, and paradigms are properly aligned. That is the common denominator for effective leadership.

For excellence in leadership to occur, you must:

- Have measures of success based on targeted, proactive goals and outcomes as stated in your Strategic Plan.
- Have an understanding of how all decisions and actions must be integrated and sequenced in order to maximize effectiveness (*performance excellence model*).
- Have the ability to integrate and focus the thinking of the organization.
- Then…success and performance excellence can become reality.

Performance excellence is not simply a "buzz word." It's a significant factor that separates the average organization from the highly effective organization.

Introduction to the Malcolm Baldrige Framework

I'm about to introduce you to the Malcolm Baldrige Framework, which is a national performance excellence system and award program. While my focus will be on introducing you to the framework and not the award, be aware that national awards are given annually by the U.S. President to the top three to six organizations in the nation that exhibit performance excellence. In addition, approximately 45 states have parallel performance excellence programs. This is not some recognition program that turns out to be a popularity contest or beauty pageant. Rather, it's an internationally recognized award with criteria that is updated annually based on what the best-of-the-best organizations do on their way to being the best. *This framework can benchmark what your organization is doing against how the "best" do it. In this way, your organization can better understand its major strengths and opportunities for improvement that can make a significant difference in its performance.* You can learn from what the best-of-the-best are doing and can then decide for yourself what changes *you* choose to make to improve performance.

My challenge is to present the Malcolm Baldrige Framework in an uncomplicated manner so you can better understand and apply the basic concepts during your leadership journey. "What" is it these best organizations do? "How" do they apply these concepts? Are these concepts interrelated and sequenced in any certain manner? Through the course of this Chapter, I will address these questions. *Once understood, these concepts could very well alter your paradigm on change and your approach to leadership.* Performance excellence has direct application at both the strategic and tactical levels. You *will* be a more effective and valued leader as you learn to apply this framework.

Overview of the Malcolm Baldrige Framework

The Malcolm Baldrige Framework, or "Baldrige," is a performance excellence model and system designed to move organizations forward *by identifying and measuring critical actions that are proven to make a significant difference in highly effective organizations.* That sounds simple enough, doesn't it! You simply copy another business's organization chart and policies and *Bang*—you have performance excellence, right? WRONG!!!! *The framework is driven by what the "best-of-the-best" organizations do to achieve success but it allows you to customize application of this* framework to your organization and to support what you decide are the key drivers for success (the Main Things). In these successful businesses, everything begins with identifying and then defining *Key Areas of Results (or Outcomes)* that will make a significant difference to your customers and to your organization. Knowing the essentials about how both your customers and your organization define success must **drive** the actions that move you toward performance excellence.

Framework for a Great Vacation

To ease into this review of Baldrige, I'll begin with an illustration of how it can be applied to a real life situation. I'll apply the "basics" to something **really** important; that is, *planning and taking your family on the best vacation ever—to Disney World*. We've all had, or at least heard of, some horrible vacation experiences. Where did the planning go wrong? Vacations with your spouse and three children can be a glorious, memorable experience or it can be a total disaster. You think you plan well for vacations, but how might your planning be enhanced by incorporating the Malcolm Baldrige Framework?

Before heading out the door to Disney, you need to lead your entire family in developing *a common understanding of "what is a quality vacation to Disney."* What *are specific outcomes* you're seeking? Identifying and defining exactly what it is you're striving to experience *before* you start the planning allows you to keep the Main Things on your vacation the main thing. How does your family define a successful vacation? I'm not asking for an activities listing or your To Do List. In order to prove you've just had the best vacation ever, you must first know how "great and quality" are defined by you and your family. The next steps will then fall into place.

Everything must be driven toward achieving those measures of success *you* and the key stakeholders (family members) have identified. *Do not let the actions or events define your success.* **You** *define success and drive every decision and action toward those success measures. Make every effort to* **create** *that success.*

The following is an illustration of how the Malcolm Baldrige Framework might be applied in planning and implementing your family trip to Disney World:

Framework for Planning—Start with the Desired Results.

Hold a family meeting to learn how each member would define this vacation to Disney World as being "wildly successful." This is "true north" for the family. Reach a common understanding and agreement as to the top five to ten indicators of success for this vacation. These are called your *Key Result Areas*. Next, under each of these five to ten Key Result Areas, identify a series of specific measures that, if met, would *prove* that each Result Area had been accomplished. *Please note that this is **not** the traditional goal setting process or "to do" list.* Rather, it's a listing of measures that, if met, assure you that you've had a great vacation. You may come up with a listing something like the following to measure a quality/successful family vacation:

- Vacation starts and ends on schedule; low stress during the vacation.

    Work schedule and school schedule allowed freedom from stress.

    No cell phone interruptions from work during the trip.

    Homework assignments completed while traveling without hassle.

    No hassles the morning you leave—on time.

    Returned home on schedule with time to unpack before returning to work.

- Travel and Returned Safely—no accidents or illness.
- Packed for All Needs—beach, rain, cold, heat, suntan lotion, sunglasses, etc.
- Excellence in Lodging and Route Arrangements—all reservations secured.
- Fully enjoyed the Disney World experience—four full days worth.
- Stayed within planned Family Budget—with loose change to spare.
- Upon return, each family member rates the JOY-LEVEL from the trip at 8 or higher (on a scale of 1 to 10). This will help identify opportunities for improvement for next year's vacation.

Step #1—*Leadership*. (Provide direction and expectations, and set the tone.)

What will you as a family leader do to make this vacation wildly successful—before, during, and after the trip? You want to instill the right tone for full enjoyment and yet have all members act with responsibility (based on age) in carrying out their duties. You keep the family focused within a no stress atmosphere. You encourage and support each family member to follow through on responsibilities accepted and keep in close communication with each member. Your leadership is driven making sure all family members plan, pack, and act in ways to achieve all Key Results measures they identified.

Step #2—*Strategic Plan*. *(Make it a coordinated effort, according to plan.)*

Who needs to do what and when? This planning step creates the more traditional "To Do List" of goals, objectives, and actions. You want to avoid trivial time wasters and energy stresses. This To Do List should include what you (as a leader) must do to support each member. All actions (Doing) are driven toward achieving those Key Result measures identified earlier.

Step #3—Customer Focus. (*Who is going to determine if this trip was a success or failure?*) You already know how the family (customer) defines success. Now, focus on how satisfied (happy) each family member is each day during the trip, and make adjustments based on any dissatisfaction feedback you receive. Are the critical "needs and wants" for *each* family member fully understood, communicated, and monitored? For example, do you need to modify your third day at Disney because the children are having a short attention span while waiting in line for some of the attractions? Your staying close to any changes in individual needs should result in modified decisions and actions that still lead you to achieving the Key Result measures.

Step #4—Information and Measurement. (*Monitor progress through feedback and gaining knowledge.*) Devote yourself to obtaining ongoing feedback on how each family member is doing leading up to and throughout the trip. How is the budget holding up? Do you have to change the hotel reservations or dining reservations for any reason? Are the children too tired to enjoy the evening fireworks? Don't become overburdened with meaningless information. All information and feedback should be driven toward measuring achievement of the established Key Result Areas.

Step #5—Staff Focus. (*Support every family member in making this trip a success based on what they do individually and collectively.*) Do you need to remind the children of the agreed upon responsibilities they were to carry out? Are you giving the children enough information to make good choices during the trip, such as how much money they have left to spend from their travel cash? You're providing family members with the support, guidance, and resources they need so "the family" can succeed in achieving the Key Result Areas.

Step #6—Process Focus. (*The Step-by-Step process of traveling and vacationing.*) The vacation activities are being carried out. Invariably, one or more of the family members will forget the Plan, get whiney, or have a lapse of good judgment. Keep a copy of your vacation plan handy or maybe you've prepared an individual listing of duties for each family member to carry with them. In case of an emergency or change in plans, does each family member understand the need for the change and know what their new role is? The daily decisions should be targeted on achieving the Key Result Areas.

Step #7—Evaluation and Feedback on Key Result Areas. *(Assessment Time; did the family actually achieve the desired vacation results of having "the greatest family vacation ever?" If so, you should be able to prove it!)* Okay, you're back home. Was it a quality vacation based on your own family measures for each Key Result Area? Upon returning home, have another family gathering to obtain immediate feedback. *How did the family prove it met (or did not meet) each of the specific measures identified before the trip and to what extent did the family feel it met each Key Result Area?* Did you have the greatest vacation ever, and if not why not? To what extent did the:

- Vacation start and end on time?
- Family travel and return home safely?
- Packing meet all needs?
- Lodging and route arrangements meet your needs?
- Family fully enjoy the Disney World experience?
- Family stay within the planned family budget?
- JOY-Rating document at 8 or higher on the scale of 1 to 10?
- Family measure the right things? In what ways could you have improved the planning and vacation experience?

Well, was it a quality vacation—yes or no? Now you can answer that question based on your family's *documented results* rather than from an emotional response because someone is tired or the children are fighting during the meeting. Second question: How could you have improved this planning and vacationing experience so you can move closer to your ultimate objective of having a "quality" vacation next year? You now have specific feedback to make improvements in your planning and vacationing next time.

What Are the Main Things?

Clearly, this was a lengthy illustration of the Malcolm Baldrige Framework, but you now have a basic understanding of how this framework flows. *It begins and ends with defining what "IT" is, with the main thing being to keep the Main Things the main things, and to measure progress in achieving these Main Things (the Key Result Areas) as you move forward.*

Organizations as well as individuals often lose their focus; they jump the priority track. It's normal to simply try to survive the daily grind by reacting to urgent issues coming at you every day. What gets lost are the important actions—the Main Things. That's why it's difficult to function under these pressures within the context of a clearly defined vision and plan.

The Malcolm Baldrige Framework provides an interrelated system or framework that *Drives* you toward success—as *you* define success. Your role as a leader is to add long-term value to the team, to the organization, and ultimately to your customers. The workplace isn't a trip to Disney World, is it! But the process, of making both trips, has many common elements, and you can learn from both.

Baldrige Application for Your Organization

This framework for change and leadership does not *begin* with leadership or process improvement or a budget or even planning. As in the Disney illustration, the framework begins with sitting down to define what the Main Things are and determining the measures to monitor progress toward these Main Things. *It requires a paradigm shift to effective listening* to your customers and key stakeholders and then acting directly on this input. *You **must** understand how they define success.*

What are the select Key Result Areas that, if accomplished, properly define success and serve to chart your pathway toward change, continuous improvement, and key results? For many businesses, perhaps yours, a set of nine Key Result Areas might include the following points:

How Do You Define Success for a Quality Organization?
(Key Result Areas)

- **Customer Goal Attainment.** Did your key customers (target markets) achieve the utility value they desired after acquiring your products and services?

- **Customer Satisfaction.** What level of satisfaction did your customers experience over time and what were their level (and areas) of dissatisfaction with your organization?

- **Customer Focus.** What percent of the respective target markets is your organization now serving and how effective is your marketing program?

- **Fiscal and Financial Performance.** What are the key indicators of budgetary, legal, and financial performance required for organizational success, including cost-benefit measures?

- **Staff Results.** What are the indicators of staff satisfaction and dissatisfaction, staff development, and retention? Is staff adequately trained to perform the assigned duties?

- **Partner Results.** What are the indicators of success for your key partners, their level of satisfaction and dissatisfaction with the partnership, and your work system performance?

- **Processes.** What are the performance excellence indicators for key processes that "drive" quality products and services to customers? Are support processes (accounting, legal, etc) effectively supporting these direct service processes?

- **Organizational Performance.** To what extent have organizational goals been attained?

- **Organizational Effectiveness.** To what extent has the organization gained operational efficiencies through changes in technology, process improvement, and staffing?

If each of the nine Key Result Areas above were adequately defined and actually improved upon annually, would it serve to elevate the level of performance for your organization? *You* define success in ways that will make a significant difference to you and your key customers. If properly defined and accomplished, these will move your organization forward. You no longer have to be directionally challenged; just lead effectively and with excellence.

Next Step: Once your organization has said "**This** is how we will define our success," you must then *determine how you will **measure** success for **each** of the Key Result Areas you've identified.* How will you *know* (or measure) that you're making progress toward each of the Key Result Areas? It's essential that you establish meaningful benchmark measures for each.

EXERCISE #32: You've just reviewed some examples of the Key Result Areas that illustrate performance excellence in high performance organizations.

- Based on the listing of nine Key Result Areas (above), write down which area or areas you would probably *not* have identified as being critical on your own?

- Write down the Key Result Areas that you believe are being monitored by and are actually driving *your* organization.

- Next, write down what you believe are the measures of success that are driving *your* team or department.

Keep your

focus.

- In your opinion, are these measures you've identified for your organization and for your team appropriate and complete? Why or why not?

Remember this: *What gets measured gets done. Your organization (or department) will become what it chooses to measure and reward.* The Key Result Areas, the Main Things, must be measured and must be priorities for action. Do not get off your path to success by hyper-focusing on actions or events or even strategic plans that do not make a significant difference in the long run. Keep your focus—keep everyone heading true north. The Baldrige Framework will provide you with a roadmap to keep you focused on what really matters to keep you moving forward.

An Overview of Baldrige
(Building A Continuous Improvement Roadmap and Scorecard)

The Malcolm Baldrige Framework is an incredible Leadership Tool for you to understand. It's not a study on *how* the best-of-the-best do things to achieve performance excellence. Instead, it is a resource for you to understand **what** *things they do—with excellence.* It forms a picture of how one change affects other key parts of the organization. This is a highly integrated model. This study in performance excellence is needed to help you *align the entire organization (leadership, information, staff, processes, results) to function with excellence in achieving the Main Things.* The framework or model is customized to meet your needs and structure.

None of us want to be an "average" organization, but we all need a framework that will help leadership move forward. How do the best-of-the-best organizations do it?

By working through the related Exercises in this section, you will learn more about your own organization within the Baldrige context. Hang in there; I'm honestly not trying to make experts out of you, but this overview will help you understand the basics of Baldrige. Look for the learning opportunities as found in this Performance Excellence Framework and these Exercises.

What follows is an introduction to the four components of the Malcolm Baldrige System for Performance Excellence:

- Organizational Profile
- Seven Baldrige Categories
- Criteria for each of the Seven Categories

- Core Values

The ORGANIZATIONAL PROFILE—the Essentials from 20,000 Feet

This Organizational Profile gives you that leadership view from 20,000 feet. It consists of a series of logical questions *every* organization should normally be asking itself. Unfortunately, most organizations do not. If you and every member of your team do not know the correct answers to these questions about your organization, you're lacking basic knowledge about how your organization functions. By asking these questions, you're beginning to inform and align staff around some of the Main Things.

EXERCISE #33: Write your responses to the following statements as found in an Organizational Profile and ask five others in your organization to independently respond, as well. Then, compare your answers. Were all of you in agreement?

- List the key customers or target customer groups your organization is serving. Which of your products and services does each customer group value the most?

- Write down the Main Things the customers "expect" in terms of product quality and service from you.

- Why are these customers still with you and not your competition's customers?

- Identify the five Major Challenges facing your organization—be specific. How widely are these five Major Challenges understood and addressed?

What if **everyone** in your organization had a common and clear understanding of each of these four questions asked in Exercise #33? For example, *what if everyone in your organization understood and was actively working to find solutions to the five major challenges you identified above?* If these five major challenges were addressed directly by the **entire** organization, chances are they would be resolved within a reasonable time period. Otherwise, they just remain challenges. If most staff are not even aware of or in agreement on these five challenges, guess where the terms "lack of alignment" or "change resisters" or "directionally challenged" originate? This isn't rocket science, but the process of asking these basic questions point out that there is much confusion and wasted energy within most organizations. Does this give you some ideas as to future leadership activities for you? Begin with everyone "understanding" key issues and customer expectations from 20,000 feet.

The SEVEN BALDRIGE CATEGORIES

The Seven Baldrige Categories were illustrated in the Disney World trip and form the structure of this interrelated framework. These Categories are highly interdependent and flow naturally from one Category to another. Together, these seven Categories form the Framework to move "willing organizations" to achieve significant performance improvement—leading the organizations toward performance excellence.

The seven Categories for performance excellence are shown on the following chart:

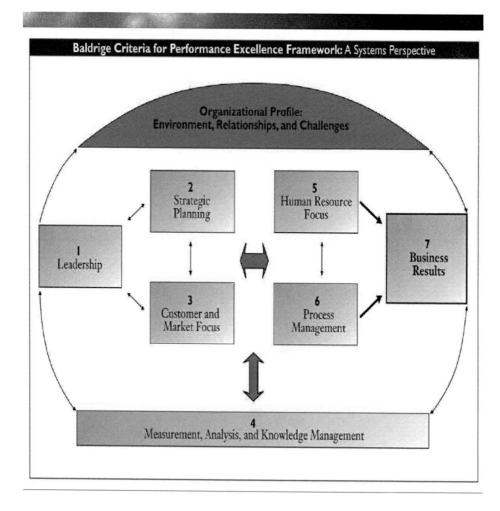

It's important to note the sequencing and interdependence among these seven Categories. While Strategic Planning is important, it cannot be done effectively without proper Leadership, and Leadership cannot be done effectively unless it knows the answers to the Organizational Profile Questions included in Exercise #33. There is much the organization can learn by viewing a framework from 20,000 feet.

The BALDRIGE CRITERIA—FOR EACH OF THE SEVEN CATEGORIES

Underlying *each* of these seven Categories (above) are a series of specific questions, or Criteria that the Baldrige process asks you to answer. There are no right or wrong answers; you're merely benchmarking against actions that high performance organizations do consistently and with excellence. By answering the more than 150 questions (Criteria) in the Baldrige process, you and your organization will learn a great deal as to your areas of strength and your opportunities for organizational improvement.

The Criteria questions do not tell you what changes senior leadership must make in your organization. You are, however, better positioned to make decisions as to areas of operation and processes you can seek to improve. You retain "choice" in making decisions to improve, but you can now do so from a new and valuable base of knowledge.

A Quick Assessment of Your Organization—Using Criteria Questions

The results of applying the Baldrige Framework to your organization are threefold:

- To provide you with self-discovery concerning your operational strengths and opportunities for improvement.

- You're given new leadership improvement opportunities that can have a significant impact on moving your organization to the next level of performance.

- You've been given a performance baseline from which you can measure your progress as you make priority improvements over time. It provides you with a *Roadmap* and a *Scorecard* for your decision-making.

EXERCISE #34: By conducting this example of a Baldrige assessment of your organization, you're benchmarking your operations against the "best" organizations, learning your major strengths and improvement opportunities, and preparing yourself to offer leadership in areas that will make a significant, long-term difference for your organization.

This is a lengthy exercise and will require you to provide "your best understanding" as you answer the listing of Criteria questions below.

- Objectively rate the extent to which your organization is doing *each* of the 30 questions that follow. Write down the numbers 1 through 30 and rate each Criteria question based on the degree to which you believe your organization functions or meets each question on a scale of 1 to 10 (with a 1 meaning "never heard of it.").

- After you've rated yourself on the 30 Criteria questions, identify five of your organization's greatest *Strengths*.

- Next, identify five of your organization's greatest *Opportunities for Improvement* based on these Criteria questions.

SAMPLE BALDRIGE-BASED ASSESSMENT for YOUR ORGANIZATION

(1-10 Rating, 5 Strengths, 5 Opportunities For Improvement)

Category 1—*Leadership*

- Do senior leaders drive the core values, mission, and vision deep into your organization?

- Are specific performance expectations for your organization set by senior leaders and effectively communicated to all employees?

- Do senior leaders establish and communicate an accurate set of Key Result Areas throughout the organization?

- Do senior leaders stay close to customers, staff, partners, and stakeholders?

- Are concerns of the local community monitored and addressed?

Category 2—*Strategic Planning*

- How well are your Strategic Plans developed and deployed throughout the organization?

- Are your customers, partners, staff, and stakeholders involved in the planning?

- How well are strategies translated into action plans and aligned with Key Result Areas for each strategic action?

- Are the five major challenges identified in the Organizational Profile being addressed in your Strategic Plan?

Category 3—*Customer Focus*

- Are the unique, value-added requirements of each major customer, stakeholder, and partner widely understood by staff?

- Does your organization determine and measure customer satisfaction and dissatisfaction, by customer segment?

- Are "standards" for customer service and customer contact processes in place, being followed, and measured?

- Does staff have a deep understanding of the marketplace and your competition?

Category 4—*Information and Measurement*

- Has the organization identified which data is most important for measuring movement toward established Key Results Areas and identified the data essential for improved daily decision-making? Is this data valid, complete, and current?

- Are management-by-fact reviews conducted on a regular basis?

- Is software and hardware kept current?

- Is feedback from internal customers used for improvement?

Category 5—*Staff Focus*

- Has your organization fostered an agility for change, do staff share information and decisions across organizational units, and do staff feel empowered to make changes?

- Are the work processes performed by staff aligned with established Action Plans and do these plans drive the organization toward the Key Result Areas?

- Do you have an effective Employee Performance Evaluation and recognition system?

- Do you determine what staff training to offer and the effectiveness of this staff activity?

- Do you have wellness plans, staff retention plans, and staff succession plans?

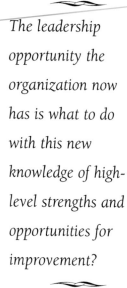

The leadership opportunity the organization now has is what to do with this new knowledge of high-level strengths and opportunities for improvement?

Category 6—*Efficient Processes*

- Are the products and services of your organization designed to meet specific customer requirements? Do you **know** the true value customers receive from your products and services?

- Do you ensure that ongoing products and services are actually meeting their original design requirements?

- Are procedures of production support services (engineering, sales, etc) actually designed, implemented, managed and improved based on production needs?

- Are procedures of business services departments (Human Resources, Accounting, Legal, etc.) meeting the needs of front line staff/operations as they meet customer needs?

Category 7—Key Results

- Do you have Key Result Areas identified that, if performed at the "excellent level," will make a significant difference for your organization?

- Do you have measures for each Key Result Areas that, if met, will make a significant difference to your organization?

- Do you monitor and compare your status with your competition?

- Do you monitor and benchmark your status against the best-of-the-best?

Okay, you've completed this quick assessment of your organization using the Baldrige Criteria. How did you compare with the best? For most organizations undergoing a formal assessment, if they score an average rating of 4 on a 1 to 10 scale they're doing very well. The leadership opportunity the organization now has is what to do with this new knowledge of high-level strengths and opportunities for improvement? If you were in charge, how would this knowledge enter into your strategic planning efforts? The goal should be to plan and then implement actions that would increase your ratings for each of thesa areas over time. You now have a *Scorecard* and a *Roadmap* to assist you in your leadership journey.

The BALDRIGE CORE VALUES

The best-of-the-best organizations have all established and actually "live" a common set of result-oriented Core Values. These Core Values are embedded deep within the culture of these organizations as they are moving forward, exercising effective leadership, empowering others to seek improvement, and introducing needed change. Effectiveness is not a slogan in these organizations—it is a way of life and is alive in all employees and in all actions. I went into greater detail on the Malcolm Baldrige 11 Core Values in Chapter 5. Please refer back to that section to review the 11 Core Values identified and the significant role each plays in organizational effectiveness. Do not take these Core Values lightly—they are the essential *Be* before you *Do* in leadership.

EXERCISE #35: If I were to be standing around the Break Room in your organization, what would I hear staff saying that might describe your organization's Core Values? Be honest now.

- Write down the Core Values you think your staff would be identifying during these water cooler discussions.

- Compare this staff listing with your organization's formal Core Values (if they exist formally). How similar are these two listings?

- Compare this listing of what you think staff would be saying with the 11 Core Values listed in Chapter 5. How similar are these two listings?

Would your staff make statements such as "I don't know where we're going anymore," or "I don't feel valued," or "I have a lot of data but no information?" On the other hand, the staff comments may reflect feeling valued, a strong sense of the organization's vision, and so on. Leadership must take a close look at the culture signals it's sending. Core Values are not the fluffy stuff around the edges of real work. They reflect symptoms of your organization's wellness and future.

Outcomes of a Baldrige Assessment (So What?)

I'm sure you asked yourself this question earlier as you began reading this Chapter: "Why should I spend time learning more about this framework?" "What will this basic understanding of Baldrige do for me as a manager and a leader?" To help you answer those and other questions now, I ask that you review your answers for Exercises #33, 34, and 35. You have completed a quick assessment of *your* organization. The question now is, what are *you* going to do with this information that *you* generated?

Let me outline some of the outcomes I see coming from a better understanding of this framework that *will* add to your leadership potential and provide needed direction for your organization. This understanding will help you in:

- Setting focused *priorities for improvement and change,* with proper alignment of staff efforts and resources.

- Providing direction for allocating *scarce resources.*

- Looking *beyond compliance* requirements towards results that make a significant difference.

- *Measuring the right things to evaluate* the effect of change initiatives and to quantify progress being made.

- Creating an environment that fosters and encourages *planned change— together.*

- *Aligning your fiscal and staff resources* toward delivering improved "value" to customers.

- *Improving your effectiveness,* productivity, and capacity.

The assessment process is a tool, which enables individuals and teams to gain a common understanding of their strengths and opportunities for improvement over time. It therefore serves as a framework and a mindset that addresses the logical and the emotional barriers that often keep an organization from growing.

In summary, what this assessment process does is to give you guidance and support in *aligning your organization's thinking and actions based on a proven performance excellence model. The ultimate goal is to help you achieve what's most important for your success—the Key Result Areas. Each of us learned long ago that improvement is not gained simply by working harder—it's by working smarter, in alignment with others, toward common outcomes.*

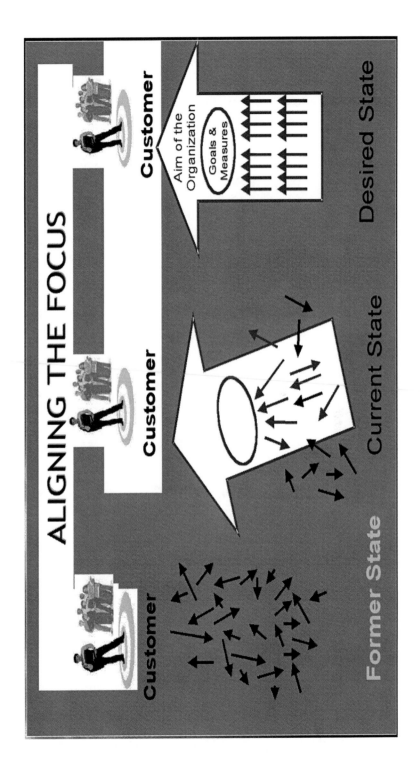

What Do the Worst-of-the-Worst Businesses Do?

In Exercise #34, you completed a self-assessment of your organization to determine what it's doing right in terms of the Baldrige Framework. In doing so, you learned more about the strengths and opportunities for improvement to better focus your leadership efforts. You benchmarked against how the best-of-the-best run their businesses. However, I want to supplement your earlier assessment with another one. Sometimes it's fun to be "master of the obvious" and in this case, *how would you benchmark your organization against the worst-of-the-worst businesses.* I hope you do "poorly" on this Exercise.

EXERCISE # 36: See the third document in the Appendix Section entitled

"Obstacles to Implementing the Baldrige Criteria." What if you wanted to do everything wrong, according to the Baldrige Framework; what all could you do wrong? Is your organization doing many of the wrong things?

- Make a copy of this three-page Document in the Appendix Section.

- Answer each question "yes" or "no" in the margin. In this exercise, a "yes answer" is bad!

- Identify and write on a separate page *five* questions you have answered *yes*, and examine "why" in further detail. For each of these five, write down what you believe to be the root of these "problem areas" and what could be done by the organization to resolve these matters?

A Framework That Makes a Difference in Leadership

Most organizations tend to plan and act in a piecemeal fashion, with one department sometimes implementing their own change priorities in a manner that then makes life for other departments more difficult. The term for this independent action is "sub-optimization." In essence, it means I do my thing and if it creates problems for you, that's not really my problem. This attitude and practice creates a serious problem with organizational "alignment" and results in a great loss of time, energy, and resources—and keeps the organization from moving forward. Highly effective organizations know how to align their resources, time, and energy. They're able to effectively engage staff when making critical improvements because they've developed a common understanding, commitment, and alignment regarding the Main Things. It's about defining success and working the system to achieve that level of success. It's about leadership as guided by a proven framework.

Directionally challenged staff is a reflection of directionally challenged leadership. **Heading true north together is not the better way to grow your business—it's the ONLY way.** For you as a Leader, you now have another significant tool for your Leadership Toolbox, and it takes the form of a framework to move toward performance excellence. I invite you to learn more about the Baldrige System and practice it.

Understand the role effective Strategic Planning plays plus the benefits of having context for this planning as found in Baldrige. I've stressed the importance of management and leadership being "together forever." I'm now suggesting that Strategic Planning and a performance excellence model are ALSO "together forever." You have an organization to lead, or at least you have a role to play in this process. Be that knowledgeable and skilled voice that will advocate for what you've learned in the last two Chapters. Lead from 20,000 feet—with excellence.

If your actions inspire others to dream more, learn more,
do more, and become more, you are a leader."

—JOHN QUINCY ADAMS

⌒

"Tentative efforts lead to tentative outcomes. Therefore, give yourself
fully to your endeavors. Decide to construct your character through
excellent actions and determine to pay the price for a worthy goal.
The trials you encounter will introduce you to your strengths.
Remain steadfast…and one day you will build something
that endures; something worthy of your potential."

—EPICTETUS, ROMAN TEACHER AND PHILOSOPHER, 55-135 A.D.

⌒

"Good leaders develop through a never-ending process of
self-study, education, training, and experience."

—MANUAL ON MILITARY LEADERSHIP

⌒

"Leadership has a harder job to do than just choose sides.
It must bring sides together."

—JESSE JACKSON

CHAPTER 12

LEADERSHIP— IT'S ALL ABOUT YOU; IT'S ALL FOR OTHERS

Leader or Not, Here I Come was written to enlighten and encourage you with the perspectives, experiences, and tools I've learned throughout my career in management and leadership. I've tried to steer clear from writing a leadership cookbook with highly structured recipes for success or a compilation of research on leadership theories. If anything, I wanted to challenge your old paradigms about management and leadership and provide you with simple but applicable Leadership Tools. My goal was to increase your capacity to grow into and through your leadership experiences, encouraging you to learn these lessons from two steps behind as you prepare to lead from two steps ahead.

In addition, the politics of leadership require that you learn a new little dance called the *Mid-Manager's Two-Step*. As you know by now, this two-step dance begins by taking your first steps into leadership, then taking one more step at a time while making periodic side steps to avoid the verbal and process stones thrown at you by your peers and naysayer's. Occasionally you'll be required to take a step backward to regroup or perform a series of vertical hops before you can once again move two steps forward. Repeat this dance as required until success is realized. Over time, your growth from these real-time experiences will expand your capacity to be an effective leader.

To place in context where you probably are in your leadership journey, I'll once again present my "non-scientific" formula for your growth in leadership as introduced in Chapter 1. By now you should be better prepared to enter that next phase of growth with new leadership skills and perspectives and with a higher level of confidence. Your journey has already begun and is about to hit second gear.

- 25% of your growth begins with a *basic awareness and knowledge of applied Leadership Tools* that will **prepare** you to move into and through the challenges of leadership (It's what **this book** has done—it's your *starting point*).

Experience the self-satisfaction of being a "leader who makes a difference."

- 50% of your growth is through those *teachable moments and powerful learning experiences* over time—growing in your leadership skills and expanding the opportunities for leadership on your job (It's what you must continue doing every day in the workplace—it's **your learning curve and your learning place**).

- 25% will be through *advanced thinking, learning, and seeing the bigger picture*, carrying you to higher levels of effective leadership. You will grow in competence, character, creativity, consideration, courage, and career. Over time, you will become wiser in seeing and capturing opportunities to lead—applying the right tools to the right circumstances (It's your search for *new knowledge, paradigms, and experiences* that will be a forever thing).

This "opportunity" to grow into and through leadership is actually *an opportunity disguised as hard work*. You will be challenged in new ways, required to assume even more responsibilities, and be pushed into risk-taking outside your comfort zone. If you find yourself waking up at four A.M. with work issues on your mind, there may be nights when it's best to simply get up and spend some good "think time" (not worry time) on these issues. As opportunities for leadership are introduced, either engage these opportunities fully or else get out their way. Much like my Leadership Rubik's Cube, you're either successful or you're unsuccessful in getting the job done. There is little room for getting leadership "half right." Effective leadership is hard work but it has countless hidden benefits, as well. Be prepared to go through that 50% stage of leadership growth on-the-job. Along the way, you too will experience success and you will experience the self-satisfaction of being a "leader who makes a difference."

Your Flight Into Leadership

We can learn about leadership from many different sources, including from Canadian geese as they fly south for the winter. The obvious lesson for leadership from geese is that once you begin flight you'd better have scheduled landings—dropping out of the sky in random fashion is not an option. You need to be committed for the long haul and keep your eyebrows up to "learn on the fly." In addition, the job isn't done once the geese arrive down south; they have to return north in just a few months. The role of leadership is never ending and the horizon is always new and changing.

I challenge you to look deeper into the 10 Basic Truths based on these Lessons From Geese:

Leadership "On The Fly"

I've come to understand that as each bird flaps its wings while in a "V" formation, it creates uplift for the bird immediately following. *By flying in a "V" formation, the whole flock adds at least 70% greater flying range than if each bird flew on its own.*

> **Basic Truth #1:** The flock must function as a true team—not independently. *Each member has a meaningful role* to play for the flock to be successful.

> **Basic Truth #2:** The team has a common understanding of *its purpose and direction*—focusing on and moving toward the Main Things.

> **Basic Truth #3:** Teams that share a common direction and sense of unity *function more efficiently and effectively* because they are traveling on the thrust of one another. It pays to be aligned.

When the lead goose gets tired, she/he rotates to the back and another goose flies point.

> **Basic Truth #4:** It pays to *take turns doing hard jobs*—with people or flying south. Cross training is a good thing and mutual support is essential.

> **Basic Truth #5:** *Empowerment* of others to get the job done is a key to success for all.

> **Basic Truth #6:** Understand your own limitations and *appreciate the strengths of others.*

The geese honk from behind to encourage those up front to keep their speed and endurance.

> **Basic Truth #7:** *Be careful what you say* when you honk from behind because you may soon be asked to take the lead (turnabout is fair play).

> **Basic Truth #8:** Be a *continuous learner* from co-workers in all situations—those in front, on your sides, and in the back. They see things you do not see from your vantage point.

The geese model leadership from 1,000 feet.

> **Basic Truth #9:** Leadership is all about seeing conditions and realities from a *higher, clearer vantage point,* and then getting the job done through and with others.

Basic Truth #10: Leadership isn't all about **you,** it's about you **and** all the others, sometimes *leading from two steps behind.*

Some believe leadership (and leaders) are for the birds. Others can't see the obvious leadership lessons you can learn everywhere—even from a flock of geese. When you boil it all down, leadership isn't really rocket science; it's natural if done properly. True leaders make it look easy. As for young geese getting ready to make the flight south, I'll bet one of the parents will say or honk: *"Leader Or Not, Here You Go!"*

Leader or Not, Here I Come—In Review

In Chapter 1, I listed eight important lessons and perspectives I believe create the "context" to guide your leadership journey—and your life's journey. It's part of the mindset that will keep you focused and healthy.

- View your daily challenges/trials from a higher vantage point. Remember your objective is to drain the swamp; don't let those alligators get to you.

- See that having choices is a good thing; then be fully aware of choices before you daily.

- Have more fun along the way than what you originally thought appropriate. Smile, people will wonder what you're up to. If you wear your intensity or frustrations on your shirtsleeve, you're an easy target for manipulation.

- Base your decisions or changes by driving toward something bigger. Make opportunity your driver, not fear. Benchmark against your passions, not the status quo.

- Go beyond making decisions based solely on what's logical—trust your instincts more.

- Understand the importance of leaving a leadership legacy *through* others.

- Focus on your journey, not just the destination.

- Receive that feeling of success and personal value from seeing *others* succeed.

Keep your eyebrows up looking for leadership opportunities and get to those higher vantage points to view the true needs, your role, and direction for the organization. Do you see that these eight (life) lessons are practical and important for you leadership journey? Every one of them help guide your thinking, attitude, and line of sight. They provide needed "context" for your leadership journey.

RECAP BY CHAPTER:

Chapter 1—Your Starting Point

Be prepared to change your paradigms about leadership and the roles you'll play. Remember, leadership is all about what value your efforts add in allowing *others* to succeed.

- Your learning curve is a forever thing. The key is learning; not just knowing.

- You don't define leadership success—*others* do.

- Your success is dependent on identifying the right opportunities, retaining your focus on the Main Things, doing the right things for the right reasons—for others.

- Leadership from two steps behind isn't a positioning statement for leadership activities; rather, it's a positioning of your heart attitude, your ego, and how you measure success.

- Whatever business you're in, your role in leadership will always be in the people improvement business and that results in organizational improvement.

- Reference the numerical listing of Leadership Tools found throughout the book.

Chapter 2—Are You Ready for The Journey?

This can be a dog-eat-dog world and I do not want you wearing Milk Bone underwear. You are not a victim and you are not the problem. You can and must be part of the solution. This book is written for **mid-managers** to develop buns of steal and to strengthen their commitment and attitude for the leadership journey. Leadership is an art to be learned and applied, not a point of knowledge.

- As a Mid-Manager, you're part of the Cheese Sandwich Crowd.

- Your attitude during this leadership journey is the critical predictor of success.

- Too many organizations are over managed and under led.

- The primary role of leaders is to identify and advance opportunities for needed change.

- For change to occur effectively, it's essential that you *first* have an accurate and complete understanding of where you are *today*.

- The result of effective leadership is change in what individuals and teams *think* (paradigms). The result of effective management is change in what individuals and teams *Do*.

- If there are major problems with inefficient processes or poor leadership, you will have a chaotic workplace culture.

- Be willing to get outside your own comfort zone.

- Be fully aware of the complexities of your organization and the risks tied to moving your thinking and actions outside the box. Use this knowledge to reduce your fear factor.

- Without risk there can be little opportunity; without opportunity there can be *no* leadership.

- With any failure comes wisdom and with wisdom rests hope and with hope you will find opportunity.

Chapter 3—Management and Leadership—Together Forever

The main thing is to keep the Main Things the main thing. Do you know the Main Things for your team and organization—are they in agreement with the thinking of your co-workers? Leadership and management are different, complimentary, and changing constantly. Look for higher vantage points from which to test your leadership wings and become a direction setter, striving to align the people, paradigms, plans, and processes. Review what you drafted in the Personal Leadership Statement exercise—and be prepared to update it soon.

- The big difference between organizations can almost always be traced back to different calibers of leadership.

- Your staff *Is* the organization's competitive advantage and represents *you* on the front line when push comes to shove. Support them as they move forward; do not abuse them.

- Leadership is not about conformance and compliance; it's about strategic change.

- If organizations don't have clear and common understanding of what the Main Things and measures of success really are, is there any wonder why we often find our hard work and decision-making in conflict with others?

- The leadership function is difficult to describe, harder to learn, and more difficult to deliver than management because it relies more on influencing than directing.

- Leadership is a *role* not a position, but the call for true leadership is even greater the higher one goes in an organization.

- It's not just a matter of the manager and team working harder that will determine success. It's management within the right framework as guided and modified by effective leadership.

Chapter 4—The Leadership Rubik's Cube

The six-sided Leadership Rubik's Cube illustrates the interrelationship between six key aspects of leadership. It's essential that you first *Be* a leader having the right paradigm and personal integrity, then *Do* the actions of leadership by setting direction, creating a positive work culture, achieving desired results, and building capacity for the future. Effective leadership does not allow you to be half right—you must know and deliver all six-sides of leadership with excellence and with a passion.

- The *traditional role* of leadership calls for you to identify an idea for change, influence others to accept it, decide to act, and to then be involved in implementing the change from your management position.

- 80% of the key to being an effective leader is found in your "attitude" toward the organization's success, your team's success, and your personal success.

- How you see your leadership role (paradigm) and your integrity will ultimately form the basis for your actions.

- Leadership requires wisdom but not all wise people are effective leaders. The key lesson: *Be* before you *Do*.

- In addition to being a leader at the strategic level, you must also lead at the tactical level. You must be available, knowledgeable, diligent, and specific in working with the various stakeholders in the change and leadership process.

- It's best to lead from a "trust model" rather than from a position of "distrusting" others.

Chapter 5—The Key to the Cube

Your *attitude, character, competencies, focus,* and *will* are reflected in each of the six sides of the Leadership Cube. Understand and grow your skill levels in the 12 Leadership Competencies.

- Remember the qualities/attributes you learned as a child—they will carry your quest for leadership forward (attitude, character, competencies, focus, and will).

- *How* you exhibit and deliver leadership competencies is as important as *what* you deliver.

- If you applied for your job today, would you be re-hired and asked to lead others?

- Leadership requires you to function effectively with your peers and partners. In addition, it requires skills in learning to lead vertically, as well as, horizontally within the organization.

Chapter 6—The Changing Face Of Leadership

You must move off the "either/or" paradigm on issues and into the "and" paradigm. It's critical that you be a Traditional Leader *and* look for opportunities to move toward the Change Leadership Model. *Change Leadership* is a cultural and paradigm shift allowing and encouraging change to be initiated from any and all levels of the organization—not just at the management levels. Empower your staff to provide greater leadership. The three R's for leading are Relationships, Relevancy, and Responsiveness, with all three delivered from a strong base of Core Values. There are unique competencies and vantage points required to support a Change Leader Model.

- One important skill set to learn is that of multi-tasking by finding easier ways to complete the growing list of tasks.

- You must be open to viewing leadership as coming bottom-up, side-to-side, outside-in, as well as, from top-down. Your role will require effective facilitation and coaching skills.

- Change Leadership, if pursued, cannot simply be a strategic initiative that's mandated. It's a model and paradigm that can only be "caught" by staff. It needs a corporate mindset, infrastructure, and recognition system that serves to create and support new leaders.

- Leadership is the process of initiating change, taking the organization on a journey toward new destinations as a result of challenging the status quo—to achieve the Main Things.

- We all have a set of Core Values that drive our thinking and actions, but are they the right values and are they consistently exhibited in the workplace?

- Change Leadership isn't a state of being; it's a state of readiness followed by action.

Chapter 7—The Crisis of Change

The process of change includes the consideration of political capital, hidden costs, addressing the change challengers, and understanding the time/change continuum. The Three C's of business revolve around the Customer, Change, and the Competition. The people side of change will present serious challenges and will require you to be thoughtful in your decision-making and assessment of staff buy-in. Your attitude and passion for change is essential but staff requires an understanding of "what's in it for me (them)." Consider the Four Levels of Staff Involvement, the Four Levels of Staff Commitment to Change, the Matrix For Managing Complex Change, and the forces for failure and success in making change.

- The change issue is not the real challenge; it's the *process* of debating, deciding, and implementing change and the perceived *results* of the change.

- Organizations, as well as, individuals become what you choose to measure and reward.

- Change will happen For you, To you, or With you—but it Will happen.

- The positioning of your eyebrows bears a direct impact on your success in leadership; you need to have your eyebrows up, looking for meaningful change opportunities.

- We talk about leadership from two steps behind, but you'd better believe your competition is learning all about your strengths and weaknesses from two steps along side of you.

- There are three phases to the process of change: Unfreezing people from today, moving people to tomorrow, and refreezing them in the new future.

- Change often occurs only when the pain of keeping the status quo is greater than the pain of making the change.

- Do not try to prepare the organization for the people; prepare people for the organization.

- Don't underestimate the impact staff attitude toward you has in the change process.

- You will seldom motivate someone to *follow* you. They will be more likely to follow your ideas based on WIIFM—"what's in it for me."

Chapter 8—The 20 Workplace Success Nuggets

Seek further understanding of the 20 Workplace Success Nuggets presented and find opportunities to pilot these tools in the near future. The more tools you have and your ability to become skilled in using each will directly impact your success over time. You must take risks in learning to use these tools for on-the-job application of leadership. Over time, increase your "success rate" from using these new tools by increasing your level of good judgment, creative thinking, proper timing, and effective communication. While some tools may have funny sounding titles, they are all extremely useful. The "20 Nuggets" fall into the categories of:

- *Awareness,* including Watch The Eyebrows, Whether Vane Test, and Four Decisions

- *Improvement,* including Slight Edge, Nurf Ball Behavior, Five Whys, and Three-3's

- *Motivation,* including Two Questions, Two Great Motivators, and The Mirror Test

- *Relationships,* including Think Like a Customer, Time Tyranny, and Sponge-Bobbing People.

Chapter 9—Seek A Leader; Be A Leader

The three keys to building effective relationships with staff are Caring, Connecting, and Mentoring in both informal and formal ways. Who is your mentor? Are you committed to being a mentor for others in the future? The mentor relationship requires a major investment by the organization and for you personally, but there is a meaningful return on this investment.

- We are *all* in the people improvement business to achieve success for the organization.

- You must go beyond simply observing leadership in action; you must learn from it.

- Leadership is *for* others, accomplished *through* others, and your success is measured *by* others.

- Build your leadership legacy based on your character, personal style, and core values. We are all (and will always be) leaders in training.

- You need context in which to manage and lead.

- Effective leadership requires mental, emotional, and physical toughness.

- The quality of boldness can also create "blind spots" as to gaps or areas of weaknesses in your style, ego, paradigm, or knowledge base.

- You can be a risk taker, a caretaker, or an under taker—but you can't be just a "taker."

- Teachable leaders are ones who never act like they've arrived, know it all, or have heard it all before.

- As you raise up others for leadership through mentoring, you're building the organization's capacity for the future.

Chapter 10—Strategic Planning In Leadership

Effective strategic planning is a necessity if you wish to create higher-level thinking and strategic-level change for your organization. Organizations will not move forward through incremental change or plans that sit on the shelf. Study the Matrix For Effective Strategic Planning.

- Highly effective organizations base their decision-making and actions with staff having a common direction, focus, and framework. That is, staff have "context" and are aligned to achieve results in areas that truly matter and serve to move toward the Main Things.

- Remember, you don't define quality—your workforce determines quality for you by the products and services *they* deliver. Your customers will tell you if the quality level is high enough.

- Don't let actions of others or events define your success; you define success by your paradigm and framework for leadership.

- It all begins and ends with defining what "It" is. The main things are to keep the Main Things the main thing.

Chapter 11—Leadership From 20,000 Feet

The Malcolm Baldrige Framework is an excellent tool to guide you and the organization toward true performance excellence. In addition, you must understand the context and role effective strategic planning plays and how it interacts within this larger framework for success.

- The framework for change and leadership does not *begin* with leadership or strategic planning or tweaking your operational processes.

- See the nine Key Result Areas (measures) that will drive organizations toward success.

- What gets measured gets done.

- The Baldrige Framework facilitates your learning and improvement initiatives based on what the best-of-the-best organizations do consistently and with excellence. It's a matter of aligning the people, plans, processes, and paradigms of your organization.

- Striving to achieve performance excellence is not a program or an add-on to work. It's central to effective decision-making, achieving high customer satisfaction, and achieving desired organizational growth.

- Unless there is a sincere leadership commitment over the long-term to making the necessary changes, the whole exercise becomes "value-subtracting."

Paradigm of Peak Performance

I've offered more than **60 new tools for your Leadership Toolbox** along with the concepts of mentoring, strategic planning, and performance excellence in application of these tools. This base of knowledge, if applied on the job, can and will move you closer to the point of peak performance and towards doing the right things for all the right reasons.

I've also shared a number of personal and leadership paradigm shifts for you to consider, but I'm about to offer three additional shifts—this time at the organizational level. As with the others, you may choose to take them or leave them. However, I believe your organization could find these new paradigms critical to their success.

1. *Shift the organization from having a focus on management to having a **focus on leadership**.* I've already made the point that organizations need both, but the question is which will carry you forward into the future? Too many organizations are simply trying to "manage harder." At stake is not just your job, but survival of the entire organization. For survival, it is a *requirement* that organizations must:

   - Become customer-driven (not just customer-focused)—act on changes that are driven by meaningful and timely customer input.

   - Have a clear and common understanding of the Main Things, and make priority decisions based on this understanding.

   - Have clear measures of success that guide actions and changes.

   - Build leadership capacity and effective management.

2. *Move from applauding just star individuals by applauding and moving toward star teams, and on to star units, star partners, and ultimately a* **star organization.**

- It's not all about you or any one individual. It's not about your team succeeding while other teams lose. It's not your unit or product making a profit while others do not. It **Is** about seeing your team, your unit, your organization, and your strategic partners outside the organization winners, as well.

- Never hire an employee unless you are assured at the 100% level that he/she will improve the dynamics, creativity, and productivity of your team.

- Never make a change unless you have it coordinated with other departments or units—avoid sub-optimizing the work of others.

- Build stronger partners; as they succeed you will succeed.

3. *Shift the organization's recognition system from rewarding activity-based accomplishments to rewarding* **result-based accomplishments.**

- Change for the sake of change is wrong just as improvement for the sake of improvement is wrong. Always assess the "so what" factor. Is the organization moving toward the Main Things or not?

- Busy-bees will not ensure survival since the focus of work remains on being busy.

- What makes a significant difference in the Key Result Areas? Discover them, focus on them, and achieve them.

Doing the Leadership Two-Step

Throughout *Leader Or Not, Here I Come*, I've made references to you leading from two steps behind and the need for mid-managers to learn the two-step dance. These are both `critical concepts to remember. Leadership is not for the faint of heart (unwilling to take a risk), not for those who are overly-humble, and certainly not for those who lack initiative. Rather, I believe true leadership is learned, especially at first, from two steps behind. This requires the proper:

- Positioning of your leadership role fully behind your CEO and other senior "leaders."

- Positioning of your *heart attitude and your ego*—the need to claim success can get in the way of achieving it.

- Positioning of your *success measures*—leadership is *for* others, accomplished *through* others, and your success is measured *by* others.

Once you are properly "positioned" as to your leadership paradigm, you must learn the two-step to move at the pace of the organization—sometimes forward, other times sideways, and other times a step backward. While I will not recap the numerous references made to the two-step in this book, simply recognize that this dance has a tune that will vary based on circumstances and the individuals involved. It can be light and flowing or it can be fast, hard, and loud—varying from a waltz, to a polka, to hard rock. It's not a dance for everyone, but if you want to be a leader, learning the leadership two-step as played in your organization is an important skill to develop. Have the patience and wisdom to learn new steps in this dance and have endurance to move into and through your leadership responsibilities with excellence.

EXERCISE #37: Write your own version of the "two-step" dance that you must perform at the workplace. I'm asking you to:

- List the political barriers and games created by your superiors, your peers, and your team members as you attempt to move forward on change and leadership matters.

- Detail three examples of when, and how others throw obstacles in your way and what you have done to successfully "dance around" those obstacles.

Five Levels of Leadership

I chose not to include my concept of the Five Levels of Leadership in earlier Chapters because I wanted you to identify these on your own—which I hope you did. I'm sure some of you are still seeking a clear roadmap or a series of specific steps to focus on initially before going on to the next steps. I can't do that. What I can provide, however, are five levels of growth in leadership that *you* must learn, apply on-the-job, and work through as you gain true wisdom in leadership. *Without achieving excellence in all Five Levels over time, your leadership growth and effectiveness will level off.*

Here are the Five Levels of Leadership I believe we must all posses for effectiveness in our leadership journey. I believe you will sequence growth in the first four levels in order. Level Five as listed might occur at any time during your leadership journey.

Level 1. *Be before you Do.* You must first have the right paradigms and integrity to *Be* an effective and positive leader before you *Do* leadership activities—as described in Chapter 4. Change and improve from the inside out. Why should your team, peers, supervisor, and senior officials choose to follow you? After your paradigm and integrity are established, you can do the *Do* sides of leadership.

Level 2. *Be a leader with and for your Team.* In Chapter 3, I referenced the need for caring, connecting, and mentoring of your front line staff. Your staff will help you become a stronger leader if you let them. At the same time, you must lead them as you strive to achieve the Main Things for your organization. As the team succeeds through your leadership, team members and the organization will succeed, as well.

Level 3. *Be a leader for your Peers; with other mid-managers.* This will likely be the hardest level so far because of different personal agendas, the culture of independence and silos between departments, and the politics of competition between equals. How can you create a win-win agenda for change that will compel your peers to join with you in moving the organization forward? This will be your truest test of leading and learning the two-step dance.

Level 4. *Be a leader who's visible and has a significant impact on the organization.* As you succeed in each of the three previous levels, senior leaders will see your role in bringing about positive change with and through others. In time, you will be offered new opportunities to assume broader leadership responsibilities. You will experience increased senior leader support as you draw on your knowledge base, Leadership Tools, and team/peer support gained along the way.

Level 5. *Be a leader outside your organization.* Business realizes the importance of "leveraging your resources" to achieve the Main Things. Your leadership skills, the success of your organization, and the success of your business partners can all be aligned and leveraged to provide leadership to your community and other organizations. Today and every day, true leaders strive to make a significant difference in the lives of others, and that will not stop at the walls of your business. *Be* that effective change leader with your suppliers and partners *and* within communities, charities, and other organizations.

EXERCISE #38: Application of the Five Levels of Leadership. Begin by writing down the titles of the Five Levels.

- On a scale of 1 to 10, rate yourself on each of the five Levels of Leadership as to how effective you are currently delivering needed leadership.

- After these five ratings, write two or three actions you might take to improve your self-rating in each Level.

Just as with the Leadership Rubik's Cube, you cannot be a complete leader if you excel in only three of the five Levels—you must continuously strive to perform *all levels* with excellence.

Your Leadership Legacy
(And Your Personal Leadership Statement Will Be...)

Remember the draft Personal Leadership Statement you wrote back in Chapter 2 that included the 10 key elements/attributes/qualities of your leadership career? Its time for you to re-write your Statement, this time incorporating what you've learned through reading this book and the new experiences gained through the Exercises. I trust you've learned a range of new tools, qualities, and paradigms that will positively "influence" the next version of your Personal Leadership Statement.

EXERCISE #39: Your first draft of a Personal Leadership Statement was a form of pre-test, and now I'm asking you to re-write and update your first draft and have it serve as a post-test. Reflect on what you've learned in this book that may have caused you to re-think and expand your paradigms and approach to your leadership journey. Write a revised, more formal Personal Leadership Statement—one that you would want your family, friends, and peers to read publicly at your retirement. What kind of leader do you want to be recognized as being and what legacy do you want to leave for others?

Begin this Exercise by reviewing your Statement written previously in Chapter 2. That earlier Statement asked you to identify your "current" leadership qualities and attributes. This time, ask yourself, "what kind of leader do I want to be recognized as being in the future?" You can't simply say "I want to be an effective leader." Describe in some detail what you think you, as an effective leader, should look like—should Be and Do—should achieve—should leave in the form of a legacy.

Specifically, I'm challenging you to write two or three pages to best present *your* Personal Leadership Statement. This Statement should contain:

- The top 10 critical elements and attributes you believe best define your leadership at the point of your retirement (at the end of your formal leadership journey).

- Describe in some detail your desired career destination (as of today), where your leadership journey will carry you—your leadership Vision.

- Identify the five Main Things you would want "others" to say reflect the "legacy" you have left for individuals and the organizations you've served.

- Write down five of the best "words of advice" you would share with someone just considering their leadership journey. This advice may or may not have been found in this book.

Please don't get hung up on format, length, wording, or even your ego. Be open as you attempt to capture your heartfelt vision, your legacy, and what leadership skills/qualities you want to acquire and deliver to take you there. Date this paper and ask someone close to you to review it and give you feedback. Remember, this is **Your Personal Leadership Statement.** *Write it in a thoughtful manner and use it for decision-making, growth planning, and career planning. While leadership is a journey, just this once, I'm asking you to think about your leadership destination.* Through the process of writing your Personal Leadership Statement, you've documented the vision for your leadership journey.

If you agree that *both individuals and organizations become what they choose to measure and reward,* choose your measures of success carefully and **Become** what you're writing about. Your leadership plan, qualities, and rate of growth are yours and yours alone. Own it and continue learning and moving toward that leadership vision. What you want others to see *In* you must become a motivating and guiding factor in your daily actions and decisions. Become that leader you truly want others to see in you.

Tools for Your Leadership Toolbox

As stated previously, I've provided you with more than 60 Leadership Tools in this book, with 20 offered in one gulp in Chapter 8. If you've been diligent in completing the Exercises relating to these Tools, you've undoubtedly gained new perspectives on the relevance of individual Tools to your workplace situations and your personal style. In addition, you've benefited from your experiences in applying individual Tools with skill and confidence.

EXERCISE #40: In this Exercise, you're being asked to reflect on the 60 or more Leadership Tools presented in this book. Based on this review, write down answers to these questions:

- Identify 10 of the Leadership Tools that you believe will be most valuable for you in your leadership journey; the ones you are committed to applying in the next six months.

- Why did these 10 tools stand out in your mind as being most useful?

- What results do you hope to see after applying each of these tools?

It's not about you knowing about the tools, it's about using the Leadership Tools on-the-job and gaining skill and wisdom in the application of each. Add new tools to your Leadership Toolbox continuously, learn to use them with excellence, assess their usefulness, and make a decision to either take them out of your toolbox or keep them. Use it or lose it.

Your Leadership Journey

By now, you've begun your leadership journey regardless of the formal position you currently hold in your organization. To continue your growth, I offer the following action statements:

- Have a leadership plan with *defined Key Result Areas and measures of success* (as benchmarks) for each—a plan and a vision with a purpose. This should be already completed if you prepared your Personal Leadership Statement.

- During your journey, *embrace risk taken with wisdom;* Deploy leadership effectively, focus on your customers, place value on having agility in making change, and understand the people and policy sides of change. You're always in the people-to-people business.

- Adopt your *plans and strategies* for addressing significant improvement opportunities within high level strategies and a proven framework for change. Be customer-driven, not just customer focused.

- Be ready to *shift paradigms*...away from managing processes and compliance requirements based mainly on internal issues and the urgent matters...to leading results and customer-driven requirements based mainly on external measures. Both leadership and the quality of your organization are measured by your customers.

- Leave a *leadership legacy* that has made a difference—through others.

To achieve the action statements listed above, remember that 80% of your success is tied to "attitude" and your paradigm for effective leadership—the *Be* side of leadership. The remaining 20%, or *Do* side, reflects how and what you do every day on the job. Are you committed enough to *Do* the right things right?

Consider pursuing the following strategies to enhance the effectiveness of your leadership in the future:

- Build effective teams.
- Build strong internal and external partnerships.
- Value your staff and your peers, and reflect this in your actions and decision-making.
- Focus on the future.
- Have a base of solid information from which to make decisions.
- Value results that make a difference.
- Talk the right game, walk it and live it consistently and with excellence.

Move Toward Becoming a High Performance Organization

In a dysfunctional or even some average organizations, the level of leadership commitment held by senior officials is far below that found in high performance organizations. The employees and officials tend to under-value and under-support risk taking while over-emphasizing the power of position and compliance to procedures. Just as with your Exercise #1 in Chapter 2 where you were asked to identify great leaders and weak leaders, you know a high performance organization when you see one. Is your organization high performance? Are you a high performance leader for others? What are the handful of changes you need to focus on immediately that *will* improve your leadership effectiveness? You should be able to answer these questions easily.

Over the years, my ultimate goal was to become an effective leader in a high performance organization—including my own consulting firm. You know what? I never worked for what I would define as a highly effective organization, but I *always* remained committed to being the most effective leader I could be, wherever I worked. The lesson I learned is that it was up to *me*, not the organization, to become that effective leader. *It Is all about **you**, with you **choosing** to be a more proactive, caring, observant, skilled, risk-taking, and creative leader.* That's how I arrived at the title for this book—*Leader Or Not, Here I Come.* Even if the organization was not fully ready for me to enter leadership, I was—and I did.

Be Out-Front

It's not "business as usual" today nor will it ever be, for you or for your organization. Are you one who believes the only way you can be a leader is to be the one "out front", being highly visible? While there are times when that's the *only* way leadership can be delivered, it's not mandatory nor is it the way most of us began our leadership journey. However, do not be afraid to deliver leadership from two steps behind—beginning from where you are today. It may be your starting point, but you do (will) move two steps out front in time. Being out front will come after you've learned your beginning leadership lessons from two-steps behind.

I'm challenging you to take the high road and make that positive difference in your organization.

The best way for **you** to succeed is to make sure *others* succeed. *Your focus on others will thrust your career ahead far faster and farther than if you make your job "all about you."* People can spot a fake, someone who's self-centered, and one who blames others to achieve personal recognition. Frankly, I'm tired of that form of petty politics and false pride, and so are quality organizations. That's why *I'm challenging you to take the high road and make that positive difference in your organization.* Take the focus off yourself.

I encourage you to step out with renewed confidence and energy. Act out the title of this book—*Leader Or Not, Here I Come!* Have the courage to *Be* that leader, today and every day. Be out-front as you're being "invited" to be a leader through new opportunities. It's a risk but so is holding back until conditions are perfect and there is zero chance for failure. *Leadership comes to those who will take it and hang on to it for all it's worth—because it's worth everything to your team and to your organization.* It's scary stuff and it's not for wimps.

While it will be a bumpy journey at times, I do envy you for the road you're about to travel. It will be rewarding in so many ways. Know that you'll be making a positive difference in the lives of others and for your organization through your leadership. The silver lining is that as others and the organization succeed, you too will succeed. I've NEVER been blindsided or double-crossed by my team when using this success strategy, although I have had experiences where one or two of my peers played negative politics regarding my role in change initiatives. But you know what, I survived and still moved ahead in my career. You can do it too. Be up-front in your intentions and be out-front in your actions.

The Leadership 12-Step Program

I cannot give a customized plan or prioritization on "next steps for you." It will vary based on where you are in leadership, the leadership opportunities that come your way on the job, and your individual workplace setting. There is no one best approach to growing on the fly, but you must grow and push through the leadership challenges, one challenge at a time. Each of you will chart your own course and proceed at your own pace. The key is that you're moving forward, even if the pace today is very slow and deliberate. Remember, this is not a race—it's about the value you can add as a leader and the effectiveness with which you perform your leadership role.

My suggestion is that you focus on the following **12-Step Program** as you progress through your leadership journey.

1. Make sure you complete the *40 Exercises* found throughout this book and seek a deeper understanding as to how and why you answered the questions the way you did. Apply the thinking, knowledge, and answers from these Exercises in your workplace setting. What additional learning can you obtain tomorrow, and the next day, and so on? Continuous learning and application is the key, and wisdom in leadership is the home run you will achieve over time.

2. Take your *Personal Leadership Statement* seriously; let it represent *the* plan for your career advancement and then commit to *working* your plan. If this is who you are or want to be—live it and achieve it. (Exercise #39, Chapter 12) In six months or a year, do not be afraid to revise this Leadership Statement—but keep a plan in front of you.

3. Apply and *practice the 10 Leadership Tools* you've made a commitment to using over the next six months, and further your learning with each. Remember to lean into the difficult and grinding experiences. (Exercise #40, Chapter 12)

4. *Establish an effective mentorship* with someone you consider a true leader. Then, commit to becoming a mentor for some other budding leader in the future. (Chapter 9)

5. Seek to better *understand the larger framework or context* that drives significant organizational improvement—The Malcolm Baldrige Framework. Use this framework to drive your Strategic Planning processes based on the larger context of improving in the Key Result

Areas and moving your organization toward the Main Things. (Chapters 10 and 11)

6. *Keep your eyebrows up,* seeking feedback on how you're doing, taking more risks as you see appropriate, learning to complete the Leadership Rubik's Cube, watching out for those Sponge-Bobbing People, and learning the two-step. (Chapters 4 and 8)

7. *Keep a balance in your life,* and remember **You Do Have Choices.** There may even be times you will have to change employers. It happens to all of us but do everything possible to stay in your current place of employment. Do not fall into burnout or bummed-out thinking. Remember, you do have choice in the matter. (Chapter 1)

8. *Further your knowledge base* about your staff, your customers, about change and leadership, and about yourself. (The entire book)

9. See the big picture and understand your role in it—lead others toward the *Main Things.* (The entire book)

10. *Be* that leader *you* would look up to.

11. Remember, it's all about *you* as a leader, but your leadership is all for *others.*

12. Believe this statement: *Leader Or Not, Here I Come!!!!!!!* Then do it— beginning now!

For some, the decision at hand remains whether or not to enter the role of leadership. It can be a big step and is certainly a serious one to take. However, if you make that proactive choice to begin your leadership journey now, do *not* look back. Others of you have already begun your journey down that leadership path, and for you, I hope this book has given you additional guidance and encouragement to continue your leadership quest. Consider your next steps carefully and use wisdom with each step along the way. I'm excited for you.

Fear should no longer control you or hold you back from learning as you progress into and through leadership. Let your passions and your paradigms drive you forward. On occasion, re-read this book to become reacquainted with some of the Leadership Tools presented and hopefully see that having fun along the way is a big part of your success. Most leaders have little trouble investing heavily in their careers, but many have trouble enjoying the trip. My hope for you is that you're enjoying the trip as you're moving forward.

ACHIEVE COMPLETE BALANCE

The final Leadership Tool is one that's highly personal to each of you but one that's so critical. It involves *achieving the Main Things in your **personal life** in addition to the Main Things in your professional journey.* In all things, be balanced. If you have a family, what legacy do you want to leave through them? How do you keep your physical and emotional engine tuned so you can invest what's needed in all areas of your life? When is enough, enough? I know that being driven to success on the job is a powerful force, and is one that can cause many of us to obsess at times. Be driven, but be smart. Do not lose your balance because you'll tip others over as you fall (your team, family, and friends).

Identify the priorities for each key role in your life: Your team and organization, your family, your career, and your personal life. Only you can decide the balance and timing of priorities for each, but choose wisely. Your family legacy, your health, and your work are highly interdependent forces. It's too easy to get out of balance with one area. As you know, it's difficult to maintain this balance—but **Do** make it a priority that you keep. You'll be a winner in both life and at work in the long run.

SUMMARY (Not Conclusion)

Thank you for being a dedicated reader of this book. Let **Leader Or Not, Here I Come** serve as a source of reference for you in future months and years. My goal was to be an enlightening, encouraging, and entertaining resource serving to help you move forward in your leadership journey. I wanted this book to guide the positioning of your heart, ego, plans, and paradigms. Set your sights high, keep your paradigms well grounded, and establish your measures of success based on those actions that make the significant differences for others and the organization. You can make a difference. You can be a leader who matters. Begin today building your leadership legacy and do it with excellence.

I've presented only an overview of leadership and have made every effort to simplify a very complex topic. Is there one simple formula to becoming an effective leader—the answer is NO. Are there actions you can begin today to move forward into and through leadership—the answer is a definite YES. As you continue progressing, be aware of the personal commitment and learning ahead of you. Only you can make the choices that are right for your career.

Let me leave you with these words of wisdom:

- Be prepared to invest heavily in your leadership growth, especially in those teachable moments and powerful on-the-job learning experiences over time.

- Be prepared to experience failures along the way, but learn as you grow.

- Develop that tougher skin to work through the down times and to control your ego during period of success.

- Logic will often be your weakest argument and your peers may be your toughest challenges.

- You must undergo change from the inside out and learn to function within constantly changing organizational and interpersonal dynamics around you.

- Be ready for leadership that comes to you as …. Ready, Fire, Aim

I've used a number of memory "hooks" throughout this book to make it easier for you to remember the key concepts presented. Let me add one final hook. Remember—*Leadership "just-in-CASE."* I've developed four summary statements on the essence of leadership that I've cleverly built around the word C-A-S-E. These statements are intended to be a reminder when you're faced with difficult situations. Consider this my parting effort to give you something that's "just in case," "just in time," "just for you" during these challenging times. Lean on your own experiences and the wisdom you've gained during your career. Have confidence in your new-found ability to succeed in spite of the challenges. You are a leader!

- "**C**"—you must be *customer-driven,* bringing about customer-driven change within the organization.

- "**A**"—you must be *action-oriented,* resulting in performance that delights customers and results in building the success capacity of your organization by achieving the Main Things.

- "**S**"—*sustainability* for the organization through effective planning, implementation, monitoring, and accountability. Build capacity in people, plans, processes, and paradigms.

- "**E**"—*employee-based performance* and delivery of quality. Your staff will drive success or failure—support them and lead them well.

There is always more that a writer would like to say but there is also a time when enough has been said. If you've read the book, completed the Exercises, applied the Leadership Tools shared, and have increased in your commitment to progress through the journey, I've done my part and you've done yours. You're on your way but you will never fully arrive. Leadership is not a destination—there will always be a bigger and better legacy to leave.

~

Every day, Be that leader you would want to follow, trust, and learn from. Every day, conduct yourself with professionalism and competence to inspire others in the organization to move toward change. Every day, focus on the Main Things. Remember, no matter what business you're in, you will always be in the people improvement business, which serves to move the organization forward. Leadership is that simple—and that difficult.

Leave a legacy that matters in the hearts and minds of staff and in the future of your organization. I envy you as a mid-manager with this future lying ahead of you. Enjoy the journey into and through leadership—make it your destiny.

Leader Or Not, Here "You" Come!!!

APPENDIX

- Biography of the Author
- Leadership Philosophy of Dennis Nitschke (1995)
- Obstacles to Implementing Baldrige (See Exercise #34)

BIOGRAPHY OF THE AUTHOR
Dennis Nitschke

SELF-DESCRIBED as:

- A "Recovering Accountant."
- An average, hard working guy, being driven to make a difference.
- A highly motivated mid-manager who, for many years, was caught in the "toasted cheese sandwich" role for mid-managers, waiting to move into leadership.
- A manager/leader by occupation but a trainer at heart. He loves to see others grow and succeed.
- Is an "eyebrows up" person, looking for opportunities and the right change ideas.
- Received his PhD in being "Pressed Harder and Deeper" involving workplace issues—not college. He spent most of his career in higher education but the true lessons of leadership did not come out of a textbook or his classroom studies.
- Someone who leans into risk-taking and a good challenge—and loves it.
- A slow learner of how to balance the "real" priorities of life.
- Driven to leave a legacy in his children and in his workplace.
- Someone who did not achieve his highest career goals but who achieved "success."
- A proud father of three, grandfather of six, and husband of one (for 40 years).

OCCUPATIONS:

- Accountant for John Deere and Company—Moline, IL
- Business Manager for Black Hawk Community College, Moline, IL
- Fiscal Analyst, Wisconsin Legislative Fiscal Bureau—Madison, WI
- Wisconsin Community/Technical Colleges—Retired College Vice President
- Part-Time Entrepreneur—Rental Property and Long Haul Trucking businesses
- Consultant and Corporate Training for Community Colleges in six states, Workforce Investment Boards, Cabela's (World's Foremost Outfitters), Outboard Marine Corporation (now Bombardier), and other organizations.

UNIQUE EXPERIENCES/QUALIFICATIONS:

- Served on two regional Economic Development Boards and elected to the Wisconsin Economic Development Association Board.
- Served on local Workforce Investment Boards.
- Elected President of a professional association having 2,700 members.
- A Wisconsin Malcolm Baldrige Senior Examiner, Team Leader, and state Judge.
- Pioneer in Wisconsin and national welfare reform initiative.
- Presenter in numerous state and national conferences on "change in higher education."
- Author: *Beginning Baldrige...For Workforce Boards* and *The Community College Role in Welfare Reform—the Wisconsin Story.*

LEADERSHIP PHILOSOPHY OF DENNIS NITSCHKE

(SEVEN KEY ELEMENTS OF LEADERSHIP)

1995 Draft—For Reference Purposes Only

1. *Have a Personal and Professional Mission that Matters* (and makes a difference):.
   - A Personal Mission Statement that I'd want read at my funeral.
   - A Personal Leadership Statement that will motivate and inspire followers, as well as, release my full potential toward excellence.

2. *Be A Big and Clear Thinker* (and have the courage and commitment to deliver):
   - Have the ability to visualize on a larger, longer-term perspective.
   - Create a clear "plan of action" based on this perspective.
   - "Work the plan" with well thought out strategies and tactics.
   - Follow-through on the plan and be held accountable.

3. *Be Able To Create Follower-ship* (on a voluntary basis—without force):
   - Become a source of inspiration to followers.
   - Understand, meet, and evaluate the needs of followers.
   - Stimulate followers to view challenges from new perspectives (new paradigms).
   - Develop confidence in followers which is based in absolute trust, in order to overcome any obstacle (internal or external).

4. *Be A Person Of Character* (Be Real):
   - Having high morals and principles, affirming the values of trust, interdependence, fairness, and proper recognition.
   - "Walk the talk"—integrity.
   - Be hard on issues but gentle on people.
   - Be a builder of team and a sense of "community" for the greater good.

5. *Be Able To Seek Renewal* (never be "frozen in place"):
   - Personally
   - Professionally
   - In the Team
   - In the Organization

6. **Develop And Keep A Sense Of Humor** (it's okay to laugh at yourself):
   - Make laughter legal.
   - Use humor to build openness, risk-taking, creativity, and teamwork.
   - Make "having fun" part of the definition of success.
7. **Achieve Unity** (in getting the job done through others):
   - Celebrate successes and build upon "teachable moments."
   - Build trust in all that is done—it's found in the small things.
   - Humility and a servant's heart to build the bridge to tomorrow's success.

Obstacles to Implementing the Baldridge Criteria

(See Exercise #34—Examples of Poor Leadership)

1. *Leadership.*

   - Senior leaders are invisible and certainly not actively committed to continuous improvement and learning.
   - Priority is clearly on meeting "Compliance Requirements" (out of fear from making a mistake) rather than "Customer Requirements."
   - Senior leaders do not assess the effectiveness of their own senior leadership system.
   - Senior leaders tend to adopt "the program of the month" as a priority and focus.
   - A clear and consistent direction (and vision) for the organization does not exist.
   - Strategic Plans do not incorporate "Opportunities for Improvement" and do not effectively align the work of the organization with its vision, mission, values, direction, and performance expectations.

2. *Strategic Planning.*

   - The Strategic Plan is not customer-focused and is written by a select few in the back room—often at the last minute.
   - Continuous improvement action plans are too vague, lack measurable criteria, and are inadequately funded.
   - Measurable outcomes (performance results) are too limited and are not assessed on a timely and ongoing basis so adjustments can be made during the year.
   - The Plan sits on some shelf gathering dust or is a good doorstop.
   - Too many priorities established.

3. *Customer and Stakeholder Focus.*

   - Quality is not being defined by the customer/stakeholders (it's driven by a status quo mindset and compliance requirements).
   - Staff and partners do not understand what service features are of the greatest value to each major customer segment—or even what the key customer segments actually are.
   - The current and potential customer and stakeholder markets are not properly identified and segmented—and are only listened to when there is a crisis in product delivery.
   - Continuous improvement/quality is *not* everyone's responsibility.
   - The organization has no formal procedures for addressing (inviting) customer complaints and for implementing process improvements as a result of the feedback.

4. *Information and Measurement.*
   - Too much data, not enough "knowledge" information.
   - The wrong activities and outcomes are measured.
   - Information is used as a power tool by certain managers for control.
   - Staff does not use the information adequately in analysis.

5. *Staff Focus.*
   - Staff is not adequately trained in problem solving, customer service, continuous improvement, and teambuilding.
   - There is no linkage between work design and the recognition and reward systems (including compensation).
   - Work is done as it was taught—five years earlier. No re-design.
   - Teams are not empowered to implement continuous improvement initiatives.
   - Staff is resistant to change.
   - There is frequent turnover of staff.

6. *Process Management.*
   - Customer and stakeholder requirements are not "built into" development of new services and support processes.
   - Current processes are never critically reviewed to identify and implement improvement opportunities.
   - There is little or no joint planning and problem solving done with suppliers and partners.
   - Too many information and communication "silos" exist between functions of departments.

7. *Organizational Performance Results.*
   - The key measures being monitored focus on how the organization is meeting Compliance Requirements established by external agencies and the organization's cash balance.
   - Measurements of customer/stakeholder satisfaction (and dissatisfaction) do not exist.
   - Benchmarking against "best practices" and your competition do not occur.
   - Measurements of the effectiveness and satisfaction of your staff activities do not exist (e.g., well being, satisfaction, development, and retention).
   - Senior leaders do not use the Organizational Performance Results and comparisons to take specific action toward improvement.
   - There is not proper "recognition" when desired results are achieved.
   - A tendency pervades in measuring the "failure factors."

A FINAL OVERVIEW

While this book will not give you the 1, 2, 3 formula to leadership success, it does give you practical, applied lessons *for* leadership. This is unlike any other leadership book you've read before. It is very practical in nature and will challenge your thinking, as well as, expand your understanding on the roles and responsibilities of leadership. *Read, Reflect, and Resolve to grow into and through your leadership journey.* It's all about you; but it's all *for* others.

#1: The "one main thing" is to keep the Main Things the main thing. (Chapter 3)

#2: It's Management and Leadership—together forever. (Chapter 3)

#3: The Three R's—Relationships, Relevancy, and Responsiveness. (Chapter 5 & 8)
The Three C's—Customer, Change, and Competition. (Chapter 7)
The Three 3's Assessment—Start, Stop, and Continue. (Chapter 8)

#4: The Four-Step Shewart Cycle of Plan-Do-Check-Act. (Chapter 2)

#5: The Five-Level Skill Development Approach. (Chapter 2)
The Five Levels of Leadership. (Chapter 12)

#6: The Six-Sided Leadership Rubik's Cube. (Chapter 4)

#7: The Seven E's to address in Political Positioning—Ego, Energy, Earnings, Establishment, Empowerment, Enlightenment, and Encampment. (Chapter 7)

#8: The Eight Drivers in Managing Complex Change. (Chapter 7)

#9: The Nine Key Result Areas for Performance Excellence. (Chapter 11)

#10: The Ten Basic Truths Learned From Watching Geese. (Chapter 12)

#11: The 11 Core Values of Highly Effective Organizations. (Chapter 4 and Chapter 11)

#12: The 12 Leadership Competencies. (Chapter 4)
The 12-Step Action Plan. (Chapter 12)

#20: The 20 Workplace Success Nuggets. (Chapter 8)

#40: The 40 Exercises for your Application. (Throughout the Book)

Welcome to *Leader or Not, Here I Come!* Remember, take time to learn, then apply (pilot), gain proficiency, use wisdom, then mentor others—and seek to leave that leadership legacy that others will want to follow.

LEADER OR NOT, HERE I COME!

ACKNOWLEDGEMENTS

To my loving wife, Bev. Thank you for being my partner and my rock for the past 40 years and for learning with me the powerful lessons of life. You've guided me as I learned the parallel lessons between leadership and those of having a good marriage, of parenting, and of growing in our faith. You are the love of my life and the bounce in my step. I look forward to walking more beaches with you and spoiling our grandchildren, as much as possible.

To my children, Lisa, Amy, and Chuck. You're grown and out on your own (thank goodness), and over the years have listened to my attempts to relate the world of work to the world of living. You've bloomed into such wonderful, loving adults–how did you grow up so fast? Remember, my goal is for you to gift Mom and me with eight grandchildren. As we speak, we have six. Chuck, we're counting on you. Who says I'm goal driven? I'm so very proud of all of you.

To my two sons-in-law, Doug and Randy, you two are the reason I'm writing this book. Over the years, the two of you and my children have asked for counsel on a variety of workplace issues and have actually listened to what I've shared. You're the ones who challenged me to put on paper some of my leadership experiences and perspectives. Well, here it is guys. Thank you for your encouragement and support—and thank you for loving my precious daughters so well.

To my co-workers and partners in the world of work. Thank you for all your teachings, opportunities, mentoring, and patience. You taught me how to survive workplace issues and how to be a better leader. I've grown because of all of you and celebrate the wonderful relationships we've developed. You know who you are. My close friends will receive a free copy of this book. If you had to buy this book—well, you know where our friendship stood (Note: Just kidding; I appreciate ALL of you.).

To all the talented conference speakers and business authors. I've learned and applied a great deal from your many books, presentations and teachings over the past 40 years. Thank you for your wit, wisdom, and wealth of ideas. In saying that, please know that I would NEVER intentionally plagiarize your wonderful stories, jokes, and insights into leadership. Do not take offense or send your attorneys after me if you see or infer references to your "words" in this book. I have not intentionally omitted referencing your name as the authors nor want to take credit for myself. I merely have these thoughts and concepts rolling around in my head and have no way of accurately recalling who should receive the proper credit or blame. I do, however, invite feedback from any reader to direct me to the origin of any concepts or phrases I've shared without properly referencing the source. Integrity dictates that I give credit where credit is due.

To my business partners. Thank you Connie, Cabot, Sandy, Al, Heath, Judy, and so many other friends who encouraged and guided me throughout this two year book writing experience. I couldn't have completed this effort without you. You've helped me realize a true passion in my life; that is, to offer assistance to those desiring to grow into leadership. With your continued support and guidance, we can take this book into the world of training to help mid-managers apply the exercises and Leadership Tools in their workplace. My hope is that our friendships and partnerships will continue and grow in the process.

ABOUT THE AUTHOR

Dennis Nitschke has consulted with businesses, colleges, workforce boards, and economic development organizations on a variety of workforce and organizational development issues. His background includes college Vice President, senior examiner for Wisconsin's Malcolm Baldrige Award, business consultant, and accountant in business. He has successfully transitioned up and through the ranks of mid-management into senior leadership. Along the way, he has learned vital, practical lessons in leadership that he shares in this book. He presents you with a set of powerful leadership tools and insights into organizational dynamics while, at the same time, offering personal encouragement as you strive to advance into and through leadership.

Dennis writes in a personal, light-hearted style that will walk you through on-the-job applications of new leadership tools. This is not a theory-based book on leadership or one that looks at leadership from the CEO's chair. It's practical and highly applicable to you, today, in your current role. The simple question addressed in this book is: "How do I become a more effective leader while I'm still in my current position as a mid-manager?" Through the *60 Leadership Tools and the 40 applied exercises* in this book, you **will** learn the front-line lessons of leadership that will also improve your effectiveness as a mid-manager. Bloom where you are today and use this book to prepare you for an expanded and elevated leadership role tomorrow.

For additional information on consulting, seminars, scheduling speaking engagement, or to write the author, please address your correspondence to:

Dennis Nitschke
P. O. Box 326
Lake Tomahawk, WI 54539-0326
www.landmarkleadership.com

In praise of
Leader or Not, Here I Come!

"Leader or not, here I come is a scary thought for most. 'Am I ready for this bold step' is the question of the hour. Not only is there hope, but content rich help exists for those placed on the cutting edge of today's management and leadership arena. In his excellent book, **Leader or Not, Here I Come,** *author, Dennis Nitschke, has developed a step-by-step guide for growing into your leadership role that's so vital in today's competitive marketplace. You and your staff will be motivated with the power that's packed in this life changing book. Leadership growth support is available to you—if you're up to the challenge. Take the challenge.*

—Van Crouch, CEO of Van Crouch Communications,
is a nationally sought after business presenter and
author of books having sold more than 1 million copies.

"Cabela's, the World's Foremost Outfitters, is proud to be using this book as text for our three-credit Leadership course made available on-line to our 13,000 employees nationwide. Our company, as with any successful organization, needs to grow its leadership capacity using the best tools and support mechanisms available. **Leader or Not, Here I Come** *is one of our vital resources."*

—Sarah Kaiser, Senior HR Manager,
Cabela's Corporate Training Department

"For success in today's corporate world, leadership skills are more important than ever. Businesses are spending millions of dollars making sure their leaders are equipped for the future and that they have an effective succession planning strategy. Without question, this book serves as an excellent leadership development tool and I look forward to using it with my own corporate staff. In addition, the book adds its own brand of humor, real life exercises, and personal leadership experiences. Both new and experienced leaders will benefit greatly from reading **Leader or Not, Here I Come.** *I personally recommend this book for my clients, many of whom are Fortune 500 companies."*

—Cabot Jaffee, President and CEO of Alignmark
(Orlando based HR Consulting Company)

LEADER OR NOT,
HERE I COME!

Your Ready, Fire, Aim Entrance
Into Leadership

DENNIS NITSCHKE

LANDMARK
OPPORTUNITIES, INC.

10 09 08 07   10 9 8 7 6 5 4 3 2 1